KT-177-039

Acclaim For
MO' META BLUES

"Questlove's truly original way of seeing, and hearing, the world and his ability to convey this on the page—these are the qualities that make MO' META BLUES such a vibrant memoir."

—*San Francisco Chronicle*

"Attention White Girls: Stop reading about vampires and read what Questlove has to say instead. MO' META BLUES is a magical kaleidoscope about a high-concept, low-maintenance genius named Ahmir. Like him, it's smart, funny, sweet and in a thousand places at once. Read it or rot on your vine."

—*Amy Poehler*

"A thoughtful, incisive analysis of hip hop—and pop music in general—from one of its foremost contemporary architects...a book with as much warmth, heart, and humor as introspective intelligence. Fanatics and newcomers to the music will both find plenty of revelation here."

—*Kirkus Reviews* (starred review)

"A hip hop thinker with historical perspective...an excellent book."

—*Philadelphia Inquirer*

"After reading it, you'll feel like you know Questlove. The book is intimate and funny. Plus, you'll come away with a crash course in hip-hop history."

—NPR.org

"Questlove recounts his musical journey...but digresses regularly with deep (and deeply funny) analyses of the artists and records that shaped him."

—*Los Angeles Times*

"Questlove is an artistic giant and spiritual genius whose roots go back to Curtis Mayfield and so many others. This book is a gem to read and a joy to feel! Don't miss it!"   —Dr. Cornel West

"Compelling... Questlove is so likable throughout, so thoughtful and knowledgeable... [It] cements Questlove as not only one of hip hop's philosophers, but as one of the pop culture's most deserved tastemakers."   —TheDailyBeast.com

"Part memoir, part music theory, part cultural critique, all Questlove... He writes with a musician's sense of rhythm and a philosopher's sense of meaning [and] colors it all with introspection and charm."   —*Denver Post*

"Required reading for fans of music... totally excellent... mostly you get Thompson's enormous brain exploring his music, his odd life, his place in the world. Long may he play, DJ, and write."   —*Austin American-Statesman*

"A fascinatingly thoughtful, sometimes nerdy and thoroughly entertaining look at life and music... as original as it is insightful."   —*Minneapolis Star Tribune*

"An unassuming, humane masterpiece."   —Grantland.com

"I truly love this book. I felt like I was having a conversation with Ahmir, and I may have even said aloud a few times, 'What? No way!' It's everything I want to know about someone who is obsessed with music... his love for music (contemporary/revolutionary/cool) is tireless. I am forever a fan of Questlove's fanaticism."   —Fred Armisen

MO' META BLUES

THE WORLD ACCORDING TO

QUESTLOVE

By Ahmir "Questlove" Thompson
and Ben Greenman

GRAND CENTRAL
PUBLISHING

NEW YORK   BOSTON

Copyright © 2013 by Ahmir Thompson

All rights reserved. In accordance with the U.S. Copyright Act of 1976, the scanning, uploading, and electronic sharing of any part of this book without the permission of the publisher is unlawful piracy and theft of the author's intellectual property. If you would like to use material from the book (other than for review purposes), prior written permission must be obtained by contacting the publisher at permissions@hbgusa.com. Thank you for your support of the author's rights.

Grand Central Publishing

Hachette Book Group

1290 Avenue of the Americas

New York, NY 10104

www.HachetteBookGroup.com

Printed in the United States of America

LSC-C

First trade edition: May 2015

10   9   8   7   6   5

Grand Central Publishing is a division of Hachette Book Group, Inc.
The Grand Central Publishing name and logo is a trademark of Hachette Book Group, Inc.

The Hachette Speakers Bureau provides a wide range of authors for speaking events. To find out more, go to www.hachettespeakersbureau.com or call (866) 376-6591.

The publisher is not responsible for websites (or their content) that are not owned by the publisher.

Library of Congress Control Number: 2013932326
ISBN 978-1-4555-0137-3 (pbk.)

Richard Nichols. You were the lighthouse. Rest in peace.

...well Tariq?

"I don't talk about the past."

—Prince

ONE

So what's this gonna be, Ahmir?

A memoir.

The fuck does that mean?

You don't know what memoir means?? A life story, told by the person who lived it.

I know what the word *memoir* means. But what about the idea? What does it mean to you?

Well, that depends. This book should be different. I don't want it to be your average book.

What does that mean?

I don't know yet. Maybe it's just an ongoing process of questions leading to more questions. I'll say this: as a reader of music memoirs, I never begin where I'm told to start. As a rule I find myself starting at chapter 3 or 4, because before that, every music memoir has the same shape. It starts off with a simple statement about childhood: "I was born in this city, in this year. My dad did this." But I don't want to start that way. I can't start that way. I won't.

Then, after that, there's a predictable move. The main character discovers music. Dude's walking past a window and hears a symphony that turns his head, or he's at a favorite uncle's house and someone puts Louis Armstrong's *Hot Fives and Sevens* on the record player and, just like that, *bam*, it's like he's been struck by lightning. His life is changed forever. That's an exciting moment, but it's also predictable and oversimplified, for sure.

So those first chapters aren't important?

How can you say what's important in a life, really? Could you sum up a whole life in twenty chapters? Or would it take twenty-one? And why is the person who lived the life the only one talking? Could you pass the mic, let someone else talk, and just shut the hell up for a minute and let them call you on your inevitable bullshit? I don't know exactly what would work, but experimenting is more interesting than just telling the story straight through from A to Z.

I'm just glad that you don't want to do a whole fucking book about obscure soul tracks. How many times can you talk about Clyde Stubblefield or Gene McDaniels and make lists for Pitchfork or *Rolling Stone*?

But sometimes I only remember things through records. They're a trigger for me, they're Pavlov's bell. Without thinking about the music, I can't remember the experience. But if I think long enough about a specific album, something else always bubbles up.

Well then maybe you should do a book that just goes through your life, year by year, using only records.

I could try to pick one record for every year of my life, but I'd have to stop in the mid-nineties, 'cause it's not the same picking records as a fan after I start as a recording artist. Would that work? It might. Think of all the different ways that stories get told. I'm working with the James Brown people on a movie that will end up being the closest thing to a biopic that can possibly exist for a man like that, who was actively working for fifty years. The story is too big to tell straight on through, so they decided to deal with it by breaking it into five different episodes, five representative short stories. Or take that Hendrix movie that André 3000 is starring in. It has nothing to do with the legend of Jimi Hendrix, really. It's about twenty-four hours in the life of a working musician, and all the stresses that come along with that—the girls, the drugs, the managers, the need to find time to breathe creatively. Or maybe there's a book that tells a story somewhat straightforwardly, but with a growing awareness that it's only telling part of the story. How can a man in his early forties hope to really talk about his life as a whole? It's like reviewing the first half of a song.

Don't people want to hear about the groupies in the hotel? Don't they want to hear about the time you got into a limo with a certain female head of state, who shall remain nameless?

Look, man, I've read plenty of hip-hop memoirs, and most of them have only one story to tell: rise, bling, fall, and lots of debauchery along the way. That's not my story. I haven't lived an interesting life in that sense. I won't pretend otherwise. I haven't had many Motley Crüe evenings...though I know those guys and I hung out with them one night and I saw things.

What kinds of things?

That's another issue. Do I keep certain stories to myself? Do I betray confidences? Does no other musician writing a book struggle with this shit? I don't get it. If I was with someone and I saw something crazy, is it really my job to tell that story and expose that person just to make other people more interested in my book? Let's say I know a juicy story about Singer X. Do I tell it? Do I keep him or her anonymous? Create a composite? Fudge the details? It seems like most of these books are content to be Jell-O from the same mold. So maybe the answer is in some unholy hybrid: some straightforward memoir, some fodder for the recordheads, some tricks and treats, some protecting the innocent, some protecting the not-so-innocent.

You really think you need a special form to tell it? Come on, dawg. At the root, why does your story require that?

Is that a joke?

Why would it be?

Because of the Roots.

You mean because of that simple pun? You think I'd stoop to something like that? What the fuck? Tell me why your story matters.

Because we're the last hip-hop band, absolutely the last of a dying breed. Twenty-five years ago, rap acts were mostly groups. You had Run DMC and the Beastie Boys and Public Enemy, and you even had bands of bands, like the Native Tongues collective, which was three loosely affiliated groups: De La Soul, A Tribe Called Quest, and the Jungle Brothers. I grew up looking at that model, at the sense of community and of a larger purpose. Even the negative things that came out of that arrangement, like competition and tension and sibling rivalry, were productive—that's what you get when you group. But today it's all solo acts. Maybe it's just simple economics. Everyone thinks, "I'm Michael Jordan and I can do this on my own and pick up the big check." And maybe you can't blame people for that. The system isn't set up to think about it, not at all. New acts worship the star system because they see the highlight films, and that's all they can see, because that's how the experience is packaged. Solo acts are also easier for labels to deal with: they're easier to control, and you don't need to do any dividing to conquering. Even if I think of this as my book, it's never only my story. It's the story of other musicians, of other hip-hop groups, of other minds. The Roots is literally the last band on the caboose of that train. But maybe I should save that for the book.

We're in the book.

We are?

We're always already in the book. We've always already been in the book.

TWO

From: Ben Greenman [cowriter]
To: Ben Greenberg [editor]
Re: Meetings

Nah, I wouldn't say that Ahmir's been scarce, just busy.
He has the Jimmy Fallon show most days and he DJs
most nights, and when the show is on vacation, that's
when they schedule Roots events like the summer picnic.
But when he isn't otherwise spoken for, he's been great
about clearing out space for the book. He's really into the
process. He talks for hours.

While we wait for his schedule
to level off, though, I've been
talking with Richard Nichols,
the group's comanager since
day one, and that's been an
experience, to say the least.
For starters, Rich has got this
great look; here's a picture
I got from Ginny Suss at

Okayplayer. Ahmir describes him as "Nipsey Russell with dreadlocks." When you start talking to him, though, he isn't like Nipsey Russell at all. (I'm guessing here: I never met Nipsey Russell.) Rich is supremely analytical, extremely verbal, and entirely determined to digest, process, present, and represent the Roots' whole experience. He has been central to the growth of the enterprise—in helping to strategize the moments when they grabbed for the brass ring as well as the moments where they sat back and thought about what the brass ring meant. He conducts an ongoing interrogation about what it all means. What's black culture? What's hip-hop? What are the responsibilities of a society and the people in it? And his inquiry isn't bloodlessly academic, either; there's something very consequential about his approach. You know how in comic books there's sometimes a supervillain who's a giant brain in a jar, and there are underground tubes leading out of that jar to the airport and the power plant and the bank to show you how he's in control of everything? Rich is like a non-evil version of that.

So Ahmir and I were talking about Rich and Ahmir had an idea. "I think Rich should have a say in the book," he said. I agreed, and outlined some of the options: an intro, an afterword. "No," he said. "I mean that he could literally speak out over the course of the book." Do you think that would work? Ahmir could be in one font and Rich could be in another, and they can be in dialogue, trying to work out their ideas. What kind of book could that be? Would it illuminate? Complicate? Clot? Whatever. Think about it. Let me know.

THREE

W here do I start?
    I was born in West Philadelphia in January 1971. My father, Lee Andrews, had been a pioneering doo-wop singer with his group, the Hearts. They had a handful of hits—"Long Lonely Nights," "Tear Drops," "Try the Impossible"—that went Top 40, or close to it. My mother, Jacqueline, had been a model and a dancer, and she and my father opened up a store called Klothes Kloset on 52nd Street. When they started their business, in the mid-sixties, Philadelphia was a colorful, peaceful place that got steadily bleaker as the turbulence of the later part of the decade intensified. Martin Luther King, Jr. was murdered in Memphis. Gangs moved into the neighborhood, and drugs came in with the gangs. My parents' store closed when their wealthy customers fled the city. At the same time, radical black political groups were taking hold. MOVE, a black liberation organization whose members all wore their hair in dreadlocks and all took "Africa" as their last name, started in Philly in 1972, and their headquarters was just a few blocks away from our house on Osage Avenue in West Philadelphia.

I say "our house" because by that time I'd arrived, joining my mother, my father, and my older sister, Donn. We had a comfortable life—our little two-story house, our close-knit family, and our music. Even though the doo-wop music my father had grown up with was long gone, music was central to our family in almost every way. We had more records than I knew what to do with, and either the radio or the TV was always on, playing music. It was soul and it was rock, and I guess some of it was proto-disco (from the Greek *protos*, meaning first, signifying the earliest or most primitive form—so it wasn't disco yet but it was getting there).

Wait, wait, stop. Let me back it up.

First there was African music. The heavy rhythmic bed. You know how Public Enemy says, in "Can't Truss It," that they came from "the base motherland, the place of the drums"? Africa, that's the place they're talking about. That was first, the world of proto-breaks, an intimate connection between rhythm and movement, between time and life. Drums, heartbeats, human clocks, dancing with your knees bent. Then those Africans were taken out of Africa, turned from people into slaves. It's a ticket you don't have to pay for, an anti-lottery. They ended up in the so-called New World, and it had new ways of hearing and new ways of being (or not being) heard. On the plantations the slave owners would take their slaves' drums away because they didn't want them communicating with other slaves. They were afraid that the drum was some kind of magic signal system, a primal, coded language, which it was. And is. When the drums were taken away, other instruments were taken up—fifes and fiddles and the rest, and they were used for celebration and lamentation both, and a new kind of song sprung up, a work song, to document the labor in the fields, to pass the time, to pass on the content of the time, so that people would know what had happened.

Slavery was abolished eventually, but enslavement wasn't, and the music they'd made kept documenting the life that was lived. And then there was money in the songs, or the want of it, and love in the songs, or the want of it, and pain in the songs, or the want of it. There was humanity in the songs, and multivocal humanity, a call and then a response, a way for the speaker to know that his speech was being heard, that he wasn't alone in the world, not in his love or his pain or his humanity. The same happened in gospel music, too, where religion was held out either as a sop to the people or a way of temporarily finding a light at the end of a tunnel of tribulation.

Someone once said that blues and gospel were fraternal twins, close in spirit, neither one wanting to admit how similar they looked. In blues the notes were flat—that's what blues notes are, flatter notes designed to get closer to the music made by voices in work songs— but the stories they told were round. And then there were records and records were round, too, and they went around, and jazz records came along to help people dance. There was swinging at the Savoy Ballroom and elsewhere. Shorty George Snowden brought in the Lindy Hop. Music made more music. History made more history. Voice warred with instruments, and instruments warred with voice, but it was a virtuous war, and a war with several cease-fires: jazz grew out of a peace between black music in the New World and white music in the Old World. And then there was electricity, and then there was swing time, and then there were the Mills Brothers and the Ink Spots singing in four-part harmony in and around Cincinnati, refining the fifties progression, and then there was my father's group putting out singles in Philly. I think I may have missed a beat or two in there, but that more or less brings us up to the present, right?

———

I was about two when I started playing the drums, but people sensed that I was headed in that direction even before that. My mom and dad said that I had a natural sense of rhythm from six months or so, and by eight months if you tapped out a pattern, I could tap it right back. One of my earliest memories of drums came a little later than that, on Christmas Eve 1973. It's probably my earliest memory in general, and it's blurry around the edges, but I remember the center of it: waking up in bed that night and going downstairs to find a toy drum kit, a xylophone, a keyboard, and a toy guitar by the tree. Nothing was wrapped yet. Donny Hathaway's second album was playing in the background, the self-titled one with the covers of "A Song For You" and "Magnificent Sanctuary Band." My parents were sitting on the couch. They didn't chastise me for getting out of bed early. They must have gestured toward the presents, and I made my way over there. Of the four instruments, I gravitated toward the drums.

That was the epiphany, the mountain coming to Mohammed—or in this case, Ahmir. Drums and I found each other just like that—BOOM!—it was like I'd been struck by lightning. If you've ever had a kid in the house or a neighbor learning drums, you know that it's not exactly a peaceful experience. But my parents never put any restrictions on my drumming—never told me that I had to stop at eight o'clock, or keep it down below a certain level. It wasn't until much later that I thought about how surprising and lenient this was; the neighbors must have heard me pounding away at all hours of the night.

———

Even though I went for the drums on Christmas, I was interested in all music. I have only a handful of memories from 1973, but all of them have a vivid soundtrack. I worry that it'll be harder for the present generation to process memory, because they have so many options to choose from, and most aren't shared in a physical space. I had two kinds of experiences that I mapped to memories: records that were played in the house or on the radio, and *Soul Train*. Every memory of mine is paired with one of those two things.

For example, my father had two ashtrays made to look like guitars. One afternoon, someone in the house was playing Bill Withers's

Still Bill. It got to the last song of side 2, "Take It All In and Check It All Out," which starts with a great keyboard part but then goes to this lean guitar line, and I started playing along on the ashtray. I was strumming like I was Bill Withers or Benorce Blackmon or whoever was playing. Except that I was playing on an ashtray, and the ashtray had a jagged bit where a chip had been taken out of the glass. It cut my hand pretty bad and I cried like crazy—like a little kid, which I was.

It's the same with my first *Soul Train* memory, which is from earlier in 1973, sometime in the winter. I was in the bathtub and didn't want to stay there. What kid does? I came running out of the bathroom into the living room and I fell toward the radiator, which branded me. For the next sixteen years of my life, there was a train-track-like burn from the radiator right up the outside of my leg. Anyway, at that very moment, Curtis Mayfield was doing "Freddie's Dead" on the TV. And not just "Freddie's Dead," but one specific part of the song, the modulated bridge where the horns come in. Even now, when I hear it, it traumatizes me. There's nothing technically scary about it, but it's forever welded to the memory of falling into the radiator. I'm not the only one with that kind of association. D'Angelo told me that to this day, he cannot listen to Marvin Gaye's "I Heard It Through the Grapevine" without feeling terror. That's strange to me, because when I hear that song I think of yuppies singing it in *The Big Chill*, reliving their youthful optimism. It's a light song for me, a party song, frothy. But for him, it's a dark place, and I'm not sure he even knows why. It's related to something in his childhood, something buried deep. I even tested him during the *Voodoo* tour. We were backstage, with people milling around, and I put it on the radio. He immediately stiffened, turned around, and said "Take that thing off."

What's funny about that *Soul Train* memory—or tragic, depending on your sense of humor—is that small memories like that can permanently distort your perspective. After the "Freddie's Dead" incident, I was really afraid of Curtis Mayfield in general. Back then, I judged records based on how the logo looked rotating on the turntable, and the Curtom logo—psychedelic lettering with a sun drawn behind the middle of the word—was a little too intense for me. And when I decided to give Curtis a second chance about a year later, I picked "(Don't Worry) If There's a Hell Below, We're All Going to Go," which was the lead track from his album *Curtis*. It was an unfortunate choice. All those echo effects and screams: that's not a sound any three-year-old wants to hear.

———

I wasn't a normal kid.

My father used to say half-jokingly that there was a little concern over whether or not I was okay. Maybe it wasn't a joke at all. The concern was about my personality, which seemed too eccentric. I don't think "autistic" was a common term back then, but I later found out that they had taken me to a doctor to see if something was really wrong.

It wasn't that I was violent or temperamental. In fact, my mom said it was a blessing because I never gave her trouble. It was the opposite—they knew exactly how to sedate me, which was to sit me in front of something that held my interest and then just leave. I'd develop a deep relationship with that thing, whether it was *Soul Train* or a record on a turntable. But that led to a secondary worry, which was that I was falling inward into some kind of trance. Once, when I was very young, my dad installed a light with a rotating shade around a lightbulb, one of those lamps that works like a kind of carousel. He pressed the switch that caused the shade to turn and, according to him, I just disappeared inside myself. Five minutes passed, then ten, then fifteen, and I didn't seem any less interested in the rotating lamp. Then my parents started noticing a broader pattern of me trying to spin stuff. I would take my sister's bike and watch the wheel go around and around. I would take my father's records and twirl them on my finger. They had a moment where they thought I might be interested in cars, because I was driving the records like a steering wheel. That was my whole entertainment for a while there, but to my parents, it was almost like a bad habit that they wanted me to drop. But I haven't dropped it, not at all. To this day, my life revolves around circles. My drums are circles. Turntables are circles. My logo or autograph, which I developed over the years through doodling, is composed of six circles. My life revolves around that shape.

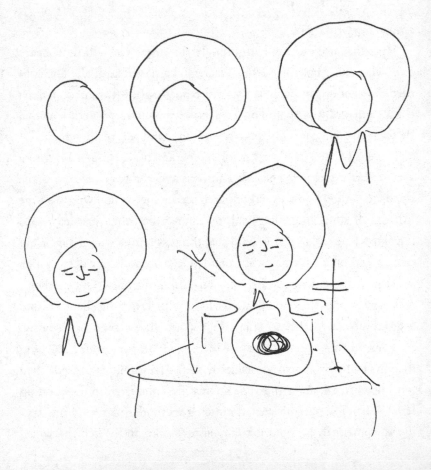

Even without the circles, I knew straight off the bat that I wasn't like other kids, not the ones in my neighborhood in West Philly. My parents wanted me to survive, to thrive, and so they sacrificed everything so that I could have the better things in life—private schools, music lessons. You always hear stories of parents who put themselves out so that their son didn't end up in jail in general population. I'm not sure that's where I was headed. I had a different set of issues. I never went outside and played. I rarely interacted with other kids. It wasn't until a little later, when I started staying at my grandmother's house, that I had a brother figure in my younger cousin Mark. That was how I learned about normal kid stuff: bikes, basketball, catch-a-girl-freak-a-girl. What kind of nine-year-old takes advice about how to get a girl from a five-year-old?

"You just go up and give her a note that says 'Do I have a chance?' and then three lines under it, Yes, No, and Maybe," he told me.

I was that nine-year-old.

———

Our house was rich with records, maybe five thousand vinyl LPs. My father took everything that interested him, from rock to soul to folk to country. If he liked it, he liked it. He was broad in his tastes in that way, although if he was left to his own devices, he went for vocals. He was a singer, and he came from the school of Nat King Cole, so his tastes veered into tasteful soft rock with clear melodies: the yacht rock of its day, decades before anyone called it that. He liked *Tapestry*, 10cc, Bread. He loved singing along to the radio, tuned to Magic 103, putting out that dentist's-office music.

The rest of the family helped to complete the picture. My sister went to all-white schools, so to blend in, she listened to mainstream rock music. She brought it all home: *Ziggy Stardust*, Queen, The Eagles. I was a very small child at that point, but all my rock vocabulary can be traced back to her and her need to be socially accepted by her circle. Later on, in fact, when I heard records like the Beastie Boys's *Paul's Boutique*, it all came back to me. And then there was my mom. If anyone in my family is what you'd think of as a crate digger, it would be her. I don't mean that she went looking for specific records, more that her judgment in music was based on the way things looked at that moment, a kind of indescribable cool. If she saw a funky album cover by psychedelic artist Mati Klarwein, she'd snap it up, so that's how the house started to fill up with all those early seventies jazz-funk records like *Bitches Brew* and Herbie Hancock and Santana. She got drawn into the package, and if the package looked cool, that was enough for her. As it turns out, many of those records would be used as break beats in the future, so in a way it was an early education for my career in hip-hop.

Even though my father worked in the music industry through the seventies and beyond, he believed that music died as a result of two crucial punches, one in 1973 and the other in 1979. The first punch came when James Brown put out *The Payback*. My father felt ripped off: it was like $17.99 for eight songs, three of which were longer than ten minutes, the longest of which, ironically, is "Time Is Running Out Fast," which is almost thirteen minutes. It wasn't running out fast enough for my father. "Where are the hits?" he wondered. "This is like one endless song." I don't mean that he wondered internally in some kind of interior monologue. I mean that he asked that question out loud, repeatedly. "Where are the hits?"

The second album that punched him in the gut was Stevie Wonder's *Journey Through the Secret Life of Plants*. It was too abstract, too spacey, too private, and not enough of anything else. All at once he just stopped buying records.

Those LPs, disappointments for him, were birthright moments for me. He just said to me, "Here. You take these." They had wounded him and he wanted to move them away from him so that he could feel right again. So I started to study them: how they did what they did, how they stretched beyond what the artists had done before. *Journey Through The Secret Life of Plants* became my *Dark Side of the Moon*, my psychedelic masterpiece. I didn't have that experience with Pink Floyd and I didn't have it with Jimi Hendrix either, but I got it with Stevie Wonder, headphones on, tranced out, moving through space in my mind.

I loved the way that music was the center of our house, though I think I knew even at the time that it wasn't normal. Something strange was happening at 5212 Osage; I was getting a Harvard-style music education in a Joe Clark, *Lean On Me* environment. If you take an inner city ghetto where there's crime and violence and drugs—and there was all that around us all the time—the last thing you think you're going to find is a family that's teaching its afro'd four-year-old son the difference between Carole King's original "It's Too Late" and the Isley Brothers' version, which is this ten-and-a-half-minute blues-rock epic that opens up side two of their 1972 album *Brother, Brother, Brother.*

And it wasn't just about listening to other people's music. My early adventures with the Christmas Eve drum set turned into something more substantial, and by the time I was five, I was taking drum lessons. Right away, I learned something interesting about drum lessons: they don't let you touch the drums. Instead, they make you take tap-dancing lessons, because tap is a good way to coordinate your hands and feet. I was a latter-day Sammy Davis, Jr., a real Philly hoofer. In fact, my very first TV interview—which was also the first time I garnered complaints from other kids' parents because their daughters were hidden behind my afro—was for a dance performance. I was interviewed by Jack Jones, a local television legend who was working for KYW-TV, the local Channel 3. (Interestingly, KYW-TV is one of the oldest TV stations in the world: it started in the thirties as W3XE, when it was an experimental station used by the Philco Corporation, which was manufacturing some of the first television sets. Anyway, maybe that interview is in their archive, along with other significant moments in Philadelphia's cultural history: Ahmir Thompson, five-year-old tap dancer.

———

I say I grew up in West Philly, but the truth is that I grew up on the road. Doo-wop had gone away at some point, like many forms of music. The market dried up, popular tastes moved on. Motown and Stax came on, and then psychedelic soul, then funk and disco. But once doo-wop was good and gone, it started to come back a little bit, and my dad had the idea to rejuvenate his music career by taking advantage of this nostalgia cycle, which was going full-blast in the mid-seventies with bands like Sha Na Na, movies like *Grease* and *American Graffiti*, and television shows like *Happy Days* and *Laverne and Shirley*. The fifties were a going concern in the seventies, and on the back of that renewed interest, my dad had a good run bringing back his group, Lee Andrews and the Hearts, along with my mom and my aunt Karen. All of them sang; all of them entertained. They were the act. In that oldies revival circuit, each group did a twenty-minute set with its five hits and other songs from that period, and then either Dick Clark or Wolfman Jack or the like comes out and announces the next group, whether it's Reparata and the Delrons or Johnny Maestro and the Brooklyn Bridge.

Even during those package-tour revivals, my dad knew it would be a limited thing. They were big in Connecticut and in the Catskills but it wasn't penetrating the rest of the country, and he wanted to prolong it. So after three years or so, he jumped off the revival tour and decided to become a nightclub act. These days, it's all DJing: I can go do a four-hour DJ gig at Brooklyn Bowl or somewhere, and there are similar clubs in every city in the country. Back then, there was a moment in history where everyone had a band, and every singer was a working karaoke machine. My father milked that circuit. It was a pretty predictable program that required him and his band to do a number of different sets over the course of the night. First was the dinner set, which went from cocktail hour until seven thirty, and that was softer music, the kind of thing you would hear on soap operas or in the movie theater before the Coming Attractions started: George Benson's "This Masquerade" or "The Girl from Ipanema" by Astrud Gilberto and Stan Getz. Then came set two, which was the Lee Andrews and the Hearts revue. My dad would sing his four songs, but my mom was the real the star of the show. She had a look and an entertainment background, and she knew how to connect with audiences. So she would do Peggy Lee's "Fever," Shirley and Company's "Shame, Shame, Shame" on *If You Can't Dance Too*, or Kiki Dee's "I've Got the Music in Me," always with a little bit of audience participation or a little bit of comedy. It's the kind of thing that June Carter did for Johnny Cash: a beautiful woman to keep the crowd happy. That lasted an hour and then the band went back to a dance set where they played whatever was in the Top 40 at the time, from "Love Rollercoaster" to "Play That Funky Music."

Finally, for the late show, my dad would do a completely different set, maybe some old soul covers, maybe some contemporary ballads. That final show was when he played the ace in the hole, which was to point at my mom. "By the way," he would say, "this beautiful woman is my wife." Then he'd point at my sister and say, "Give it up for Donn, my lovely daughter." This was a huge hit with audiences. My mother and my sister defied time. They looked like sisters. Other groups with bigger hits, like the Coasters, used to get angry because we had this added dimension. There was a period when my sister and I stayed in Philadelphia to attend school, and my parents went back out on the road to support us. Then a little later on, the family was reunited on the road, and there was another wrinkle in my father's last-set speech: "Give it up for my son, Ahmir, on the drums."

The result of all of this was that I ended up with what you might call a distorted worldview. I thought that living in a Howard Johnson's was normal. I thought everyone had ice machines in the hall and a swimming pool in the middle of a courtyard. One afternoon back in Philadelphia, I was out in the street with some kids, talking about first-class airplane meals or room service or something. And one of the kids on the block looked at me like I was an alien.

"What the hell are you talking about?" he said.

I started to explain: you know, when you get on the plane, and you see the tray of food, and you know that it's for coach instead of first class because it has the paper salt and pepper instead of the little glass shakers. At that moment, my mom appeared and told me to go in the house. Seven-year-old me wasn't registering that she was trying to protect me from a beatdown or trying to limit my involvement with kids who were headed down more dangerous paths. I didn't know, at the time, that she was trying to prevent it from turning into a game of catch-the-snob. Later on, she explained to me that I had been given access to certain experiences that granted me a different perspective than other kids in Philly had.

"Most people never leave this neighborhood," she said. "You're lucky you get to be out there seeing the whole country. But you can't talk about Muncie, Indiana, or Jacksonville, Florida, like they're neighborhoods right next to West Philly. They're not."

———

These days, when celebrities travel, they stay at the Four Seasons or some other high-end hotel. Back then, we stayed at airport Sheratons, and not just for a night. We camped out there while my father entertained. During our stay, we would see other acts come through, and not just musical acts—football teams like the Pittsburgh Steelers, the Kansas City Chiefs. Boston, the arena-rock band, was there, and of course, KISS.

Have I mentioned that I was a KISS fanatic? My obsession with the band was damn near legendary. Any trip to Sears or K-Mart started with me making a beeline for the KISS records. I was both obsessed and frightened at the same time. I never heard a note of theirs for years, but I compulsively studied all the record covers. They had such a weird set of records early in their career, so many in such a short time span. In 1977 I remember seeing *Dressed to Kill* and *Destroyer* and *Love Gun* in record-store bins, all at more or less the same time. I learned everything I could, all the nuances and details: what Gene's makeup looked like, what kind of shoes Peter was wearing. For a while there I had "Christine Sixteen" on heavy rotation. That became my favorite song.

One night in the hotel in Buffalo, I was watching live music performances on TV as usual. There was a guy named Dan Hartman who had written "Free Ride" for Edgar Winter; later on he had a big solo hit called "I Can Dream About You." In the late seventies he recorded a disco song called "Instant Replay." He followed that up with a single called "This Is It." I remember being freaked out by that video specifically. It was the last song on *Midnight Special* that night, and something about it kept me up. It was one in the morning and I was thirsty, so I said to my sister, "I can't sleep. I'm thirsty."

She said, "Get the money off the dresser and go get yourself a drink."

I went into the hallway, which was a circular corridor that ran all the way around the hotel. I got a soda and walked back to the room. Just as I passed the elevator, the doors opened. Bing. Eight years old. And what I saw there was my worst nightmare come to life. It was Ace, Paul, Gene, and Peter, all in the elevator, with bodyguards. I don't think they were in full costume and makeup, but maybe they weren't totally cleaned up yet, either. At any rate, I knew it was KISS. Who else could it have been? I was excited and terrified and generally overloaded, so I let out the most high-pitched, bloodcurdling scream you can imagine. I dropped the soda and ran so fast that I went past the elevator three times. The neighbors woke up. I was the little boy who cried KISS. I got to my room breathless.

My dad took me down. It was one forty-five in the morning. Much of my life has been like that: go to sleep strictly at nine, but wake back up at midnight. I put my clothes on and went down to this lair, a kind of green room. The ratio of women to men was like eight to one. The room had two pool tables and a sit-down pinball machine that Paul Stanley was playing. It was a "Mean" Joe Greene moment.

My dad said, "Excuse me, I'm Lee Andrews." He pointed at the poster. I couldn't stop staring, and I'm betting my mouth was wide open.

Peter Criss looked at me and said, "Oh, yeah. Little screamer guy."

The whole band gave me autographs. They couldn't have been nicer. No one could believe it when I got back to school. KISS was at the apex of their power, and I was at the apex of mine because of them.

———

When time for elementary school came, I was terrified. Up to this point I had lived most of my life out on the road, with my family, and the idea of staying in Philadelphia seemed almost like a punishment. In reality, it was about the softest landing I could have hoped for: a private school for the performing arts. It was a large campus in City Center that contained all of the grades, not just elementary school, but also a junior high, a high school, and even a college. I was interacting with older kids and adults from the very start. Even though they weren't about to let me play first chair in chamber—during orchestra time, I think I got the triangle—I got to see it all up close. That first year, I was the only male in my grade: the rest of them were Hungarian or Russian girls whose parents had them marked for ballerina fame or violin fame or piano fame. They weren't so big on acting or contemporary music.

From the beginning, I did well at the music part of school. I was technically mature. Socially, though, it was a different story. The only people

I had interacted with at that point were my parents, my sister, and my father's band. To go from that world, the only world I knew, into this dark brown building was like entering some kind of house of horrors. Not to mention that the first person I ever met was a girl named Jill, who is still a great friend of mine today. She has a neurological condition, and I had never met or seen anyone like that in my life. My first words to her were "Do you bite?" She spoke to answer me, probably to try to kindly correct me, but I heard her voice and freaked out. It was all every kind of overload. I went running for cover and ended up in the art teacher's basement, which was filled with all these Bill Plympton–inspired drawings of distorted faces and frightening gnomes.

It was a horrible, surreal experience, and as soon as I got home I told my parents that I was never going back. I cried, I protested. But they knew the way to my heart. They promised me that if I went back they would take me record shopping.

———

Ah, records. I was there when they premiered the Sugarhill Gang's "Rapper's Delight" on WDAS, 105.3 on your FM dial. I was at home with my sister, and the two of us stared at the radio the whole time it was happening; it was our equivalent of the old radio drama *War of the Worlds*. All the black kids in Philadelphia who were listening to the radio that day have the same story. It stopped us in our tracks. I was paralyzed. It was like we had all been struck by lightning. I remember thinking about whether I had time to go downstairs to get the tape recorder, or should I just let the song run? I ran calculations in my head. It sounded like it might go on for another five or six minutes. I went for the tape. I got it into the machine just as Wonder Mike starts his story about his dinner: "Have you ever went over to a friend's house to eat and the food just ain't no good? / I mean the macaroni's soggy, the peas are mushed, and the chicken tastes like wood." I must have listened to that tape thirty times that night. The next day in school I was a hero. I could do the whole thing. Three kids had heard the song, and they couldn't believe what I was doing. Within a week everyone had heard "Rapper's Delight," and the world was different forever.

It's hard to overstate what a change it was. The day before the song premiered on the radio, our hero was Michael Jackson. The single "Don't Stop 'til You Get Enough" had come out in July, and then the *Off the Wall* album in August, and that had hit us in a very big way. Everyone knew Michael's vocals and Michael's lyrics and Michael's dance moves. Then one day in November, we turn on the radio and there's this new thing. It was like magic. Years later, I talked to Jimmy Fallon about this and he said that he remembers doing the same thing with comedy albums—replaying them at home until he had them committed to memory, and then the next day go and performing them at school. If it was a new birth for music, it was also a new birth for me. I found my identity through hip-hop. It made me popular, and immediately I started buying it.

The first order of business was to get my hands on the "Rapper's Delight" LP, and I had a foolproof strategy. I knowingly used Steven Savitz's obsession with my sister. Steven was a handsome guy, maybe a jock, maybe an actor, a twelfth-grader with an immense crush on Donn. American society was decades away from *The Game*, but Steven Savitz had an idea of how he was going to get close to her, and it involved being cool with me. My first manipulative move was to ask him to buy me the record. He agreed immediately so we walked to Listening Booth on Chestnut Street after school, where he purchased my very first twelve-inch. It cost only $2.99 plus tax, $3.17 total. It was the first pressing, and amazingly, I still have it. All that was left was to figure out how to keep that gravy train going, but the Steven Savitz Method of Record Purchasing dried up pretty quickly. Every Monday there was a new rap single, so my goal was to find thirty-two dimes within a seven-day period so I could buy the next twelve-inch. If I saw a dime on the floor, it went into my pocket, and I was one tick closer. If my mother asked me if I had put the dimes in the collection plate at church, I said "Yes, ma'am," but they were in fact going to another higher power: a fund to help me buy records. And just like that, my record-buying obsession began.

? ? ?

Quest Loves Records, Part I

"When you live your life through records, the records are a record of your life."™

1971: Stevie Wonder, *Music of My Mind*

I know this record was played right around the time of my birth, and for years after that. I encountered it very early, at a point when I was still judging records not by how they sounded but by how they looked, and I didn't like what I saw. Motown wouldn't commit to one factory plant— they used twenty plants regionally—and that was very troubling for me as a kid, because it resulted in inconsistent ink quality. Some of the records were printed too dark and some of them were printed too light. There was a man my mother brought into the family as a kind of grandfatherly figure, Mr. Lewis, and he was very dark, of Cuban background. He laughed like Geoffrey Holder, which scared me a little bit: "Ha, ha, ha, how are ya, man?" To me, his teeth always looked like the Tamla logo, which was on all the Stevie Wonder records. I wasn't a fan of photo collages either, and that cover is a photo collage. Records whose covers scared me would be buried in the bottom of the pile—the opposite of crate digging. There are also records from that period that my father thought I liked for the profanity. "Sweet Little Girl," from *Music of My Mind*, is one of them. Stevie's talking smack to his girl for not giving him some, and as the song is fading out, he says, in this puffed-up, aggressive voice: "Get mad and act like a nigga!!" I thought that was the craziest, most hilarious thing.

Extended Playlist

There were other songs that year, but I was too young to remember them. When I add songs, I don't want to fake it—I want to make sure they're really songs that were important to me.

1972: Sly and the Family Stone, *There's a Riot Goin' On*

Though it came out in 1971, I remember hearing this record in 1972 and embracing it for the wrong reasons. My sister was giving me a bath, and when she was washing my afro, soap got in my eyes. I went running downstairs, screaming uncontrollably, and it just so happened that "Just Like a Baby" was playing in the background. It's not the most inviting or jovial song to start with, and there I was as my mother, my sister, and my aunt Karen held me down so they could flush out my eyes. Anytime I hear it now I wish I had Johnson's No More Tears. That's another record with photo-collage art, which made the eerie experience of the record even scarier. I was creeped out by Rose Stone's singing in "Family Affair." It sounded strange to me. But I used to love emulating Sly on "(You Caught Me) Smilin'." I'd use any excuse to make my voice raspy.

Extended Playlist:

I heard these on the radio, which my father controlled.

...Aretha Franklin, "Daydreamin'"; Melanie, "Brand New Key"; O'Jays, "Backstabbers"; America, "Horse with No Name"; Johnny

Nash, "I Can See Clearly Now"; Three Dog Night, "Black and White"; Billy Preston, "Outa-Space"; Carly Simon, "Anticipation" ...

1973: Rufus, *Rags to Rufus* / Sly and the Family Stone, *Fresh*

I have an obsession with the song "Sideways" on *Rags to Rufus*, which was almost just an interlude. It's like a jam session where you're hearing the band from outside the club, the sound all muffled. Then all of a sudden the song opens up, clears up, and Chaka Khan is singing some jazzy stuff. Evidently it went on too long and no one stopped the tape, because then you hear her say, "The food is here?" There's also a great tremolo effect on the cymbals—I went through a phase where I loved to make that noise on my drums, that high hissing. And I loved *Fresh*, but I especially loved side 1. I treated it like a full song-suite, the way other people talk about Marvin Gaye's *What's Going On*. I never really played side 2 until I was an adult. "Frisky" is especially great. There are vocals and arrangements on there that you can't even imagine. Ironically, the song I gravitated to the least was its hit a single, "If You Want Me to Stay." I was always an album-cuts person, even back then.

Extended Playlist

My father had a warehouse where his band rehearsed, and there was an area in the corner with a stack of 45s and a mono RadioShack portable record player. It was my playpen.

... Tony Orlando and Dawn, "Tie a Yellow Ribbon ('Round the Old Oak Tree)"; Roberta Flack, "Killing Me Sofly"; Paul McCartney, "My Love"; Stories, "Brother Louie"; Cher, "Half Breed"; War, "The Cisco Kid"; The Temptations, "Masterpiece"; Edgar Winter Group, "Free Ride" ...

1974: Bill Withers, +'*Justments*

Sly and the Family Stone's *Small Talk* came out that year, and the title song features a baby crying. By that time I was going to the studio with my parents. I thought the baby was me. This is a tough one, but I have to go with Bill Withers. He was my idol. I embraced all his records. But +'*Justments* is especially vivid. Sundays were a sad day in my house. When my parents were going away on tour, they would wait until Sunday afternoon to tell me and my sister. "No!" I'd cry. "When are you coming back?" +'*Justments* was playing during one of those Sundays in 1974. Later I learned that the record was kind of Bill Withers's version of *Here, My Dear*, Marvin Gaye's 1978 divorce record for Anna Gordy for his own wife, actress Denise Nicholas. "Railroad Man" is the happiest song on +'*Justments*, and it's about a train that decapitates a swindler.

Extended Playlist

A majority of these were when I discovered music on television, especially by watching variety shows. Everyone had a variety show.

...Barry White, "Love's Theme"; Gordon Lightfoot, "Sundown"; The Spinners, "Then Came You"; Joni Mitchell, "Help Me"; Tom T. Hall, "I Love"; Average White Band, "There's Always Someone Waiting"; Curtis Mayfield, "Mother's Son"; 10cc, "I'm Not in Love"...

1975: The Ohio Players, *Honey*

This record, like many Ohio Players records, is famous because of the cover, which shows a naked woman holding a spoon up to her mouth, glowing honey dripping from it. It's famous to me because I got it for my fifth birthday, along with *Moving Violation* by the

Jackson 5. There was a note, "Happy 5th Birthday from Mommy and Daddy—we love you very much," taped right on the honey jar. Later on I asked my mother: "Come on! How did you approve of that cover?" She explained to me that their eyes weren't open to the evils of the world until years later, when Prince came along. In a way, she was right. I didn't see it as salacious or sexual at the time. After all, at that age most kids are playing dress-up or house. Me? I played record store. There were three mom-and-pop music stores on 52nd Street in West Philly, and the most notable was King James. It had these incredibly curated displays in the front, with *Caught in the Tracks* by the Commodores suspended high in the window and *Up for the Down Stroke* by Parliament hanging on a thread. I memorized the layout of the window and went right home and set up my own record store. I put Lou Rawls's *All Things in Time* out in front, which meant that *Bert's Blockbusters* from *Sesame Street* had to go a little further away: children's section. I thought I would do the corner displays just like they were done at King James. I put *Honey* up there. But at the record store the edges of the covers were curled. What I didn't know is that King James wasn't using actual album covers—they were posters from the record company. You can curl and bend posters from the record company. You can't bend record covers with discs in them. So, yeah: I cracked *Honey*. There's no tragedy like your first broken record. And it wasn't like broken records got replaced. I know the entire Ohio Players catalog like the back of my hand. Except *Honey*.

Extended Playlist

My father had a Granada with both a cassette player and an eight track. It was very rare to have both of those things. He made mix tapes.

...Bee Gees, "Nights on Broadway"; The Eagles, "One of These Nights"; David Bowie, "Fame"; Donna Summer, "Pandora's Box";

Carole King, "Chicken Soup with Rice"; Earth, Wind & Fire, "New World Symphony"; Funkadelic, "Be My Beach"; The Isley Brothers, "The Heat Is On"; The Ohio Players, "Fopp" . . .

1976: Stevie Wonder, *Songs in the Key of Life*

I'm a person who loathes everyone who name-checks Stevie Wonder like there was nothing else to listen to in the seventies, and yet he turns up on my lists over and over again. *Songs in the Key of Life* is especially inescapable. It came out at the beginning of my first-grade school year, which I know because on the first day of school our music teacher told us to have our "mommies and daddies" buy us the record. To ask your parents for that record in 1976, that was a major event. We went to the record store to get it. I was thrilled, although I didn't like the cover art. I thought he was drowning in donuts. In school, we studied the liner notes. It was the first time I read liner notes obsessively. And then the teacher started us on side 4, on "If It's Magic," so we could hear Dorothy Ashby playing the harp. Then we went to side 2, to "Pastime Paradise," to learn about eastern finger cymbals, and to "Love's in Need of Love Today" to learn about harmony. That record was my textbook.

Extended Playlist

My father upgraded to a van. This is when I started to take charge of what people listened to. My sister was also an influence—she loved yacht rock.

. . . Average White Band, "Pick Up the Pieces (live)"; Phoebe Snow, "Cash In"; Al Jarreau, "Letter Perfect"; Paul McCartney and Wings, "Silly Love Songs"; Fleetwood Mac, "Rhiannon"; Elton John and Kiki Dee, "Don't Go Breaking My Heart"; The Miracles, "Poor Charlotte"; Starbuck, "Moonlight Feels Right" . . .

1977: Rufus, *Ask Rufus*

I'll put this album in Questo's Top Ten of All Time every time. By 1977, we had four record collectors in the house, and I wasn't even officially one of them: Mama on funk, my aunt Karen on funk and jazz, Donn on eclectic rock, and my dad on easy vocals. One day my aunt went out to the record store without me and came home with a number of records, including this one. I loved it. It wasn't a jazz record, but it wasn't a soul record, either. Chaka Khan undersang everything. She wasn't up to her usual wailing tricks. The most notable presence on *Ask Rufus* was Clare Fischer, the uncle of the drummer, André Fischer, and a legendary string arranger in his own right. Orchestral work in black music is nothing new—Philadelphia created an entire genre based on adding orchestral arrangements to songs. But there's something about the beauty of darkness that Clare Fischer adds to these records that's just haunting. This was also a Sunday record in my house. My parents were going to do an extended trip to Louisiana and Miami, gone five weeks. When they told me how long they'd be away, the string breakdown of "Egyptian Song" came on. It's a soundtrack moment, a perfect illustration of childhood sadness, lush and spare and at the same time, creepy. And then the story got sadder, at least for me. In Louisiana, Aunt Karen met a man at a restaurant. It blossomed into romance and they decided to get married. When the grown-ups came back from that trip, my parents gave us another talk: We're not going back out on the road again, no, but Karen's leaving. She took the record with her.

Extended Playlist

This was definitely the punishment period. I would get records, and get in trouble, and lose them for months. Many of these I heard on my clock radio, with the volume turned down.

...Bill Withers, "Lovely Day"; Bootsy's Rubber Band, "What's a Telephone Bill?"; Brothers Johnson, "Q"; Commodores, "Fancy Dancer (live)"; Heatwave, "Put the Word Out"; The Isley Brothers, "Climbin' Up The Ladder"; Kraftwerk, "Trans-Europe Express"; Bob Welch, "Sentimental Lady"...

1978: Average White Band, *Warmer Communications* / The Jacksons, *Destiny*

This was the first year I had a major punishment. I wasn't misbehaving in school, not talking back or fighting or anything, just not exactly paying attention. Like I said, I was an indoor kid with a tendency to fall inward. To lay down the law, my father banned me from getting any new records. That was terrible for me. But he had his own music, including the Average White Band album, which he played in the car when we drove. Still, there were new rules: I wasn't allowed to look at the cover art and I wasn't allowed to sing along. Eventually, maybe after a month, I was off punishment and the first record I bought was the Jacksons' *Destiny*. That's another scary cover: the group is sitting on top of the album title, which is like a seawall, and there's a tsunami beating on the letters, threatening the *D* and the *S* and the *Y*. There's also incoming fire or meteors or something. That album was the first time the Jacksons took control of their own music, and it was a huge success, with "Blame It on the Boogie" and "Shake Your Body (Down to the Ground)." "Blame It on the Boogie" is confusing, because it's a cover of a song by Mick Jackson, an English singer whose real name was also Michael Jackson. He had a version of the song out at the same time, and British newspapers and radio stations took sides: some of them liked the Jackson version, while others liked the Jacksons' version. They called it "The Battle of the Boogie."

Extended Playlist

My parents went away on Mondays, so Sundays were sad days at my grandmom's. And my uncle's tastes came into play, too—he had more avant-garde records.

…Angela Bofill, "Under the Moon and Over the Sky"; The Bar-Kays, "Holy Ghost"; Commodores, "Fire Girl"; Nina Simone, "Baltimore"; Raydio, "Jack & Jill"; Sun Ra, "Twin Stars of Thence"; Switch, "We Like to Party…Come On"; Gerry Rafferty, "Baker Street"…

1979: Stevie Wonder, *Journey Through the Secret Life of Plants*

I know, I know…another Stevie. But every time I hear "Seasons" / "Power Flower" I'm right there, all over again, walking home with Donn from Broad Street, passing through the urine-soaked subway that leads to the trolley that eventually takes us to 49th Street, to my grandmother's house. There is snow on the ground, maybe even in the air, and posters for the Steve Martin film *The Jerk*, which is coming out at Christmas. And it's late, too, on into evening: at the performing-arts school I go to, the bell rings for the end of the school day but that's just a signal to hang out with my friends, to go to the band room and watch the older kids practicing their ensemble version of Eric Clapton's "Cocaine" *ad nauseum*, to see the dancers out in the hall tightening up their choreography. I wait for Donn, and then we go out into the winter.

Extended Playlist

This has to do with watching *Soul Train*, which by this point had shifted from noon until 1 a.m. My sister would wake me up after *Saturday Night Live*.

…Chic, "Le Freak"; The Jacksons, "Shake Your Body (Down to the Ground)"; Michael Jackson, "Don't Stop 'Til You Get Enough"; The Doobie Brothers, "Open Your Eyes"; Cheryl Lynn, "Star Love"; GQ, "Disco Nights"; The Sugarhill Gang, "Rapper's Delight"…

FOUR

So, that's what made you feel like the world had become a better place **?**

"Rapper's Delight"? I forget that you were eight at the time. The lyrics must have spoken to you: "At the age of eight I was really great," "At the age of nine I was right on time."

You had to be there.

I *was* there, my dude. I was thirteen years older, maybe not quite, but already a little world-weary. At that point in my life "Rapper's Delight" hit me like some coonish pastiche, with all its tales of chicken eating, "super sperming," white Sasson wearing, Cadillac driving, and love of country having. It was black Americana and hard to take at face value—Dewey "Pigmeat" Markham's minstrel shtick come back to life and set to a cover of Chic's "Good Times." It was a final piece of punctuation ending the polymorphic dictation of the sixties.

Really, Rich? It was music. It was fun. I liked it. Besides, who was talking about the sixties anyway? This was 1979, remember?

I know, Ahmir. It might've been '79, but the seventies were like the aberrant child of the sixties. And 1979 was the year that the seventies left home, not just literally, but also in a spiritual sense. Gone was the existential longing that you could find at the core of songs like "Dock of the Bay," "What's Going On," or "Higher Ground." I figure it this way: when Sam Cooke sang "a change is gonna come," I didn't foresee that change being one that would allow for niggas to be rapping about "busting bitches out wit dey super sperm." I just felt a kind of revisionism kicking in with this *up jump the boogie to the bang bang boogie*–ing. I had already pretty much stopped listening to radio some years before, so hearing "Rapper's Delight" simply strengthened my resolve. But as retrograde as that was, there was something progressive in the world, too. When I was thirteen, my brother-in-law took me to see Rahsaan Roland Kirk at a West Philly bar called the Aqua Lounge. The performance was nothing short of amazing. I knew nothing about Rahsaan at the time; I just thought he was some blind nigga playing at a local bar. But that show, and that music, taught me just how elegant the quotidian lives of black people could be. That moved me, and then moved me over convincingly to jazz. Later on I had a weekly radio show on Temple's jazz station for about ten years.

Jazz? We were talking about hip-hop, weren't we?

Hold up. Let's go back before we charge forward. I grew up in Philly, too, about fifteen years earlier. That puts me in a different generation, younger than your father but older than your sister. From early on, I was listening to music, partly because it was such a rush. Think about how much music

changed in that period. When I was three I was dancing to
Ray Charles. Louis Jordan was in the recent past. Five or six
years later there was Motown, which seemed modern even
to an eight- or nine-year-old. And then just four years after
that there was the Beatles, and then Sly, Stevie Wonder, Jimi
Hendrix. Music was picking up steam. I had a brother who
was in the service, and one year he came back with a real
stereo. It had a reel-to-reel player and a weighted turntable,
real speakers, and real headphones. This was like in the mid-
seventies, right around the time Stevie's *Music of My Mind*
came out. For me, the combination of that record and that
real—and I mean *tubes* real—stereo was magic, man. We'd
just go into his room and turn on the fan and chew on ice and
listen to records. It was beautiful. Of course, twenty years
after that, I was with your ass and the Roots on the tour bus,
watching y'all get your heads around this same music, and it
was annoying.

Annoying??

By that time it was all on CD and you could easily skip tracks if
you wanted or change the order. Even more annoying, you guys
reprogrammed all my associations—now it's just stinky socks
on a fucking tour bus. This whole shit is made worse by the fact
that music is now available to everyone, all the time, in every
place. That doesn't necessarily reward real connection with
music. When I really like something, I tend to never listen to it
again. I want to remember the feeling even more than I want
to remember the music. If you get that record back out, you
risk learning that it's not as good in reality as it is inside of you.
Better to have the memory than to go back and have to adjust

your truth. And even if it is every bit as good, you're just going to deconstruct it, like this. You're going to use your brain instead of your feelings. As you get older, feelings are hard to come by.

But you had those feelings, right?

Fuck yes, I had them! All my life. That's what I was saying about my brother's room and ice and the fan. Weren't you listening? But after that period came along a kind of vacuum. Disco was cute at first, I guess, but it rolled into this very unthinking and unfelt R&B, and what was beautiful in popular music started to become less and less present. That's when I stopped with the radio and moved over to jazz, real outer-space stuff.

So you weren't listening to "Rapper's Delight" at all?

Fucking hated it. It was awful. But I kept hearing things like it, and soon enough I had a sense that this was something new that was breaking the back of the generic shit that was happening in black music. I became especially interested once the sampling came around. I mean, look at the difference between Public Enemy's first album—which was okay, maybe a little old-school noisy—and *It Takes a Nation of Millions to Hold Us Back*, which blew my fucking wig back. And then you had groups like De La Soul, who could certainly rap, but that wasn't the only point, was it? They had that whole Native Tongues alliance with A Tribe Called Quest and the Jungle Brothers. That's what I was looking to get out of it, a bit of a black cultural paradigm. People would see me coming from the record store and I would pull out an MC Lyte record along with Cecil Taylor or Big Daddy Kane.

And that made you want to be part of it?

It didn't hurt. I got into hip-hop because of what wasn't there yet, because it was nascent. I wanted to be part of it and the production process. Because of the whole MIDI revolution, even as an untrained musician you were able to create. I loved music, but I had missed the boat on being a trained musician. I was studying electrical engineering. I wanted to make toys and games for a second. I studied poetry with Sonia Sanchez for five semesters. She'd put you through your paces both academically and spiritually. Every class was like this crash course in life lessons, and every week you left the room a different (dare I say better) person. My experience with her was about the words. From the words came this language and from that language came a music, an expansive music. So, the actual music that I was interested in was this distinct thing, falling far off any sensible career path and even further off from what I was actually capable of doing. I loved Dolphy and Ayler, Monk and Hemphill, Strayhorn and Shepp, but I was never going to play with that level of inspiration. And then there was hip-hop, perhaps the most elemental, black DIY music since the days of the proto-blues. Hip-hop attracted me as someone who loved music but whose facility was a precious little thing. I began to realize that hip-hop was something old, something new, something borrowed, and something blue. It had my attention and my attention was enfolded into that of an entire generation.

FIVE

What do you do when just listening to the music you love isn't enough?

I guess you do what I did, which was to become a serious music-press nerd, the kind of kid who collected back issues of *Rolling Stone* and memorized all the record ratings. The magazines soon became as important to me as the albums they were writing about. I loved the Robert Risko illustrations in *Rolling Stone*, the portraits that accompanied the lead reviews in each issue. On the walls of my bedroom I created a kind of Risko wallpaper made from hundreds of reviews. And every Saturday I would go down to the Philadelphia Main Library's reading room and go through back issues of *Rolling Stone*. It was so ancient back then: you had to request the periodical and wait for it to come out to you on a microfilm reel, after which you hooked it up on the reader, which was kind of like a reel-to-reel tape recorder, and found out what critics had written about the records, whether it was Hall and Oates or Cameo or the Zombies or Warren Zevon or Parliament. Take *Her Satanic Majesty's Request*, the Rolling Stones record from 1967. It wasn't very acclaimed at the time, because it was considered derivative of the Beatles' *Sgt. Pepper's Lonely Hearts Club Band*. I had my own ideas of the record that came from listening to it, but I also wanted to know the ideas that other people had at the time. I immersed myself quickly, and I don't think I've ever really gotten dry.

There are artists who will tell you that they care what a record sells, or whether they get to put their video in rotation at this channel or website or whatever. I can say with confidence that I'm indifferent to those things. Even today, my esteem comes from record ratings. When I started out with the Roots, *The Source* was the standard, but for me, *Rolling Stone* was still the mountain that had to be climbed. In my head, I imagine that when I'm dead, when I can no longer defend my records or explain them, the periodicals will stay forever, like they did in the reading room at the Philadelphia Main Library, and those reviews will become the final word on the things that I've created. Maybe I imagine it this way because I expect that the people of the future will be people like me. Who's to say that when it's time to look up the history of the Roots, and some kid wants to learn about *Phrenology*, that *Rolling Stone*'s review, or *Spin*'s review, or the *Source*'s, or Pitchfork's, won't tell that kid everything he or she thinks? Those words will still be there. The words are always there.

Even so, I don't want to suggest that I'm totally beholden to what reviewers believe. I have a strange relationship with good and bad reviews. If a great artist makes an album that critics don't like, or that they're suspicious of, I make a beeline straight for that record. I'm the music snob who takes up the "wrong" records, like U2's *Rattle and Hum*, which was maligned at the time for being slavishly imitative of American music. That game—trying to guess how a record will be received, and why, and if it'll be overrated or underrated—has always appealed to me. When I was a kid, I used to listen to records before I read the review and try to guess what ratings that record would get from major magazines. No—it was worse than that. I would have a friend tell me what *Rolling Stone*'s lead review was, and then I would get the record and figure out in my head what rating I would give it. Sometimes my review was too high, and I'd read to find out why. Sometimes it was too low, and I'd see if I bought the critic's rationale for the higher rating. When *Ragged Glory* came out in 1990, I didn't know much about Neil Young. I think that was the first record of his I bought. I listened to it and I knew it was strong: lots of guitar noise; a big, thick, sludgy sound; a kind of clear-eyed darkness in the lyrics. I did my internal calculations and thought to myself that it was probably a four-star record. Then I checked *Rolling Stone*. The headline was "Neil Young's Guitar Ecstasy," and the writer, Kurt Loder, gave the album 4½ stars. That blew my mind. Holy shit, I thought, they just declared him the lord Jesus Christ.

I was and am so devoted to the review process that I write the reviews for my own records. Almost no one knows this, but when I am making a Roots record, I write the review I think the album will receive and lay out the page just like it's a *Rolling Stone* page from when I was ten or eleven. I draw the cover image in miniature and chicken-scratch in a fake byline. It's the only way I really know how to imagine what I think the record is. And as it turns out, most of the time the record ends up pretty close to what I say it is in the review.

———

That's the kind of kid I was, even early on, trying to balance the pleasure I felt in hearing music with the pleasure I felt knowing that certain albums were considered critically superior. Soon enough, this led to a pretty strange set of preferences. I remember being a teenager and being ashamed of my musical tastes, at least some of them. My Brian Wilson and Beach Boys fandom, which is as important to me as anything else, was almost like a porn stash. Hide that shit, someone's coming! You couldn't look like me and be black in West Philadelphia and love the Beach Boys the way I did. I remember the first time I really came out of the closet for Brian Wilson. It was years later, after the

Roots were already going. I was with J Dilla and Common and suddenly realized that there was a loop I wanted from "There Must Be an Answer." When I pulled the record out, they just looked at me like I was crazy. *Pet Sounds?* They probably thought I had put my hand on the wrong record. Now that kind of thing is cool. Everything is accepted as part of everything else. There's a broad hipster continuum. But back then, there were so many times that I had to explain to myself why "I Just Wasn't Made for These Times" meant so much to me.

So there was my obsession with Brian Wilson. There was Led Zeppelin. There was Miles Davis. There was Michael Jackson, of course—there was always Michael Jackson. But as much as I loved all those artists, as much as I saw their genius, the fact of the matter is that for a while, there was only Prince. It may be hard for kids now to recover a sense of how out there Prince was in the early eighties, how far above the crowd he was operating, especially since the Prince today is kind of the opposite of the Prince then. But in the early eighties, people spoke of him as a genius, and they weren't kidding, not even a little.

I have a vivid memory of reading the review of *Dirty Mind* in *Rolling Stone* in 1980. Ken Tucker wrote it, and he said something about how the record was an example of lewdness cleansed by art, and about how it was dirty but it certainly wasn't pornographic. I had been following Prince since his first album, and I knew the second record pretty well, with "I Wanna Be Your Lover," but it wasn't until *Dirty Mind* that it hit me—he was big news. The fact that a relatively new, relatively unproven artist could get a 4½ star review from *Rolling Stone* blew my mind. It must have been around that time that I started to take the idea of a review seriously. I had a germ of an idea in my mind even at that age, and it came into focus pretty quickly, that I wanted to make records that were part of that same set, records that critics would admire and that would be marked as important. You know: 4½ star records. A few years later, even though my whole room was wallpapered with *Rolling Stone* reviews and Risko draw-ings, I reserved a special place for Prince: I put his reviews right over my bed, on the ceiling, where I could see them all the time.

———

The same way I had become an independent businessman to get my hands on "Rapper's Delight," I started to come up with schemes to get Prince albums. It wasn't like it is now. You couldn't just go online and have access to all the music in the world. You had to go to record stores, with money in your pocket, and acquire albums. If they were out of stock, come back next week. When Prince's *1999* came out, back in 1982, it touched off a saga that lasted a half-decade. I would say, conservatively, that I purchased that record eight times between 1982, when it first came out, and 1987, which is when I stopped get-ting on punishment for having it. Every time I bought it, my parents managed to take it away from me, and then I'd have to go and get it again. It was a war of attrition, and the only one who won was Prince.

The story of that record and how my parents and I saw it so dif-ferently is the story of my family, in a sense. When I was young, in the mid-seventies, my parents were how I've described them to this point: this funky, hip, post–civil rights, postrevolutionary bohe-mian black couple. They listened to all the cool music and wore all the cool clothes and had all the cool attitudes. In the early eighties, though, something switched over in them, and they became the black Ned and Maude Flanders. Beginning in 1983, they listened only to Christian radio, which included whatever soul stars had moved over to religious pop—Donna Summer, say. It wasn't that other music was banned, exactly. We still listened to Stevie Wonder, but there were other acts that were clearly on the other side of the line. By this point, I had rejoined my parents for tours sometimes, and one night in Myrtle Beach, South Carolina, we were in a hotel room on the road.

Some TV show, probably Burt Sugarman's *Midnight Special*, showed Prince's "I Wanna Be Your Lover" video, and my father was jaw-dropped. "Is that boy in his diapers?" he marveled. I thought it was strange for him to fixate on that, because it wasn't exactly unprecedented: P-Funk had a guy who was always wearing a diaper, and that hadn't seemed to bother him. But Prince was just too salacious, and you couldn't call it.

Pretty soon, my parents weren't the only ones noticing, and the opposition to Prince hardened. It accelerated because of church, obviously, and how the people there acted after Michael Jackson's *Thriller*. That was right around the same time, and it had to do with the title track: they couldn't take "Thriller" as a campy Halloween song. For them it was a Satanic message straight from the gut of Hollywood, a warning sign that made it more important than ever that parents pay attention to what their kids had on their stereos and in their headphones. A few months later, there was this other guy named Prince, and if you wanted to see how dangerous *he* was, well, just take a look at the cover of this *1999* record. Turn it upside down, for starters, and the title changes from something futuristic and fun, to *666*, the mark of the beast. Oh and also the part of the title that's not Satanic when you turn it upside down, the *1*, well that's clearly a drawing of a penis. This went out on the church wire as something to be worried about, and my mother recognized it as something from my collection. "You have it," she said. Of course I had it. Everything I learned about sex was from Prince. That was the first time I heard the word "whore," and probably a whole lot of other words, too.

At any rate, my mom found the record and threw it away. This would have been in the fall of 1982—the record came out in October and I had it maybe a month before it got tossed. Then winter came, and I shoveled snow until I got enough money to buy it *again*, at which point she found it... *again*. This time she was tossing records by Prince and any of his associates, like The Time and Vanity 6. Vanity was especially problematic, as she was already getting a reputation as a scandalous, highly sexual performer. My mother had probably heard about the Vanity 6 album by then, with "Nasty Girl" and "Drive Me Wild," and she certainly wasn't going to let me keep that. I forget how I scraped together the money to replace it that time, but I had a sinking feeling that they'd find something else to object to. The third time I think it disappeared the same day I got it. The fourth time my father just cracked the album over his knee—the second disc, sides 3 and 4. He destroyed it right in front of me, and slowly. He must have been so angry that he forgot it was a double album, and I kept the first disc and hid it in my room, between the mattresses. Four months later, my mom was in my room to clean it, or at least that's what she said. (My theory is that parents don't want a room to be clean so much as they want to know what you're into when you're in there.) She found that hidden disc. That was like, another month of punishment. A few years later, I wised up. I found a friend who was an even bigger Prince freak than I was, and I bought the twelve-inch singles and brought them over to his house, where he would make me cassettes of the music. Even that wasn't the extent of the concealment operation. Since I had three floor toms, I took the one I liked the least and bought two Remo drumheads. They were from the Ebony series—black and opaque—and I loosened the heads and stashed a bag of clandestine Prince cassettes inside them. Even then, I could only listen when I snuck a Walkman to school or when I was practicing my drums, when I would hear Prince through my headphones and play something totally different so that no one knew what was happening.

———

That same year that *Thriller* and *1999* came out, something happened that was a tide-changer and was, in some sense, the true beginning of my life. Up to that point, I was a cute little kid, obsessed with music, in love with TV, carefree, traveling with the family band from hotel to resort, and attending an exclusive performing-arts school. But toward the end of sixth grade, I put a foot wrong, and the world tilted.

It wasn't my fault, exactly. I was at the drugstore with my mom after school and I naively asked her for two dollars for glue. That went fine. "Sure," she said. She probably didn't even think twice about it, and if she did, she was thinking about airplane models, or an arts and crafts project. Then, in full view of her—and, more importantly, within earshot—I asked for an extra paper bag. You should have seen her face. That was the beginning of the end.

Let's back up a day. Two of my friends were clowning around in school, and suddenly they nominated me for this secret project: get Testors model glue, get brown paper bag. What they neglected to tell me was that it was a secret plan for glue sniffing. I should say right off the bat that they probably weren't serious. They were little kids just like I was, preteens. I doubt they ever considered going through with it. Still, they went through with phase one, which was to acquire glue and bag. Or rather, they had me go through with phase one. And, as I proved in the drugstore, I didn't have any idea what I was doing. I probably had never heard of the idea of sniffing glue. Sure, there were drugs in the neighborhood, but I didn't really go out in the neighborhood much. I was an indoor kid, and mostly in my own head. My friends really picked the wrong guy to satisfy their glue-sniffing needs.

The glue did it, though, right then and there. That alarm was rung, and all of a sudden they became hypersensitive to everything else I was doing. For instance, I was a video game freak. Every kid was. Maybe I was a little more of a freak than most, because I liked studying patterns. My arcade favorites were Pac-Man and Ms. Pac-Man. I read books about them, studied them like they were the Bible. I got to the point where I could stretch twenty-five cents out forever, but I still needed a steady supply of change, so I started inventing ways of separating my parents from their quarters. "Ahmir, run out to the store and get me some bread." Ahmir runs to store. "Where's my change?" Ahmir shakes his head like he doesn't know. There couldn't have been anything more innocent than that, but after the glue thing, to my parents, I seemed like an eleven-year-old on the leading edge of more serious trouble.

And that was that. Within the month, my parents had a plan to take me out of performing arts school and put me in a conservative Baptist school. And it wasn't my grandmother's Southern Baptist, with Bible thumping and hooting and hollering in choir. This was Baptist schooling, South Philly style. My old school, the private performing arts academy, had been on the corner of Broad and Spruce, right next to Philly International Records. It showcased everything about Philadelphia that was cosmopolitan and forward thinking. The new Christian school where I was sent for seventh grade was in deep South Philly, Italian Philly.

In retrospect, I realize that it wasn't just about the glue. In my parents' heads, they felt like the performing-arts school was going to create a certain type of child, one who was supremely prepared for entertainment and the craft of making music. But at the same time, my parents had aspirations for me: they wanted to raise a future *Jeopardy!* contestant instead of a future *Jeopardy!* clue. I was doing fine, grade-wise, but they wanted me to know more about the world, to be more generally sophisticated. And, just as important, they wanted me to learn in a Christian environment.

Arriving at that new school in the fall of 1982 was culture shock and then some. The place I had come from had every diverse cultural background represented. From first grade I already knew a goth kid, a gay kid, a kid with a neurological condition, a thug-ass graffiti writer who was ashamed to let people know he could do fine art as well. It was a bunch of talented misfits inside this artificially charged, highly rewarding environment. The new school, though, was hard-core. It wasn't easy to make friends, especially because I was the new kid. It was also the first place I encountered all the things that make junior high nightmares for millions of kids across the world. There was a school bully. There was overt racism. It was kind of like *Everybody Hates Chris*. Ironically, the evil influences that my parents sought to shield me from—the big, bad, outside world—hit me full force, all at once.

To say that I wasn't happy there at first is an understatement. I cried and complained, but most of the time I wasn't even coming home to my parents, but to my grandmother, with whom I was staying while my parents were out on the road. A new chapter of my life had started, and for the first time I wanted to slam the book shut on it.

———

I was rescued by music again, though in a completely different way than I had been at performing-arts school. Toward the end of 1982, Michael Jackson had released *Thriller*. That's both a straightforward statement of fact and the beginning of an amazing, almost magical sociological process. Over the course of the next year, *Thriller* was everywhere. It became inescapable. It was, for a little while, American life, and during the year that it occupied the center of popular culture, it united everyone. Who liked *Thriller*? *You* did. White people, black people, skinny people, fat people, straight people, gay people, punks, rockers, hip-hop kids, thugs, nerds. You. Everyone alive. After Michael did the moonwalk on Motown's twenty-fifth anniversary television special, the sense that everyone was the same became even more pronounced. The Jets and the Sharks put their weapons down. For me, the same kids who had sneered at me and kept me from feeling good about my new school became, by some invisible *Thriller*-powered process, my good new friends. It's corny to say that it was a lesson about how music can unite people no matter their superficial differences, and I'm not so deluded as to compare myself with Michael Jackson. But it reminded me that music has powers that sometimes extend beyond the notes and the lyrics.

————

The Great Christian School Experiment lasted through seventh and eighth grade, and then for ninth grade I went on to another school that my best friend at the time was attending, City Center Academy. It was a Christian school, too, but even more rigorous than the junior high, with only twenty students in every class and math and science curricula that were more advanced than anything I had seen.

High school marked the beginning of an intellectual awakening for me, though it wasn't necessarily the one the school had in mind. There's a song on Stevie Wonder's *Songs in the Key of Life* called "Black Man" that ends with a kind of educational call-and-response section, where a chorus of students announces the name of a figure in the arts or sciences or politics, and then the rest of the kids detail that person's achievements and identify him or her as a minority writer or scientist or whatever. The kids on Stevie's record came from a Marva Collins school. Collins was a Chicago educator who became famous in the mid-seventies for taking kids from poor neighborhoods and beginning to educate them in a classical fashion. She opened her first school, which was called Westside Prep, in 1975, and there was a vogue for that kind of school across the country.

My high school had opened right in the middle of the Marva Collins era, and everything there was oriented toward ancient Greece and Rome. There was an Eidolon club. The basements were called catacombs. We were led to believe that those societies were the alpha and omega of civilization, so to speak. For me, this was confusing, because I was just starting to listen to Afrocentric rap, and the music was telling me something different than the teachers. In my headphones, I was learning that modern mathematics began in Egypt, but then in the classroom it came from an Anglo-Saxon philosopher building on the thinking of the ancient Greeks.

The school was determined to turn us into intellectuals, but because I had discovered hip-hop and a handful of rappers who followed Clarence 13X and the Five Percenters, I had an alternative curriculum, at least for a little while. I was listening to Jungle Brothers, though they were subtle about their teachings. I was listening to Lakim Shabazz, who was rapping pretty straightforwardly about the Nation of Islam on songs like "Pure Righteousness" and "Black Is Back." I was listening to the first Public Enemy album. Music, which had always been my primary teacher, was pushing me toward a greater appreciation of African civilization, and soon enough my head began to turn a bit. I wouldn't say that I was rebelling, at least not overtly, but school started to feel like someone else's mind superimposed over mine, and my grades suffered accordingly. My parents, as I have said, were fairly devout Christians at that point, and the running joke about my religious life was that I became born again the Sunday before third-quarter report card. That's when the D in chemistry was coming. There was one year, believe it or not, when I got straight Fs, which would make me the worst student in the world.

———

I had reached the end of my road with that school, and in fact with private school in general. I wanted to get back to public school. At first, my mother resisted the idea; she was protective of me, and worried that if I went back to public school I'd get torn apart, or become a drug addict, or get stabbed in the lunchroom.

What got their attention, I think, was that my lack of effort started to show up not just in classroom performance but also in music. I started talking about it less. There was less light in my eyes when

I talked about records or watched bands on TV. I started slacking off on rehearsing. Even though I was still actively drumming in my father's group and in church, I didn't seem to have the same devotion to it. They started to sense that I was losing my spark, that I was shutting down, and when I told them that I wanted to get back to music in a more focused manner, they listened.

Around that time, a plan came together. There was a local TV dance show in Philadelphia called *Dance Party USA*. It's the program that made Kelly Ripa famous: she hosted it in 1986 for her first real television job. A few years before that, when I was in high school, it was called *Dancin' on Air*, and it came on every day at 4 p.m. We all watched it religiously. It was like a local *American Bandstand*—or, more accurately, *Bandstand*, which was the name of *American Bandstand* in the early fifties when it, too, was just a local Philadelphia show.

My best friend at the time, Mark Mansaray, watched *Dancin' on Air* with me every day, and we loved the music and the sense of community. Most of all, though, we loved the girls, two in particular. He had a crush on one named Melissa, and I had a crush on one named Domeeka. Over the summer between ninth and tenth grade, we decided that we were going to write letters to our girls, and so we did. "Dear *Dancin' on Air*, my name is Mark [or Ahmir], and I'm a big fan of the show. I think that Melissa [or Domeeka] is very pretty." They were your basic fan letters, very innocent, and we certainly didn't have any thought of actually meeting these girls. At most we thought that the letter would be read on the air.

Amazingly, my girl Domeeka responded to me. She called me on the phone and we sparked up a friendship, though it never developed into anything romantic. I think she thought I was a dweeb. Mark's girl, Melissa, didn't write back, but I somehow found out that she was a student at the Philadelphia High School for the Creative and Performing Arts, or CAPA.

I went straight to Mark and told him, "Look, man, I know what I have to do. I have to go to CAPA. Melissa goes there. If I switch over there I can meet her and get the two of you together. I can hook you up in time for prom." It was like a romantic comedy plot: "Would you throw away a potential college career for your best friend's crush?" The truth, of course, was that I had found a lever that I thought I could lean on to liberate myself from City Center Academy.

My parents didn't resist the idea of CAPA, but it quickly became apparent that I had decided too late. I hatched my Mark-Melissa master plan in July, but auditions had been held all the way back in January, and my application was rejected almost as soon as I submitted it. That's when my father stepped in and played the Lee Andrews card. It wasn't the kind of thing he did very often, but when he did, it worked like a charm. I didn't even have to audition.

The first few days at CAPA redefined "culture shock" for me. I went from a small school of twenty to a school of two thousand, and the first day alone was surreal. It's like I had been transported into the movie *Fame*. Look, there's a knot of goth kids. There are some ballerinas over there in the corner. There are jazz students with their instruments out in the lunchroom.

It bore some resemblance to the school I had attended when I was a little kid, but with one important difference. Back then, I was just an observer—I went there because I was interested in music, but also because my sister attended, and as a result I existed on the edge of her social sphere. At CAPA, I was on my own, and the newness of it all washed over me like a flood. I was like a country boy in a movie about the big city, looking all around me, gaping at the tall buildings.

My mission was to find Melissa. I heard that she worked in an office on the second floor. She was a student volunteer who handled transit tokens, which seemed tremendously exotic to me. Free tokens for students? That would have been unthinkable at a private school. I asked around to find out what I needed to do to get them, and people told me to go to the second floor, ask Melissa, and pick up my two packs of free tokens.

When I saw her, I couldn't believe it. There she was, in the flesh, the girl that I had promised I'd get for Mark. Predictably, I was tongue-tied. I managed to mumble something about tokens, and she smiled and told me that I was a little early. "Just sit over there on the bench," she said, "and they'll bring them along in a few minutes."

And that's when my mission changed, though I didn't know it at the time. I was out there sitting on the bench, waiting for token delivery, when suddenly a non-teaching assistant (or NTAs, as they were known at the school) burst into the room holding a kid by the ear. The kid, the perpetrator, looked like a serious roughneck, with DMC glasses and a crazy box haircut. When my mom worried about the kinds of kids I would meet in public school, this was exactly who she had in mind. He was thugged out to within an inch of his life.

The NTA threw him down on the bench next to me, and we got to talking. "Motherfuckers," he said. "Fuck this shit. Fucking NTA jealous because he can't get no pussy." That was how I met Tariq Trotter.

Motherfucker. Fuck this and that. Fucking NTA jealous because he can't get no pussy. My eyes were as wide as saucers. "What happened?" I asked. He explained that he was in the bathroom with a girl, and that the NTA had inconvenienced him by interrupting his tryst.

I don't even remember whether I got my tokens that morning. I wandered out of there in a daze, and by lunch I realized that I wasn't the only one who was obsessed with the story. The word spread like wildfire about the freshman who was getting some from a girl in the bathroom. And not just any girl. She was super bangin', a ballerina. What were they doing? No one knew for sure, so they let their imagination do the talking. By the end of the week, Tariq had a hero's credibility. He was an overnight legend.

———————

It's probably a stretch to say that we were friends right away, but we were something to each other from the start. It was like the prince and the pauper, a sheltered Christian kid and a cool, rebellious thug. To say that I was intrigued was an understatement. My dad would have beaten my ass if that incident had happened to me, but for Tariq it was a badge of honor. He had no dad around; his father had passed away when he was two years old. Then Tariq had burned the family house to the ground. His mother had a troubled life herself, and she moved to South Philly while he was sent to live with his grandmother.

He was at CAPA because he was one of those thug creatives, a kid who kept up street appearances and projected toughness but who was also immensely gifted as a visual artist. He could draw, paint, sculpt. He could do anything. It's strange to think about now, from a distance of more than twenty years. I went to CAPA to be a musician, and that's exactly what happened. He went to CAPA to become an artist, and became a lyricist. If we hadn't started the Roots together, if he hadn't become a hip-hop star, I wonder what he would have done in the visual arts.

———————

Tariq got suspended for the incident with the girl in the bathroom, and he was gone for much of that first semester as I made my way through CAPA. When he returned, it was like one of those scenes in a movie when a guy comes back to the neighborhood after doing time. We were happy to see each other, but pretty soon we settled into our roles: I was the dweeb and he was the cool kid.

Because it was high school, much of the social capital came from fashion. My mom was a great help in this regard: she always had a hip, East Village kind of fashion sense. She would take me to thrift stores and when I would complain, she'd explain to me that the people kids idolized, the fashion trendsetters of the day, weren't doing their shopping in the mall.

My role models were musicians, and the world of rock and soul fashion was changing fast. Prince had gone through his hippie phase with *Around the World in a Day* and was starting a kind of paisley junkyard aesthetic for *Sign O the Times*, and I was emulating that as best as I could. And then there was the Time, and Morris Day's whole zoot-suit look. Under my mother's tutelage, I figured out that the cool baggy pants Morris Day was wearing could be had for three dollars at Goodwill. The same way that rap had helped me find my identity in 1979, when "Rapper's Delight" came out, fashion started to separate me from the pack. I didn't have Lee jeans, or Sergio Valente, or Jordache. I had jeans with holes in the knees, jackets accented with splashes of paint.

A few years later, the teasing would stop when De La Soul made that kind of thing popular. But the teasing started with Tariq, who dressed in Run DMC sweatsuits and whatever else was considered authorized thug fashion. It's strange to think about it now, because we've reversed: he'll think nothing of paying some crazy amount for a mohair suit, and I've gone back to casual. But that was the way our styles shook out then, and he mocked me mercilessly. He told me that I was a man out of time. He wondered if I was trying to be white.

Trying to be white? What the hell does that mean? I've never understood that. How could anyone be white when they aren't white? Seems like a simple enough thing to prove, right? Hold out your arm next to someone else's arm and do a simple swatch test. Of course, what people mean when they say that is that there's some kind of authentic black experience that the accused isn't properly expressing. But what is the authentic experience? Clothes that wannabe gangbangers wear on the street? Hood style? What's authentic about that? For that matter, is fashion even a good marker of authenticity or race, anyway? Aren't clothes a second skin you wear over your real skin to obscure who you really are? Can they also express who you really are? My mother told me that you had to go to thrift shops to find your own style, which made more sense than going to stores, but weren't both forms of borrowing where you were always aspiring to have something that was truly your own? The question marks were piling up and I wasn't even ?uestlove yet.

But Ahmir had questions, too, and the fishhook of the punctuation wasn't catching anything, and it wasn't straightening out either. I remember once, when I was a kid, hearing Johnny Winter singing "Tired of Tryin' " with Muddy Waters on guitar, on the *Nothin' but the Blues* album, and hearing him sing and liking what I heard and then looking at a picture of him on the album and double-taking, maybe triple-taking, and then wondering what it meant to be black (or white, or albino) and play black music (was it?). And was Johnny paying tribute to Muddy by recording a takeoff on "Tired of Cryin'," by Howlin' Wolf, one of Muddy's personal and professional rivals— and, while we're on the subject, one of the most authentically black voices in the history of popular music? Except that the closest artist to him vocally was Captain Beefheart, one of the whitest—if by "white" you mean the kind of fractured art rock he was practicing— except that he was playing the blues, and the blues are black, except that he was white and the blues were his, so maybe there's no color in it at all except the color you put there. The exceptions don't prove the rule. They shame it. They banish it. In one of Beefheart's songs, "Dirty Blue Gene," he explains why black and white are never black-and-white: "The shiny beast of thought / If you got ears / You gotta listen." You heard the man. You gotta listen.

Were there answers underneath the questions? Was there a light at the end of the tunnel? Maybe, but I wasn't old enough or wise enough to look for them, not then. The answers had to come to me. And right around that time, one of them did. It came to me like it came to everyone. We got Prince. More to the point: We got *Princed*. The kids of the eighties were just sitting there, minding our own business, when all of a sudden the same artist who had freaked out our parents with his unholy mix of sex and salvation on *1999* returned to action with *Purple Rain*. That record took whatever categories remained and burned them all down. He says it right at the beginning of "I Would Die 4 U": "I'm not a woman / I'm not a man / I am something that you'll never understand." (Of course, later on in the song he says "I'm not a human / I am a dove," so maybe it's not a good idea to take the lyrics at face value.) But aside from gender, he split the difference in so many other ways, too: race (people said he was half black, like the character in the movie), fashion (Was he a leather-jacketed punk? A French aristocrat with frilly cuffs? Was that eye makeup? Lipstick?), and of course, musical genres. I once read an academic paper that argued that the song structure of "When Doves Cry" is modeled on female rather than male desire, because it has a relatively flat melody rather than the surging arousal-to-climax pattern that would mark it as masculine, not to mention that it is stripped of all bass (more masculinity surrendered in the instrumentation) and that most of the tension comes from the call-and-response arrangement of the vocals. But flat notes? Bare instrumentation? Call and response? Sounds like blues to me.

But whatever it is—and I'm sure it's nothing that it's said to be, and everything, and more—that song, and that album, did more to bring together freaks and geeks and thugs than almost anything else from that decade. Tariq and I could agree on it, and we could both agree with the hulking football player who was coming up the street, headphones on his ears, Walkman in his jacket pocket. Prince was a unification treaty written on sixty-two inches of purple parchment.

? ? ?

Quest Loves Records, Part II

"When you live your life through records, the records are a record of your life."™

1980: Diana Ross, *Diana* / The Commodores, *Heroes*

I spent the entire summer of 1980 living in the Virgin Islands at a resort called Frenchman's Reef while my parents gigged nights. The *Diana* record was the only contemporary record that I heard during that period, because the owner of the nightclub where my parents were playing had it on continuously as filler music between my father's shows. It was also the first summer I earned real money for myself—I was doing lights for my father's band, working the spotlight and that kind of thing, making sixty-five dollars a show. By the end of the summer I had over $1,000, and he promised me that I could buy a bike for myself when we got back to the States. So we went to Kiddie City to get my first ten-speed Saxon bike, and next to Kiddie City there was a chain called the Listening Booth. I bought the *Diana* record there, on cassette—that was the period of phasing out LPs and eight-tracks. I also bought the Commodores record. My father loved the Commodores. He loved Lionel Richie and was doing many of his songs in his show, whether "Three Times a Lady" or "Still." Of the Commodores' platinum sellers between 1976 and 1981, *Heroes* was kind of the dud in the collection. They wanted to get closer to their gospel roots, but that meant that instead of a slow, sappy love song they had a slow, sappy gospel song, "Jesus Is Love." I liked it because of the consistency of the logo. I was always liking records for the wrong reasons.

Extended Playlist

The next-door neighbor's older brother was a DJ, the first I observed. He let me sit and watch as long as I wasn't in the way.

...Michael Jackson, "Rock with You"; Styx, "Babe"; Ambrosia, "Biggest Part of Me"; Kenny Loggins, "This Is It"; Jermaine Jackson, "Burnin' Hot"; M, "Pop Muzik"; The Rolling Stones, "Emotional Rescue"; Rupert Holmes, "Him"...

1981: The Time, *The Time* / The Jacksons, *The Jacksons Live!*

This was the beginning of a dark period of my life. My grades had taken a dive. I was getting in trouble in school and on punishment frequently. I was doing uncharacteristic things—nothing extreme, violent, or criminal—but things that simply weren't in keeping with my character. There was a kid in sixth grade whose mom allowed him to bring his boom box to the cafeteria. He had a cassette of the Time's first record, and this was the first time I heard anything coming out of Minneapolis that wasn't an early Prince single, "I Wanna Be Your Lover" or "Soft and Wet." When "After Hi School" came on the boom box, we thought it was the coolest thing ever and we were dancing to it. At the end, though, I tripped over the cord and knocked his boom box onto the ground. "You destroyed it," he said. "You owe me money." He wanted twenty dollars for it. Now, I went to performing-arts school. There was no thug element there, not really. But this kid came from the streets—he could act his ass off, but he was at heart a tough kid—and I didn't want to get in trouble with him. I had to get that money by any means necessary. I knew that my dad kept at least $4,000 hidden in the library. I figured, *I'm just going to take a twenty*. A perfect crime. I took twenty-five instead. I supposed

I would get *The Jacksons Live!* and then *Voices* by Hall and Oates and a Rick Springfield record, because there was a girl I knew who liked him. My plan failed. My dad was a meticulous counter. He even knew how many inches high the orange juice was in the jug, so he could tell when someone had drunk some. I had been disciplined with whippings throughout my life, but when he found out I had taken the money it was that and then some, a Kunta Kinte/*Django Unchained*–like whipping. That incident set the course for our relationship and how it remains today. My father and I are not particularly close. It's strained at best. And that defining moment came in the name of records. More ironically, it came in the name of a Jacksons record: If Joe hadn't given his kids all those whippings, they would have never made the record, and I would have never gotten my whipping.

Extended Playlist

I'm on my own now. Donn is with my parents in the show. This is where school and friends started to influence my tastes.

…Boz Scaggs, "Miss Sun"; Devo, "Through Being Cool"; Rick James, "Super Freak (Part II)"; The Time, "Cool/After Hi School"; Grandmaster Flash, "The Adventures of Grandmaster Flash on the Wheels of Steel"; Patti Austin, "Betcha Wouldn't Hurt Me"; The Afternoon Delights, "General Hospi-Tale"; Earth, Wind & Fire, "The Changing Times"…

1982: Prince, *1999*

I have written about the difficulty of keeping Prince records in the house, especially as my parents became more religious. What that also meant was that I got better at distracting them at key moments in songs. In "Lady Cab Driver," on *1999*, there's a Jill Jones/Prince dialogue that starts innocent and then gets sexual (and spiritual) fast.

At that time, black radio was doing live remote shows from clubs on Saturday nights—"Come party with us at Richard's on Broad Street from 9 p.m. until midnight," they'd say. "Our DJs are compensated for appearances." One Saturday, that song was on the radio, and I realized they were about to play the 90-second sex part. I needed a distraction. I didn't want to run to the radio and turn it off, shrieking the whole way. Instead, I ran to the kitchen, where there was a bowl with some salad leftovers from the night before. I sacrificed the bowl. Down it went to the floor and shattered. By the time we got back from cleaning it up, Prince was on to the guitar solo. Over the months, I developed similar tricks for distracting: lots of coughing, lots of wheezing. Once I pretended I stepped on a thumbtack.

Extended Playlist

We finally got our second urban radio station in Philadelphia, Power 99. It was all-inclusive. Donald Fagen should have named his song "What a Beautiful World." It would have been easier to find.

... The Time, "777-9311"; War, "The Jungle: Beware It's a Jungle Out There"; Donald Fagen, "I.G.Y."; Cheri, "Murphy's Law"; Chaz Jankel, "Glad to Know You"; Joe Jackson, "Steppin' Out"; Kool and the Gang, "Steppin' Out"; Grandmaster Flash & The Furious Five, "Flash to the Beat" ...

1983: The Police, *Synchronicity*

We had a drummer named Frog in our group whom my dad always saw as a screw-up. My dad didn't dig Frog because he thought he didn't have it all upstairs. He saw him reading Jimi Hendrix books, which he associated with drug culture, and I think one of the words in the title was "voodoo," which he associated with devil music. One day we were driving to a bar gig in Pennsylvania. We had two vans by this point. The family was in van one and the band was in van two. When we pulled up alongside each other, Frog was listening to "Mother." It's a strange experimental song with Andy Summers screaming his vocals. "Turn that devil shit off in front of my son," my father said. "No, it's cool," I said. "It's the Police." But my father was one of those people who, when he was wrong, was more right. "Turn it off," he said. I was twelve, so whatever he thought was a no was, in my mind, an instant yes. A few days later I ran into my best friend at school, John Cavallero. "What's that song?" I said. He played it back to me on his Walkman and I went out and bought the record the following Saturday. It was the first rock record I bought on my own, without my sister's aid.

Extended Playlist

The first time we got MTV, we were at Poconos resort. But our MTV was sort of broken—you could either listen to the music or watch the visual. I would leave it on so I wouldn't miss "Billie Jean"; that's how I discovered these songs.

...The Police, "King of Pain"; Musical Youth, "Heartbreaker"; Frida, "I Know There's Something Going On"; Newcleus, "Jam-on Revenge"; Hall & Oates, "Family Man"; The System, "You Are in My System"; Prince, "Little Red Corvette (Dance Mix)"; O'Bryan, "Soul Train's A-Comin"...

1984: Sheila E., *The Glamorous Life*

By this point, much of the music I loved was contraband in my house. But I had successfully convinced my parents that even though Sheila E. sounded the same as Prince, she had nothing to do with him. (It's good that he used pseudonyms—he was listed as the Starr Company on that one—because they inspected the credits carefully.) Plus, she was a drummer, so it fit in with their idea of my education. That was the only album from the Purple empire that I kind of flaunted. But then I fucked up, or the record let me down. There's a line from "Oliver's Party" where she says, "She got drunk and called me a bitch just 'cuz I kissed him," and that was that. Good-bye, Sheila E.

Extended Playlist

The majority of this was stuff I had to listen to in the basement, while I practiced drums. I couldn't play it outright. The Prince performance was on TV and I snuck down and recorded it off the set onto a cassette.

...Deniece Williams, "Black Butterfly"; Sheila E., "Shortberry Strawcake"; UTFO, "Roxanne Roxanne"; Prince, "I Would Die 4 U/Baby I'm a Star (Video Version/Live in DC)"; Diana Ross, "Telephone"; Jermaine Jackson, "Come to Me (One Way or Another)"; Glamour Girls feat. M.C. Craig G, "Oh! Veronica"; The Beastie Boys, "Party's Getting Rough/Beastie Groove"...

1985: Jesse Johnson, *Jesse Johnson's Revue*

Prince's development during the mid-eighties was interesting, and not always satisfying to his hardcore fans. He wanted to be a star, but when he had his big breakthrough with *1999*, it turned out that wasn't enough. He wanted to be a movie star, but when he conquered the film world with *Purple Rain*, it turned out that wasn't enough. He wanted to be a celebrated, universally loved singer-songwriter. He wanted to beat the Beatles at their own game. *Around the World in a Day* was his bid. I dug it. I loved it. I actually loved the B sides and twelve-inch singles more. But I also missed the straight, stripped-down Minneapolis funk, and that's why I gravitated toward Jesse Johnson's first record.

Extended Playlist

> I went to California to visit relatives, and that is where I heard "Batterram" by Toddy Tec. It was West Coast hip-hop, a regional hit, and when I got home no one had heard it and no one cared.

> ...Schooly D, "P.S.K."; Toddy Tee, "Batterram"; Doug E. Fresh, "The Show"; Stevie Wonder and the Huxtables, "Jammin' on the One"; Sting, "We Work the Black Seam"; The Family, "Susannah's Pajamas"; Jesse Johnson's Revue, "Can You Help Me (Extended Version)"; Fishbone, "Modern Industry"; Sheila E., "Yellow"...

1986: Janet Jackson, *Control*

At some point, my mom let me join Columbia House Record and Tape Club, which meant that I could get a dozen records for a penny, which meant that lots of questionable pop and adult contemporary started to enter the picture, from Anita Baker's *Rapture* to Debbie Gibson's *Out of the Blue*. Some of it was okay: I was actually not mad at the first record by the Jets—to this day, I will say that "Curiosity" was one of the best Prince-cut songs that he never got to write for any of his female foils. And then there's *Control*. From a creative standpoint, I preferred Prince and the Revolution's *Parade*, but I will admit that *Control* was the standard-bearer of mid-eighties funk. Jimmy Jam and Terry Lewis were fired from The Time and had gotten their revenge. And I was a Janet fan. I had her self-titled first record, which is a boogie classic, and *Dream Street*. I DJed for her three times, and she just shit when I put on "He Doesn't Know I'm Alive," which is one of the few songs from that record that didn't become a hit. I wasn't doing it to shock her or anything—I wanted to show her that she was important to me, that I remember when she sang "The Magic Is Working" on *Diff'rent Strokes*. In a way, that's the best thing about having achieved a measure of fame: I can be near the people whose work I love. I can be a superfan with the best seat in the house.

Extended Playlist

I bought songs after this and taped them off the radio. I loved songs. But it was a little different after this—high school, peer pressure, hip-hop radio. After this it was more of an apprenticeship, less innocent. So I'm going to end the extended playlists here.

... Prince and the Revolution, "Alexa De Paris"; The Beastie Boys, "Paul Revere"; Sade, "War of the Hearts"; The Jets, "Curiosity"; Oran "Juice" Jones, "The Rain"; Run-DMC, "Peter Piper"; Peter Gabriel, "This Is the Picture (Excellent Birds)"; Luther Vandross, "So Amazing"...

SIX

What's the single most influential moment in the history of hip-hop?

It's not an album release. It's not a video. It's not a concert tour. To my mind, hip-hop was changed forever by the episode of *The Cosby Show* in which Stevie Wonder's driver crashes into Denise and Theo. Why do I say that this episode changed hip-hop forever? Simple: it was the first time that 99 percent of us who went on to be hip-hop producers saw what a sampler was. Go look at the episode, you can find it on YouTube or Netflix. At one point Theo says "jammin' on the one," and before you knew it, Stevie Wonder had sampled it and inserted it into a song. It's not an exaggeration to say that this episode was the incident that truly sucked me into hip-hop production. It was the first time I saw anything like that, and I've surveyed the rest. It was the first time J Dilla saw a sampler. It was the first time Just Blaze saw a sampler. There wasn't a sense yet that it was truly revolutionary, in the critical sense, that it would explode old ideas of structure, sign, and play. At that point, it was just something cool on a sitcom, and in response to it, in awe of it, an entire generation of talented, ambitious black kids leaned forward in their chairs to the point of falling out.

And then, on the heels of that, fantasy became reality. The Casio equivalent of that keyboard, the SK-1, came out right around that time. There was a TV commercial with a clean-cut suburban kid in his bedroom, playing some kind of New Orleans jazz on his little keyboard. Suddenly, he has a brainstorm: he'll include his dog Rufus in his music. The dog barks while he presses the record button on the keyboard and then, just like that, as if by magic, the keyboard barks back. The dog is shocked and possibly impressed. "You know, Rufus," the kid says. "This could be a single." It couldn't, but still, by mid-1987 that keyboard was what every music kid wanted for Christmas. I was one of the lucky few who got what he wanted. You know that feeling when you're young, the moment when you realize what present is inside the box, and you have to make a choice between covering up your mild disappointment and covering up your insane enthusiasm? I had to cover up my insane enthusiasm. I am not sure I succeeded. If it happened now, I might be one of those kids on You-Tube shrieking and running in circles around the room until exhaustion got the better of me.

I was still drumming, mostly, but when I got that keyboard, it changed my life. In retrospect, it was mainly a conversation piece. You could record yourself saying "shit" and then play it back in every key. But that exercise was more than trivial. Much later in life, I had a friend who tried to explain Roland Barthes to me; not all of it, of course, but that one little principle about how a text is not a unified thing, but a fragmentary or divisible thing, and that the reader is the one who divides it up, arbitrarily. Reading is the act that creates the pieces. I wasn't totally sure I understood it—I'm still not sure—but it sounded like what was happening with the SK-1. You, as the listener, pick a piece of sound, a snippet of speech, or a drumbeat, and you separate that from everything around it. That's now a brick that you have in your hand, and you use it to build a new wall. It also lets you take things that were transparent, that were previously thought of as words and sounds that you look through to see other words, and make them opaque. You can take the invisible and make them visible. This was especially useful to me, because I wasn't the kind of kid who listened to the obvious parts of songs. Take Prince's *1999* (again). When I first listened to it as a kid, I fixated on songs like "Something in the Water Does Not Compute," with its crazy drum programming and dissonant chords, or "Lady Cab Driver," where the snare drum is played live but the rest is programmed. I played the record constantly, but more often than not I found myself drawn into the more experimental material over on side 2, all the while ignoring the fact that what made *1999* a cultural phenomenon was the trip of huge hits that kicked off side 1: the title track, "Little Red Corvette," "Delirious."

And I was like that long before *1999*. As a child, my parents noticed that when I listened to songs, I never focused on the obvious melody or the lead singer. I almost seemed deaf to what was out in the front of the mix. I was searching for a part of the song that was buried, a rare treasure that no one else knew about. The SK-1 was just a toy, but it was perfect for bringing with me on those kinds of expeditions.

When I figured out the SK-1, I became the man to Tariq. He had started down his path as a lyricist, though maybe that's overstating the case a bit. He wasn't exactly writing, but he had developed his reputation at the cool-kids table as a dozens player without compare. He would sit back and coolly dissect everyone else with a quick wit and deadly aim. Somehow, from talking trash with the guys and messing around with the girls, he evolved into a kind of verbal athlete. I remember one kid whose sneaker sole flapped around loosely. Tariq told the kid that his shoes were talking, and then, before you knew it, the talking-shoes insult became a rhyme. There's a clip of the Roots online where we're in an alleyway. I point at random objects and Tariq invents a rhyme on the spot. Sink, fish, bolt—whatever I give him becomes a brilliant freestyle verse. It's gotten some currency online as proof of his talent, and it was certainly a moment where he was in the zone. But for me, I don't need that as proof: I go right back to CAPA in 1988, watching Tariq dismantle kids at the lunch table, to the point where other guys wanted to fight him. I saw the power of words wielded in that way. He was amazing.

And as amazed as I was by his verbal dexterity, that's how amazed he was by my prowess with the SK-1. Before me, they would back him by tapping out a lunch-table rhythm. Then suddenly there I was with a James Brown sample, and what was a casual game a moment before became a kind of performance. So I started to passive-aggressively inch my way into the cool-kids circle. Soon, they were asking me for backing tracks. Tariq might ask me if I could do "Top Billin'" by Audio Two, and I'd run from the eighth-floor cafeteria all the way down to the basement, where the studio was, where I could drum out the beat. They wouldn't let you use the elevator, so I went down the stairs, out of breath, played the break beat from "Top Billin'," put it in the SK-1, and ran back upstairs, only to find out that Tariq had changed his mind and that now he wanted Busy Bee's "Suicide." The next day, maybe, he'd want Big Daddy Kane's "Wrath of Kane," and I'd have to run down to the studio room and get it ready. Soon enough, that was my job—and I was working in a growth industry, because Tariq was battling everyone. People started coming by with prepared rhymes and he'd take them on one by one. He mowed them down over my beats.

At the time, I didn't think we were starting anything. I thought we were just local dozens specialists. Part of the reason for that was my father already had a plan worked out for me. He wanted me to focus in orchestra class so that I could go to the Curtis Institute of Music in Philly, or even Julliard, in New York. His dream was that I'd call him from the road and tell him I was playing session drums for Luther Vandross or Anita Baker. He knew Bernard "Pretty" Purdie, the legendary session drummer who played with James Brown and Aretha Franklin and Steely Dan and hundreds of other artists, and whenever we ran into him on the road, my dad called Bernard over to tell me "how he keeps food on the table." Bernard simply said, "The two and the four."

Once again, things ascended to the next level because of a girl. Her name was Amel Larrieux, and she ended up having a Top Ten hit, "Tell Me," a bit later with her group Groove Theory. But at the time, she was just a beautiful, kind girl in high school. She was like an unattainable golden girl. One day, we were waiting in lines for tokens—much of my life seems to have happened on or near the token line—and she was talking about Prince's *Parade*. I got in on that conversation, because I was a card-carrying Prince expert, and the conversation evolved into a discussion of student groups. Suddenly I heard words coming out of my own mouth. "I got a group," I said. "Yeah. With Tariq."

"Oh?" she said. Her posture changed in a way I liked. "Are you going to do the talent show?"

I looked around and took a quick breath. "We're going to do it. Sure."

And so I was trapped.

Later that day, I ran into Tariq. Remember that at this point we had no real relationship. We knew each other well, but I was just the kid who got him samples. My mind was running full-speed, trying to figure out how I could break the news that I had lied to Amel about this group he and I supposedly had together, and I wasn't really listening. When I brought him into focus, though, I couldn't believe what I was hearing. His playful arch-nemesis at the time was a guy named Wanya Morris, and he had a singing group that was always practicing in the bathroom. Tariq was fuming. "Wanya ain't going to take [enter Jawn's name here] away from me," he said. "Let's start a group." Wanya's singing group, by the way, enjoyed some success a few years later. You may have heard of them: Boyz II Men.

So we had the beginnings of the beginnings of the idea, and then I had to flesh it out. My first trip was to the jazz kids. Other high schools are dominated by jocks, or by student government, or by cheerleaders. CAPA was dominated by jazz kids. But even within that group, there were two distinct camps. On the one hand, we had kids like Christian McBride, who played bass, and Joey DeFrancesco, who played organ and trumpet. They were traditionalists who believed that jazz had entered a fallow phase thanks to fusion and that it needed to be rescued by purer figures like Wynton Marsalis. On the other side, there were kids like Kurt Rosenwinkel, self-styled outsiders who argued that Wynton's music was retrograde, the kind of "Salt Peanuts" bebop that had no place in the world anymore, and that the future belonged to iconoclastic rock experimentalists like Frank Zappa. The two groups were Bloods and Crips, in a way, but they were united by a common hatred for hip-hop. So here I came, wading into the middle of that divide, to ask them if they would be a backing band for me and Tariq at the talent show. It wasn't an easy sell, though I could con McBride into playing a loop from "Get on the Good Foot" by James Brown without telling him that it would be a sample from a hip-hop song.

And so that was our live band for the talent show. Tariq and I played our first pre-Roots gig, as Radio Activity, on Valentine's Day of 1989. I'm not sure I saw a future in it, but I saw a present in it. And the jury's still out on whether or not it impressed my future prom date, Amel.

———

When I graduated high school in 1989, my plan for myself was essentially my father's: to go on to Julliard or to the New School for Music, to continue to learn theory and arranging, to make my way as a professional musician. But I couldn't afford it, and I settled into a kind of limbo in Philly. I was taking courses with Joe Nero, who was the head of percussion at the University of the Arts. He was keeping my chops sharp. I enrolled in a program called the Philadelphia Settlement Music School, which was one of the largest community-based continuing-education programs in the country. Other alumni of the Settlement Music School included Chubby Checker and, if you can believe it, Albert Einstein—he played the violin in chamber groups—though I obviously didn't take classes with either of those guys. (Too bad, really: I could have learned how to dance from Chubby and copied off Einstein's tests.) I was living at home and when I worked, it was for my father, who paid me about $200 per gig. I had a normal job, briefly, selling death and dismemberment insurance. It was not very much fun. But in my mind, whatever I was doing was still pointing me toward the ultimate goal of Julliard.

At the same time, I sensed there was a new culture coming together and going strong. On a family trip to California in the summer of 1990 I stood in line for what must have been six hours just to get into *The Arsenio Hall Show*. All of the celebrities I saw going in and out of the studio got my attention—I saw Sheryl Lee Ralph drive by the corner, and I saw Warren Beatty, who was a guest that night—not to mention the fact that the music they were playing, Ice Cube's *AmeriKKKa's Most Wanted* and A Tribe Called Quest's *People's Instinctive Travels and the Paths of Rhythm*, was confirmation that a new generation of hip-hop had truly been set in motion. There was a Warner Brothers representative giving out prizes to the people who were waiting in line. I got the Time's "Jerk Out" single, which was a huge surprise to me. I didn't even know that they had reunited. To this day, whenever I drive down Sunset toward Gower, I make a right turn and then two lefts rather than simply turning left into Roscoe's Chicken and Waffles heaven. My reason for taking the scenic route never makes sense to anyone I'm with, but it does to me: I'm paying tribute to Arsenio and to the show and to everything that it represented about pop culture, and black culture, and hip-hop culture, and my memories. And to "Jerk Out."

But that California trip was just a flash in the eye of that year. The rest of the time, I hung in purgatory, playing talent shows and showcases here and there, living like a normal teenager in Philadelphia. Or maybe I should say living like a normal *black* teenager, which meant that aimlessness was accompanied by a certain unique set of risks. One night, I was out driving with a few friends of mine when the police pulled us over. We were told we fit the description of someone who had committed a robbery or stolen a car, though I don't really know what kind of description that could have been: three black kids in a Hyundai blasting U2's *Joshua Tree* on their way back from Bible study? The officer actually drew a gun. I was terrified. The worst part of all was that when I saw the police in the rearview mirror, I started thinking that maybe I *had* stolen the car. I don't know what the psychological phenomenon is called, exactly, but when you encircle someone with suspicion, the idea of guilt just starts to appear within them. It was a terrible feeling and it's a terrible process, and it was another reminder that the life I was leading, while superficially uneventful, had the potential to turn against me at any moment.

———

All the while I was hoping that something was going to happen with Tariq, with the music career we so desperately wanted. During those years, Tariq's *afterschool* job was washing dishes at Pizzeria Uno. He would work until closing, from *ten until three in the morning*, and then he'd go home, grab a few hours of sleep, and try to make it back for the opening bell of school. At some point, like many young black men of his generation, he decided to explore various aspects of recreational drug culture. One day he was out on the corner with the wrong kind of guy, and one of his uncles drove by and saw him standing there. That uncle went instantly to his grandmother, who called another uncle to drive down to the corner and grab Tariq. An hour later he was packing a bag, and the next day he was on a plane to Grosse Pointe, Michigan, to live with some rich relative. He got Fresh Princed. I didn't know that he had gone to Michigan. I was minding my own business, literally, working in insurance. But I found out soon enough.

These days, I'm one of the go-to guys when someone wants something done musically in Philly, when they want a band for a big public event or a youth music program. At the time, *the* guy was Bill Jolly, who had a trademark piano-patterned scarf. He had a studio in his basement and he charged about seventy-five dollars an hour, and Tariq and I would go down there and loop beats or put down vocals. The money, for the most part, came from my insurance career—whatever I made went directly to paying for sessions. The day after Tariq's misadventure, we had a session booked, and I went over to Tariq's house and waited for him. He didn't show. Eventually his grandma looked up at me and said "Tariq's gone."

"What?" I said. "What do you mean? He went on ahead to the recording session?"

"No," she said. "Gone. He's in Detroit."

I went directly home and collapsed. I was devastated. I had been counting on my life with Tariq, even in this germinal form, to deliver me from a life of being a session musician or an insurance salesman. My father wasn't entirely sympathetic. "Serves you right," he said. "I never liked that rap stuff, anyway."

And just like that, a year went by. I continued working in insurance. I went to jazz and composition classes at Settlement. Other than that, there was nothing. Tariq and I talked every once in a while, but he wasn't exactly forthcoming about what was happening in his life, and neither was I. It might be strange for other people to hear that, but it's the way things have always been between us, and especially for him. It took our first *Rolling Stone* feature for me to really find out how his father died. He had been part of the Black Mafia, a crime organization that grew out of the Nation of Islam that was responsible for lots of the South Philly and Germantown drug trade. He was murdered when Tariq was just a baby—the same thing that would happen to Tariq's mother when we were in high school. His life, which was surrounded by crime and violence, was so fundamentally different from mine that it created a kind of attraction. We were like negative images, each of us seeing something in the other they had never seen before. I saw this kid living on the edge, dabbling in all the dangerous areas of urban life. He saw an awkward black kid with an optimistic outlook, a sheltered Christian devoted to clean living, naive about girls, not really able to participate in thug life at any level. At the same time, I saw his sensitive side and he saw that I had a hidden self-confidence and self-possession. In that sense, it was a perfect kind of sibling relationship. To my parents, though, he was a liability. Tariq loved them. He enjoyed my mom's cooking and the affection he got from them; when my mom would hug him, he would light up. But he was the first person I ever brought home who had anything remotely "street" about him. Most of my other friends were white dudes or, if they were black, other musicians. When he was gone, I missed him, but I also felt like a part of me was missing.

And then the wheel turned again. Someone in the neighborhood where he was living went after him. She was a troubled teenager, apparently, and the pressure of having extra people around was too much for her. She attacked Tariq with some kind of weapon and he came right back to Philly, where he enrolled at Germantown High School. I was two years older and well out of school by this point, but we were back in the same city again, back in the same band again, and that was enough for me.

———

In 1992, I heard about a scholarship program at the New School for Music. I went to New York to apply and audition, and Tariq came with me. On the way back on the train, we started talking to a girl. "Hey," she said. "You look like that kid from the commercial." I knew what she meant immediately; there was a Spike Lee commercial that featured a street musician named Chocolate who played buckets as percussion instruments.

The next day, Tariq and I were watching *Soul Train* and that commercial came on. We sat there, staring at the guy that the girl thought I was. And then, all of a sudden, Tariq had a moment of irrational bravery. "Hey," he said. "Why don't we just do it?" The second he spoke, the whole idea came spilling out of him. Meet me on South Street at five, he said. You bring the pots and pans, he said, and I'll bring my grandmother's chitlin' bucket, and we'll play. It was Greek Week in 1992, and we set up on Passyunk Square, and he was freestyling, and I was playing. We had a crowd right away. It was a busking trick, but a great one: we were recycling great break beats and giving the people top-notch spontaneous lyrics. You could see it in their faces—they were getting something they weren't expecting and it had value to them. That's the seed of any entertainment, and their energy energized us.

The cops eventually stopped us, but in the nicest way possible. "You can't make noise here," one of them said. "But—word to the wise—if you come back at a different time, like noon, we let street musicians play."

We thanked them, but when we counted our take for the day, we had eighty bucks, or forty each. Our goals at that time were pretty modest: we wanted to have enough cash to go down to Wawa and get a quarter pound of honey-roasted turkey, a quarter pound of pepper-jack cheese, iced tea or lemonade, and a roll. If you got that for yourself and for a girl, that was date money. Forty dollars of cash in your pocket was more than enough. You could really take a girl out.

I went back to Settlement Music School, flush with cash, thrilled with my good fortune, and ended up telling the story of our South Street score to a bass player named Josh Abrams. "That sounds dope," he said. "Are you going to try again next week? Can I join up?"

———

The next week, Josh came to pick me up in his station wagon and I walked out the front door with my buckets. "Hey," he said. He was looking at me funny. "What's up with that bucket? Why don't you bring your real drums?"

"My dad would kill me," I said.

"Is your dad home?" he asked. I shook my head. "When is he coming back?"

"Around midnight," I said.

"Well," he said. "We have to stop playing at six, right? We'll have everything back in order by the time he's back. He'll never know a thing. Get your drums."

I was a sucker for logic. We snuck out of the house and loaded my drums into Josh's station wagon. My father wouldn't have understood. He thought hip-hop was one big nothing, a bunch of nonmusical nut-grabbing. And he sure didn't think much of Tariq at the time. In a way, it was understandable. My dad was old-school to the extreme. He had undergone this extended education in the business, learning to clean his suede and to cut light gels and to adjust monitors and to count his cash before the show. As far as he was concerned, he had spent years busting his ass so that I could go to a private music school and then a private Christian academy. He was getting me the best education that he could so that I could go on to become Bernard

Purdie, not so that I could stand on stage while my punk friend said, "Bitch, suck my dick."

With the drums loaded in Josh's station wagon, off we went to South Street. We were beginning to be something. Over the next few months, a group coalesced around us, people who would come and watch us all the time and sometimes even participate. For example, there was a kid named Kenyatta, a classmate of Tariq's from Germantown High we called Crumbs. He wasn't a great MC, but he had youthful energy, and he was a regular, and we took him on. We were inspired by the Native Tongues collective and their idea of a broader identity that hangs over all the individual acts and unites them. By the fifth week out there, we even had a name for that overarching umbrella, too: the Foreign Objects. It was mostly playacting, I guess, the idea of thinking of a band name and a name for the group that united all the acts in your orbit, but it also kept the idea real, and that's what we needed more than anything. If the idea was real, then there was the chance that the thing inside the idea would one day become real.

Around that time, we met Joe Simmons, who went by the name AJ Shine. Joe was our hero, Philadelphia's Stretch Armstrong and Bobbito García all rolled into one. He had a local college radio show called "The Avenue" on WKDU that we listened to religiously, because it was one of the only places in Philly that you could hear rap music.

Joe came to one of our shows, and then a few weeks later he came back and brought his partner, a guy named Richard Nichols. I already knew Rich, although I didn't know that I knew him. When we would finish our South Street sets, which went from noon to five, we sort through our money and find that we had acquired a half-dozen business cards offering us more gigs. Sometimes it was a young woman wanting us to play her poetry slam; sometimes it was an African-American group wanting us to come over to UPenn. Sometimes it was a big keg-ger at Drexel. So we spun our afternoon South Street sets into nighttime shows, and when those shows ended—or, in the case of the Drexel keg-gers, when the cops busted them up—we would drive over to Wawa for turkey and pepper-jack cheese, and then drive around at night lis-tening to the radio. What was on then was a super-experimental, super outré jazz show called "Jazz 90." The DJ was this guy who would play the craziest shit imaginable—a half-hour improvisation by Rahsaan Roland Kirk, the most outlandish Sun Ra space jazz, violent spurts of saxophone. But I didn't know the DJ in person at all, so when Joe Sim-mons came to our show with his partner, Rich, I had no idea that I was meeting the guy from "Jazz 90." I had even less idea that I was meeting the guy from my future.

SEVEN

From: Ben Greenman [cowriter]
To: Ben Greenberg [editor]
Re: Refining the approach

No. I wouldn't necessarily say that the book is coming into
better focus, though I would say that my excitement over
the nature of the blurriness is increasing.

But yeah, to answer your question, Rich and Ahmir do
play off each other well, but they also play on each other.
Sometimes it seems like Rich is a voice in Ahmir's head,
a correction or an echo, and sometimes it's the other way
around. Sometimes they remember the same event in
exactly the same way, and sometimes their accounts are
pretty divergent. It's intellectual and cultural isometrics,
creating strength by pitting one set of muscles against
another. At one point the other day, Rich mentioned
something about how he used to go into his older brother's
room and listen to Stevie Wonder records on his brother's
stereo. But with Rich, because of the way he's wired, the
conversation immediately took a turn into the nature of art

in memory and memory in art. He went on to say that he listened to those same records in different circumstances over the years—maybe in the car driving, or on the tour bus with the Roots—and that the second and third and fourth occurrences didn't reinforce those original feelings and emotions so much as they eroded them. He was going a mile a minute, like he does, but at one point a silence swelled the line and Rich said, "As you get older, feelings are harder to come by." It was so simple and poignant.

That stark reflection on memory, by the way, came in the middle of one of those triathlete-level phone calls that always surprise me because they start the way that any other phone call starts. I dial the previously agreed upon number at the previously agreed upon time. He answers. I say hi. He says hi. But then, before you know it, there's an epic disquisition that winds through hip-hop, unemployment, unskilled labor, youth culture, regional identity, market research, post-structuralist theory, documentaries on industry, and the history of political subversion in Russia in the late nineteenth century. I was scared to look at the clock because I was sure that the hands had fallen off. Then, the very next day, with that conversation still ringing in my ears, Rich sent a quick, compact email in which he let me know that Ahmir was skeptical of the book becoming too straightforward a memoir, but that he (Rich) also thought he (Ahmir) would come to terms with it eventually because "I" (Rich) told him that "you" (me) were building in dialogues that would situate the more memoiristic material in a broader context. The day after that he (Rich) wrote to say that he (Rich) wondered if his dialogues with him (Ahmir) were yielding diminishing returns, and that he (Rich) had another idea for how to enter his (Ahmir's) line of vision. Not for nothing, that email also contained jokes about and/or allusions to Quentin Tarantino, Jean-François Lyotard, Ishmael Reed, Henry Ford, and the Petrashevsky Circle.

EIGHT

S o what happened with "Jazz 90"?

Well the station was WRTI. It was Temple University's
public Radio Station, which had an all-jazz format. Its
location on the dial was 90.I so sometimes peeps called it
The Point (deep huh?) or simply Jazz 90. My show didn't
have a handle. It just sort of was: it was an avant-leaning,
stream-of-consciousness, Jazz tradition-ing, sleight-of-hand
thing. The music director at that time was Steve Rowland,
a tall, affable, intellectual Jewish guy who people would
consistently mistake as a light-skinned black dude. Three
slots had just opened and he recruited me, the visual artist
Homer Jackson, and Ludwig Van Tricht. (Believe it or not,
Ludwig was a nigga. His pop was from Suriname and Ludwig
looked like Alexandre Dumas or maybe like a black Count
of Monte Cristo or some shit, but he was a real dude and
fellow admirer of the jazz avant-garde). Homer was still in
art school, sported a ragged, deconstructed afro, and could
often be found going off the top about Gabby Marquez or the
Marquis de Sade or Foucault or Fanon or the like. There was
also Miyoshi Smith, who, while not an on-the-air person, was

every bit a member of our collective (maybe more so than us even). So that was my inside-outside crew. Our mission: to rage against the machinations of conventional wisdom and culture. Ironically, conventional wisdom/culture raged against us. I quit the station in 1990 (the crew's last man out/ dead man walking). This dude from the Midwest took over and showed us how they got down in Missouri. He had everything programmed by computer and he told me that I had to follow the computer. "I'm not gonna do that," I said, which he seemed to take well for a little while, but then he started telling me that I had to vary my show. Mine was a real DJ-driven show. If I wanted to play only Cecil Taylor from 12:00 to 12:28 on a Sunday, I would. He wanted me to do more programming, and I remember he had one question for me, which was, "If you have to play Mel Torme in some specific time slot, would you play it?" My answer was no. I'm not going to fucking play it ever. I'll play Lambert, Hendricks and Ross as a one-off, but that's about as far as I'm going to fucking go. What's the point in being here if you have to follow a computer? What is this, a fucking Turing test in reverse?

So you left.

I left. And pretty soon I started hanging out with Joe Simmons, who was over at WKDU. (Jazz had seen its better days and now hip-hop was all grown up and shit.) One night, Joe went to a talent show at Prince's Lounge. He came back and told me that there was something interesting there: a drummer, an upright bass player, and a guy rapping. The guy on the bass played the *Inspector Gadget* theme. He was excited by them, and the way he talked about them piqued my interest.

A month later he invited me to come along with him to a local spot called The Chestnut Cabaret to see these "wunderkinds." So we went, but the affectless black "electric" bassist who was there was clearly not the inspired white "acoustic" guy Joe had described. The vocalist was spitting some rappering shit, railing against Kriss Kross of all fucking groups. I remember the chorus was "don't jump, don't jump, don't jump" (geez). If the shit wasn't so absurd I would have simply been disappointed. As it stood... I was mildly amused.

We came backstage, I remember.

To explain to me and to Joe that the bassist wasn't your regular guy, that he was off at college and would be back on break in October. On the way home, I asked Joe, "Uh, are you sure these guys are cool?" He was sure, and I decided that we might as well record a song. I had a relationship with the studio. If the Squares sucked I would have simply wasted a hundred and fifty bucks. So then the three of you came to the studio in the suburbs in Bensalem. There were two songs, "Anti-Circle" and "Pass the Popcorn," along with a "Pass the Popcorn" remix. It wasn't rocket science. We recorded it and added a keyboard overdub. And I remember thinking to myself, "These motherfuckers are all right." It was different, not quite there but nonetheless approaching inspired. And we went the next day and mixed it.

And then Tariq asked you to manage us?

Nah, that was months and months later, but I do remember him asking me some point-blank shit. I was driving him home after the mix and, like it was directed to no one in particular,

he said, "I heard about you. You've worked with a bunch
of rappers." I didn't bother to respond, it felt like a setup.
Then he blurted out, "We're the best damn group you ever
worked with, aren't we?" At first, I was a little thrown off by
his blatant hubris, but after I thought about it for a couple of
seconds, I said yeah. "You guys are the best, but at best that's
a dubious distinction." Things evolved from there, and there
were shows and shows that begot other shows that begot
other shows. I liked the early recordings a lot but the peeps
that I let hear the shit were fairly dismissive and the whole
"dubious distinction" thing seemed firmly in effect. The show,
on other hand, was frenetic, a revisionist yet progressive
affair. At once homage and karaoke, it had this proto-hip-hop-
revue thing that was consistently working. Even the patrons
who initially looked askance at the band ended the set as
part of the nod factor. And what was success, anyway? In
many ways, I was still using the jazz avant-garde model as
an approach to financial success on the fringe. As a younger
man I used to help out with concerts in the Philly area. My
job, among other things, was to drive to New York and pick
up the artists. I remember going to get Lester Bowie. He lived
in a nice place. His floors were shellacked. They had African
sculpture. His wife had a minivan. I would see Lester playing
at the Empty Foxhole and there would be maybe thirty people
in there smoking reefer, and somehow he managed to get
enough money to keep a wife and a minivan. That was my
entire sense of things at that point. I never thought the Roots
would really get on the radio, at least not then (and now not
ever). Industry types thought the Roots brand to be some
unstructured freestyle-based shit. All heart on empty sleeves.
It didn't matter to me, really (well, maybe it really did). I still

dug it because I knew there was something there (even if that something was an afterthought).

So you knew that we were—

You know what? I've said too much.

About what?

About my own life. If you don't want this to be a straightforward account of your life, I'm sure as fuck that no one wants it to be any kind of account of mine.

So you're just going to leave the book?

No. I'll keep going, but I'm tired of being here, in bold type, like this. It's too straightforward when I want to be coming from the blind spot. It's too flat-footed when I want to be arch.

NINE

What were we before we were the Roots? Lots of things. For our very first gig, at the high-school talent show, we were Radio Activity, but that name had a short life— or a short half-life, as the case may be. (That will be the first and last radioactivity joke in this book.) After that, we went into seclusion briefly and reemerged as Black to the Future. Then directly back into seclusion, and then back into the light as Square Roots. Each of the names came from Tariq. He would just show up to practice or to South Street and announce that we weren't who we were anymore. Each of the names had something to do with the hip-hop that was dominant at the time. Radio Activity reflected his two Queensbridge idols, Big Daddy Kane and Kool G Rap, because G Rap had said were "radio-activated" once. Black to the Future came around in 1989, at the height of *Do the Right Thing*–influenced Afrocentricity. And then we settled into the Native Tongues groove, which is where we probably most belonged from the start, with Square Roots. It sounded nerdy, which (let's be honest) was clearly what we were at the time. I felt that was an accurate portrait of us. It fit.

The way we arrived at our name was representative of how we operated generally at that time, from the outside in, trying to find a package that made sense. Much of our time and trouble was spent figuring out what kind of act we were. I knew I wanted a record deal, but I wasn't sure that I wanted that record deal to center on our live act. I knew that we'd almost immediately be compared to A Tribe Called Quest, because we had the same sensibility, give or take, and I wanted to make sure that we distinguished ourselves.

To get a clear sense of who we were at that time, it's important to look at who we weren't: in other words, to shine a light on the Philly music scene of the early nineties. It was more than a little strange, a bit of a crazy quilt. The biggest phenomenon at that time—and they had such popularity in Philadelphia that it's not inaccurate to say that they rose to local Beatles status—was Boyz II Men. Tariq and I knew the guys from the group, Wanya and Nathan Morris, Shawn Stockman, and Michael McCary. They had been our classmates at CAPA, and in fact I'm in their very first video, for "Motown Philly," which was a Top Five hit in January of 1991. I have a prominent solo shot wearing a T-shirt so distinctive that Tariq liked to insist that I wore it just so people would notice. It worked, and then some. People would say, "I know that shirt from somewhere... Oh, my God. It's you." Boyz II Men went so big so fast that even being a minor figure in that video made me recognizable.[1]

Beyond them, the Philly scene was eclectic, to say the least. DJ Jazzy Jeff and the Fresh Prince had released "Parents Just Don't Understand" back in 1988, and then Will Smith went off to television to do *The Fresh Prince of Bel-Air* in the fall of 1990. By the time they had their biggest hit, "Summertime," in 1991, it didn't even seem

---

1. Ahmir, do you fully remember what videos were like back then? People were losing their damn minds over the fact that all of a sudden there were black videos on TV. It's not that there weren't black TV stars or actors at that time, but you just didn't see black people in a more-or-less natural element. I remember how, once, a girl in the neighborhood who was friends with my then-wife came into the house and there was a video with black people playing on TV. She fell to the floor and started crying. It had that kind of impact.

like Philadelphia music any more, not really. It was Hollywood music born of Philadelphia. Then there was Schoolly D, who many people believe to be the first gangster rapper; he had released some classic music, like *Saturday Night! The Album* in 1987, that had the sparse beats, the obnoxious comedy. The Beastie Boys owe their first three years to him. There was Three Times Dope, a great early hip-hop group led by EST, whose real name was Rob Walker. He had the best rap voice and was the standard of straight hip-hop in the city. Then there were MCs like Steady B and Cool C. They imitated Philadelphia drug dealers and they did it very convincingly—the two of them tried to rob a bank in 1996, and Cool C shot and killed a police officer. He's on death row, and Steady B is serving a life sentence.

So that was the world we were trying to break into, and to our eyes it all seemed kind of provincial. We were looking outward, to De La Soul and the Jungle Brothers and A Tribe Called Quest, who were New York bands but, more importantly, Native Tongues bands. We brought that into Philadelphia, which meant that we dressed up in khakis from Banana Republic and presented a certain style. People looked at us like we were from another planet. And it wasn't just the pants. When I braided my hair in the summer of 1990, it was more radical than anything you could have imagined, even more so than a giant Afro. It was out of step with the times, not accepted as nostalgia or cultural outreach or forward thinking, and I had to suffer lots of teasing. Philadelphia was a small big city, which meant that the scene was close-knit and loyal, but also not very culturally progressive. Every step forward was followed not by a step back, exactly, but by a suspicion that the step forward was somehow going to leave the city behind.

———

Around that time, I went to work as an intern at Ruffhouse Records. Two local guys, Chris Schwartz and Joe Nicolo, had founded

In 1971, Philadelphia, with my best gal.

I was six months old when this picture was taken in our house on Osage Avenue. The Sears photographer actually made house calls back then.

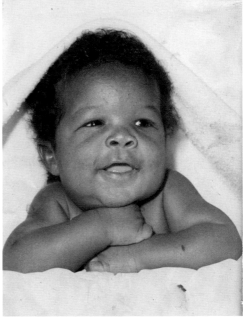

My sister and I in the New York studio where I would spend most of 1974 and meet Bernard Purdie, who consistently hammered home the fact that I had to keep it "on the two and four."

Playing on the floor at my Grandmother's Compton, California, house. This is where I stayed when my parents were recording their *Congress Alley* album in 1972.

Three years old, standing with the man who taught me everything about the music business—Lee Andrews, my father.

In my backyard in West Philadelphia. I was four years old here.

Sitting on my favorite item in the world—my father's "Don't You *Dare* Touch My" stereo.

Before luxury tour buses, most bands either traveled in broken-down Greyhounds or ancient school buses. Here I am with my father's band in Richmond, Virginia. That's my mom, Jacqueline, sitting at the far right, with my aunt Karen next to her. My sister Donn is to the right of me. It should be noted that this is the period when I picked up my habit of wearing my favorite band's iron-on logo on my T-shirts. If you squint, you might be able to see that I was in my Average White Band phase.

My parents would do season-long residencies at different resorts and casinos. The entire summer of '76 we were in Miami. I still can't swim.

Me at age five in Muncie, Indiana. It's Saturday, October 16, 1976. The reason why I know this is because the "Emotions/Rimshots/Ritchie Family" episode of *Soul Train* was playing in the background.

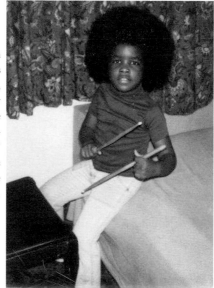

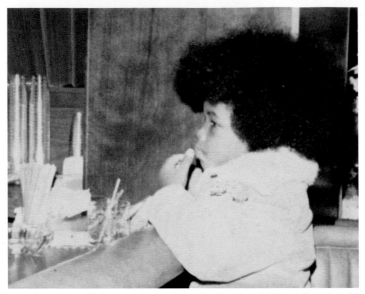

This photo is notable because this is when I developed my habit... of learning the family trade. This particular Valley Forge Sheraton hotel is where, at the tender age of six, I would learn to iron suits, cut light gels, and operate my father's light and sound system. So after a hard day's work, I was allowed to relax and have a drink at the bar (don't worry, it's a Shirley Temple).

I rebelled against wearing a suit and tie knowing that some thirty-five years later, when writing my memoir, it would be way more impressive to have taken this photo wearing a Bee-Gees T-shirt rather than the suit and tie.

This is all a ruse. Inside of that black floor tom to my left lies all the Purple contraband that I was not allowed to listen to in my then-Christian household.

The Internet has already seen my senior prom photo with Amel Larrieux. Ever the completist, I give thee my junior prom photo. For some reason, I can't find a picture with my date, but I swear that she existed.

My senior graduation photo. My shirt is made of cardboard. No seriously, my shirt is literally made of cardboard. And believe it or not, my senior quote that went along with this photo was: "Yeaaaaaaaaaaaaaaaaaaaaaahboy-eeeeeeeeeeeeeeeeeeeee!"

This was our first year as the Square Roots, with Joshua Abrams on bass (toward the top left), Kid Crumbs as the sidekick (sitting on the right in the hat and vest), me on drums, and Tariq on the mic. For every performance, we'd buy twenty large bags of popcorn and throw them at the audience. Club owners in Philly were not amused. *Credit: Mpoži Tolbert*

Ruffhouse back in 1989 as a joint venture with Columbia Records, and immediately the label started to churn out hits and top artists. Kriss Kross was their biggest signing at the time, two little Georgia kids who were discovered by Jermaine Dupri at a mall, earned a spot on Michael Jackson's *Dangerous* tour, and went to Ruffhouse, where they released the *Totally Krossed Out* album. It was preceded, slightly, by the single "Jump," which came out in February 1992.

Philadelphia has its own Hall of Fame, which is like a miniature version of the Hollywood Walk of Fame: notable figures in music, movies, literature, and so forth in the concrete. That year, my father was inducted, and at the ceremony, I met a woman who worked at Ruffhouse. I was starting to take steps to move out of insurance and get more involved in music. I had shifted my hours at the company from a daytime, ten-to-five schedule, to a nighttime one, and I planned to use the days for music. I explained that all to the woman from Ruffhouse, and she told me that they needed an intern. "You can start tomorrow," she said.

When I got to Ruffhouse, I made a point not to tell them what my true aspirations were. I didn't want to be known there as an aspiring hip-hop star or a drummer or even a musician of any kind. I was there to learn the business. And what the business involved, I soon found out, was lots of street-level energy. This was before Sound-Scan, before the whole record business became computerized and predictable and—some would say—lifeless. We would call mom-and-pop record stores across the country and ask them if they needed more posters, more cassettes, more CDs. And then we'd tell them how to answer the question we were asking. It seems so quaint now, but I would actually have to call up these stores—say, Funk-O-Mart Emporium on 13th Street—and finesse the numbers. "Look," we'd say, "when *Billboard* calls you to find out how the record is doing, we need you to tell them that you did thirty-five pieces of product."

"Well," the store manager would say, "I only did fifteen pieces."

"That may be," we'd say, "but we need you to report thirty-five."

Then there would be a pause. Thinking was happening. "Well," the manager would say, "that's fine, but if that's what I'm going to tell *Billboard*, I'm going to need two tickets to the Johnny Gill concert." It was the lowest level of payola, wheeling and dealing to try to give these indie records a chance. Those few months at Ruffhouse taught me how the old record business worked. You had to barter and pay for your position, develop relationships, shake hands, kiss babies.

Ruffhouse also stripped away another layer of my naivete. There was an artist then who was well known in the Northeast. I can't be any more specific than that. But the man was a star. He projected an image of family values, wife, kids, pillar of the community, that kind of thing. One of my first days at Ruffhouse, someone told me to go into the supply closet and get a stack of Kriss Kross posters. I went in and found the posters and then, right next to them, this famous artist fucking a girl who was definitely not his wife. I don't know if they saw me. I took the posters and left quickly and quietly.

———

One day, one of Tariq's rhyming buddies, Malik B, met a prominent jazz bassist at his mosque. This bass player, Jamaaladeen Tacuma, told Malik that he was looking for a rap group to take to Germany for some kind of rap-jazz thing. Malik offered us up right away: "I'm down with the Square Roots," he said, as if Jamaaladeen Tacuma knew who we were. But he trusted Malik, and he told him to feel us out to see if we would be interested.

But who were we, exactly, at that point? At the beginning of the summer of 1992, the Square Roots consisted of me; Tariq; Josh, the bass player; and Kenyatta, the other rapper. But then the stresses of a fledgling music career started to take their toll. As September approached, Josh's parents became adamant about him going back to school to continue his education. Kenyatta, who was becoming more involved in his Muslim faith, began to have a problem with the way that hip-hop was evolving, specifically in terms of the racial makeup of the audience. He started to feel like we weren't black enough as artists, or that hip-hop was being distorted and distended by its broader acceptance among white kids, and he left, too. It's hard now to recreate the strangeness of that moment. *The Source* magazine reamed Cypress Hill's "Insane in the Brain" for appealing to white kids. De La Soul stifled their hippie side so that they could appeal to black kids. The idea of doing a show and seeing more white kids than black kids in the audience was a crazy mindfuck, and it was happening more and more.[2]

We had a catalog, so to speak, the few songs that we managed to get down on tape with Rich and Joe that first night of recording: "Pass the Popcorn," "The Anti-Circle," and "Popcorn Revisited." Joe had thought that he would be the producer of the actual record and that Rich would handle management, but as it turned out, Rich was a very good engineer. He was the king of vocal takes, which is something that I'm horrible at, and he was excellent at mixing, which I didn't know how to do yet. I didn't know much, to be honest. I sat behind the drum set unaware that I was supposed to do anything other than

---

2. When I went to jazz shows, especially avant-garde jazz shows, there were never really any black people in attendance. Hip-hop venues varied. In the earliest stages of hip-hop, the shit was almost novelty music. But then the downtown art scene granted it credibility, and that meant a changing audience. By the time you had records selling two million copies, you had white people listening—there just wasn't any other way to account for those sales. I remember being somewhere painting someone's house and there were some white kids listening to Public Enemy's *Fear of a Black Planet*. It didn't seem that strange. There was a connection between them and Anthrax for a reason. The noise felt post-punk and metal-ish. It tapped into an adolescent discontent that was universal.

tune the drums or tape them. I didn't even use a click track. We just performed like we did on the streets of Philadelphia, and luckily it sounded awesome on the recording.

But we still only had three songs when Malik got us that gig with Jamaaladeen Tacuma, and it didn't seem like we were in a position to get many more. For starters, we were down to only two permanent group members—Tariq and I. We quickly picked up a replacement for Josh in the person of Leonard Hubbard, whom we called Hub. Hub was a trained musician who gave us a strong foundation with his bass playing. He was also a little older, and he had in experience what we had in enthusiasm. Malik officially came on board as a second rapper. And then, because of the fascination that we all had with "4 Better or 4 Worse" by the Pharcyde, we became obsessed with the idea of putting a Fender Rhodes piano in our songs. That was the sound we wanted. When we said that, Rich told us that he knew just the guy. There was this lanky white kid named Scott Storch who used to hang out at Rich's place. He was a walking karaoke machine, and we were all fascinated with his keyboard skills the same way that Tariq had been fascinated with my drum skills in high school. Scott knew every Stevie Wonder lick, every Bernie Worrell part, everything Junie Morrison did with the Ohio Players. It was a trip to see my record collection come alive inside this guy's fingers.

In this new configuration—me, Tariq, Malik, Hub, and Scott— we started playing around town. We opened for the Goats, who were an overtly political group signed to Ruffhouse. Their debut, *Tricks of the Shade*, was a sprawling, ambitious record that had lots of promise, but they soon faded out when groups with a clearer political agenda, particularly Rage Against the Machine, came onto the scene.

And we went back into the recording studio. Rich had this brainstorm that we needed to build a buzz. He said that we would use the trip to Germany to sell our debut record and become the kings of

America. We thought he was crazy. We didn't have a hit. We didn't have a song on the radio. We didn't even have a full album. But he led us back in, Pied Piper–style, and after four marathon nights in the studio we had eighteen songs. We made finished work of everything we had jammed on during the summer. We mastered the record, made a simple text-treatment cover that was very similar to the Beatles' *White Album*, called it *Organix* (we wanted to emphasize that we were playing real instruments), and just like that, we were legitimate recording artists. At that point, we made the final evolution in our name. It wasn't completely voluntary: There was a folk group in Philadelphia called the Square Roots, and even though they hadn't copyrighted their name—it was an expensive proposition—they went a cheaper route and registered it as a fictional character for use in a theatrical artwork. Whatever the case, they blocked us, and we dropped the "Square" off the front of our name. Sometimes less is more: Silver Beatles to Beatles, Square Roots to Roots.

It was a stroke of luck. Names are a big deal for bands. They aren't just something to fill the line on the poster over the band you're opening for, or a way to take up space on an album cover. They're an attempt to make sense of something that's often so chaotic and dynamic that it's hard to capture, let alone label. But "The Roots" was tight and streamlined where "the Square Roots" had been blocky and felt unwieldy. "The Roots" made us look cool, whereas "the Square Roots" had made us look, uh, square. Most importantly, it created the impression that we were musical conservators, that we respected the past and kept a stubborn hold on the funk and soul that had come before us.

———

And so, off we went to Germany to play the jazz-rap festival with Jamaaladeen Tacuma. If we had been more experienced, we would have traveled small, but we traveled large: it was me and Tariq, Malik and Hub, Scott, Rich, and Joe, but that was just the beginning. We took along a rapper named Shortie No Mas, a client of Rich's who was associated with De La Soul and was scheduled to release a record that year. We took along a kid named Lord Aaqil, who had just put out a twelve-inch of his own called "Check It Out." And, most importantly, we took along a woman named Miyoshi, a friend from Rich's jazz radio days who had a credit card and was, as a result, our life preserver. We lived off of Miyoshi's credit card for that entire trip.

The trip seems like centuries ago. This was back when you could still smoke on a transatlantic flight, and I remember watching people light up nervously in the smoking section. I watched my first Bollywood film on the screen set into the seat in front of me. When we got there, the show was big—a stadium show where we were on the same bill as the Last Poets, and for some reason we were the headliners. I don't think it reflected our fame, or even Rich's idea of our coming fame. I just think that there was some worldwide cachet at that point to being an American rap group. If you were from the States, and you were a hip-hop act, you were important. We did the show and came back out for one encore, and then a second, and then a third.[3] We sold our *Organix* CD backstage and throughout the festival. Then we came home for the beginning of the label wars.

---

3. It's not a mystery why the crowd stood up. Imagine listening to a bunch of abstract music or old-ass fucking boppers and then a band comes in with youthful energy. Plus, Scott didn't know how to do a solo, so he would just string together thirty fucking pop songs, which at least gave them melodies they knew. The people there had probably been at that festival for a number of days and here you come playing actual pop music. It's like Stanley Crouch said when he turned his back on the avant-garde: People say they like that shit, but nobody gets off their feet until they play 4/4.

The Native Tongues bands were the first wave of hip-hop, at least from our perspective: albums like De La Soul's *3 Feet High and Rising*, Tribe's *The Low End Theory*, and the Jungle Brothers' *Done by the Forces of Nature* set a standard for what we wanted to do, and how it could be done. The second wave started in 1992, with Arrested Development and the release of the "Tennessee" single. I had a strange reaction to the song. I wondered if it was really rap. There were samples, but the cadence of the vocals was more like singing than like MCing. I decided, at the time, that they may or may not have been a rap group, but that they were definitely the hippest R&B group around. In fact, I looked at Arrested Development, I'm afraid, the way that people now sometimes look at us, like they were the gay cousin at a Bible Belt family reunion—kinda like "deal with you at arm's length" conditional love back then. The hip-hop journalist Harry Allen later wrote something about us that feeds right back into that question: "Are they simply R&B's hardest group or hip-hop's softest?" Arrested Development was followed closely on their heels by Digable Planets, who put out "Rebirth of Slick (Cool Like Dat)" in 1993; I got a test pressing of it the day we recorded "Pass the Popcorn." In my mind, and possibly in hip-hop history, we were the third group of that second wave.

Well, we were about to be. We weren't signed yet, but Rich's plan was starting to happen. During high school, whenever I invented band names, record titles, album art, I always put my group on Def Jam Recordings, because they had a mystique about them. They had signed only six acts, including Slick Rick, LL Cool J, and Public Enemy, and they stood pat on that original set. Breaking in at Def Jam was like climbing the mountain.

And just like that, they were the first label to come calling. Russell Simmons and Lyor Cohen, who ran the label, paid for a Roots showcase in New York City. It was across the street from their old offices on Varick Street, and we went to New York in style: Flintstones style. With the "profits" from Organix, Rich bought a station wagon for *three hundred bucks*. It was great—except for the fact that the backseat had no floor. You had to lift your legs up so they didn't hit the pavement rushing by beneath. He put a rug down for cosmetics and safety. Even with the rug, I couldn't sit there. I was too big. But we all packed in, three people in front, four of the skinniest in the center, and the rest of us Middle Passaging it in the back, lying across the top of our equipment.

I wish I could be there for every band's label audition. I wish I could serve as a kind of fairy godperson. What I'd tell them is that all those tricks you're thinking about using, all the razzle-dazzle—set it aside. Leave your innovations at the door. All a label wants are songs they can sell. Our calling card at the time was a kind of freestyle exercise where Tariq would scat to different topics, and that was a showstopper. And Def Jam loved our musicianship and our vision and our energy. Still, they passed. As much as they loved the idea of us, they said, they didn't know how they were going to market that idea.

In a sense, we fell into a crack in the history of hip-hop. Had the showcase occurred in 1991, or early in 1992, we would have been signed instantly. But something had happened in the interim that changed the face of hip-hop, and that was the release of Dr. Dre's album *The Chronic* in December 1992—and, more to the point, the way that *The Chronic* dominated hip-hop sales and radio play and video play through 1993. *The Chronic* gave a credible artist a taste of massive, multiplatinum success. And while I have nothing bad to say about the Young MCs, Tone Lōcs, and MC Hammers of the world, Dr. Dre had an obvious cultural pedigree as a pioneering gangsta rapper and top-flight producer. None of that changed the fact that I felt as mixed about *The Chronic* as I had about Arrested Development. I was as freethinking as the next man, but I liked my hip-hop a certain way, and this was obviously different. I treat important hip-hop events like they're *War of the Worlds*, and there have been many times when I have stood there open-mouthed before a turntable or a CD player, asking myself if I can be trusted to believe what I have just heard. Usually, if I have to ask, those albums end up being masterpieces, but at the time I never know how to feel. That was definitely the case with *The Chronic*. That album sounded so clean and pristine, so anti-hip-hop. I just wasn't sure if anyone was allowed to *do* that or not. I was so conflicted. And add to that the fact that I had a strange connection to the record: My father, my mother, and my aunt had recorded an album under the name Congress Alley in 1973, and there was a song on that record called "Are You Looking?" that was sampled in *The Chronic*'s first single, "Nuthin' but a 'G' Thang."

Within about six months, I had come around, and I recognized the genius of the record. But it caused a problem for me as an artist, or at least as a potential label signing. Because *The Chronic* had so much success, labels were focused on getting comparable acts, credible artists who could also sell huge numbers of records. We weren't that act, and Def Jam recognized that, and when they passed, that dream vanished.

Then the parade started. We had dealings with Tommy Boy, the home of De La Soul and Digital Underground; with East/West, home of Das EFX and Snow. Ruffhouse, ironically, never gave us an offer—though even if they had, I probably would have passed. I felt like I knew them too well, and I didn't want to stay in the neighborhood, so to speak.

Then Mercury Records surfaced. One of their flagship hip-hop bands was Black Sheep, a Queens group that was the unofficial fourth member of Native Tongues. They were the first hip-hop artists to appear on *The Tonight Show* with Jay Leno after Johnny Carson gave up his host chair, and their debut album, *A Wolf in Sheep's Clothing*, remains a classic. (The opening track, "U Mean I'm Not," is a parody of gangsta rap in which one of the Black Sheep rappers, Dres, narrates a killing spree only to wake up and realize that it was all a fantasy.) We met Ed Eckstine, the label president (and son of legendary jazz vocalist Billy Eckstein) who was very interested in us. We met the man who would be our A&R guy, Kenyatta Bell. Yes, another Kenyatta. He seemed extremely excited, too. They took us to the video shoot of "Jingle Jangle," by the Legion, which featured a verse by Dres. We left the Mercury meeting with a strong sense that we had found a home.

The following week, they sent contracts down, and somehow all of our names were misspelled: mine and Tariq's and Malik's. I don't know the technicalities of what contracts require, but I was told that had there been one mistake, we could have just initialed it and corrected it. With three, though, we had to return the documents to the label and wait for them to supply new contracts. It was on a Friday, and Kenyatta's assistant didn't turn the paperwork around quickly enough. Then that Saturday, Brad Rubens, our lawyer, called, and asked us what we thought about Geffen. Wendy Goldstein, the woman who signed Snow to East/West, had just left for a head position at Geffen, and she was still interested in us.

We laughed. We were virtually on Mercury, the deal as good as done. But we knew this might be our last chance to be courted by a label, and so we entertained them by letting them entertain us. Wendy took us to dinner, which meant steak and lobster and friends tagging along and ordering extra food to go. We really took advantage. Then Rich and I had a radical idea. Ever since Michael Jackson's *Bad* came out in August of 1987, I had been obsessively reading *Billboard*, and in early 1992 I read about this alternative metal band named Helmet that had released a single and an album independently and then attracted the attention of Interscope Records. They got caught up in the grunge craze, and it was rumored that when Interscope signed them, each member of the band got more than $1 million.

"Rich," I said, "why don't we pull a Helmet?"

"What?" he said. "What do you mean?"

"You know," I said. "We should ask Geffen for huge money and studio equipment and whatever else. If Wendy says no, we just go to Mercury."

"It's never going to happen," he said.

I conceded. Never going to happen, never going to happen, never going to happen. And then the call came in. It happened. Geffen wanted in. They were prepared to give us everything we asked for. I had thought the parade was over, but it was still going.[4] It was

---

4. I don't know what parade you were at, holmes, but that float was a bier. Triumphantly returning from Germany's Moers Festival, niggas saw nothing but halcyon days ahead. What we got instead was straight Sturm und Drang. As the fanfare of Dusseldorf faded, all that remained was this troupe of unemployed negroes with heightened expectations (too heightened) and a black cover demo in CD format. I had worked with a bunch of rap acts before (remember) and now I was beginning to experience a dreadful déjà vu. You know: the loop of the also-ran, the point where a young artist's expectations outpace their youthful enthusiasm and a manager's finances. During the summer of 1993 *Organix* was, at best, a pictureless curio floating around the bottom of industry A&R bins. It may have made sense to sell at a European jazz festival, but back in the United States it got lost in translation. It was swag deficient, lacking the grit of sample, microchip, and identifiable urban narrative that, to this day, define the genre. It was who you guys were and everything you weren't and so there were no takers, just diminuendo in freefall. Then, a little interest from Bill Stephany's smallish imprint, and even though he passed one of his reps told Kenyatta, who was the Mercury A&R head, about this demo "which was actually on CD" (novel right?). Bell got my number and called about a potential licensing deal. I feigned disinterest, telling him that we were looking for an actual deal and not trying to just put our demo out. He led with $40K, stall tactics got him to $80K, and word spread to East West's Merlin Bob. Then Epic called and Kenyatta arranged a showcase for Ed Eckstein. You niggas brought your hunger game that night. I knew it was in the bag when half way through the performance I saw Ed mouth "sign them" to Kenyatta. The next day they had me come to the office to work out the details. Lisa Cortes, the VP or A&R, started at $160,000 and ended at $200,000, which was the biggest deal for a Philly rap outfit...ever. Crescendo: we had arrived...or so I thought. But then

November 1993, and all of a sudden Mercury was gone, and we were signed to DGC, a subsidiary of Geffen that was better known for alternative-rock acts like Sonic Youth, Weezer, and Beck.

---

came Geffen. Based on the success of Arrested Development the year before, Geffen chairman Eddie Rosenblatt hired Wendy Goldstein away from Elecktra for the express purpose of signing a rap act "that played their own instruments and didn't talk about guns." Fran Spiro, from Rush Management, told Wendy she had just the group for her but that "they were in the midst of a bidding war" and she would "have to go big or go home." When I got a call from our lawyer Brad Rubens about Geffen's interest it seemed more than a bit odd. With literally zero niggas on their artist roster, it was a label Daniel F. Malan could be proud of, but yet they beckoned. For the most part, we granted this eleventh-hour look on a lark. I told them to bring Wendy to our rehearsal studio for a run of show. She was scheduled to come through one Saturday in October but was running late. Tariq had to leave and then everyone else did, too, and I could see that she was thrown off when I told her that the band was gone and had no plans of returning. I was sure that the Geffen thought experiment was dead as soon as "no plans of returning" rolled off my tongue, but Wendy regrouped and said she would come back the next day. The next day you guys were in rare form. Midway through, I remember thinking to myself, *Yeah, these are the best motherfuckers I've ever worked with*. Wendy was wowed as well. She asked what would it take to get the deal done, and we gave her our go big number. She got back to us some days later with some game-changing shit. Not only had she got Geffen up to our number, but she dropped another $50,000 on top. We were ecstatic but humbled—it was like niggas were actually waiting for Lena Horne to pop up and sing "Believe in Yourself." There was one downside (at least for me): I was going to have to give the what's up to Lisa Cortes at Mercury. When I got there, she was all big-momma smiling and welcome-to-your-new-home-ing, and then I hit her with the bad-news bear. She looked stunned. She told me it was a mistake. She was a second away from saying "David Geffen doesn't like black people." Instead, she poignantly asked, "Are they going to take racial sensitivity classes?" I got stuck for a bit, I really did know what she meant—there was a sense of an apartheid roster thing popping over there—and I had mixed feelings about turning my back on the Mercury guys, all of whom were black. But, with visions of *Nevermind* in my head, I thought those thoughts, told her I appreciated where she was coming from, and left. Okay back to the floats.

We entered Geffen's orbit at a strange time in their history, and in fact a strange time in the history of rock and roll. The label was able to give us a gargantuan deal because they were flush with cash from a trio of rock acts: Aerosmith, Guns N' Roses, and Nirvana. Those three bands were selling tens of millions of copies every time they released an album, and as a result Geffen could throw money at us without even thinking about it.

We were their guinea pigs. We knew it. They knew it. At least they had the decency to be straightforward about it. They set us up as a semiautonomous unit, without a real A&R person attached to us, and we were one of the last groups to get one of those old-style development deals where a label invests in and brings a group along without paying too much attention to the numbers. Geffen told us that they would put out our first record but urged us not to worry too much about sales, because they would release a second, and a third, and a fourth. "Stay diligent," they told us. "Stay the course. By the fourth record, you guys are going to be monstrous, and by the sixth record, you'll be household names. Look at the Stones." That's what they always said. "The Stones?" I said. I tried to keep the disbelief out of my voice. I told them that seemed like a strange example to me in a world where most rap groups disappear after three records, tops. They shook their heads. "Stop thinking like that," they said. "You guys are beyond that. The only reason why you guys should not make a twentieth record is if you yourself sabotage your progress."

In a way, it made sense. I knew plenty of top-notch rap groups, from De La Soul to Group Home, that were making records for relatively cheap, and I think that Geffen thought we could do the same thing, deliver them a great album at an affordable price. But I never felt like a tax write-off. I was slightly concerned with the fact that the label didn't really have a dedicated urban staff, but even that turned out to have a silver lining, because the people who ended up staffing the urban division borrowed from other labels, moonlight labor. So maybe it would be a street team that had experience at Def Jam and a guy from Loud/RCA who would help radio outreach. They were experienced in the genre and very enthusiastic about us and what they thought we might become. (In the wake of signing us, Geffen did start to acquire other hip-hop acts. GZA's *Liquid Swords*, one of the defining documents of the first wave of the Wu-Tang Clan, was released on Geffen just a short while after our debut.)

The Roots were ready to go into the studio, but the Roots were changing again, bringing in new personnel. During the period where we were flirting with Mercury and marrying Geffen, we forged a good relationship with Bobbito Garcia, the writer and DJ who hosted *The Stretch Armstrong and Bobbito Show* on WKCR in New York. Bobbito let us know about an open mic event called Lyricist Lounge in New York. Rich and Joe went up there a few times; I think I may have joined them once or twice. A little after that, to make some money on the side, Hub and I joined up with a gospel tour; he had a friend who was a gospel singer who was barnstorming the country, and we were invited along to be their rhythm section. It wasn't enjoyable. We spent three weeks packing eight people and their gear into a fifteen-passenger van, hoping for the best; some nights getting small crowds, some nights getting none at all. The only real highlight of that period, from October through November of 1993, was the *Sons of Soul* album by Tony! Toni! Toné!, which is either the last real R&B record ever made or the first R&B record of the new era. I listened to that record constantly, especially "If I Had No Loot" and "Anniversary."

Meanwhile, the other half of the band—Tariq and Joe—were going to Lyricist Lounge. We'd speak to Rich nightly, and he would fill me in on the things that they were discovering. One night the call came in. I said hello.

"Yo," Rich said. "I found a secret weapon."

Rich and I have always talked this way, always thought in terms of how a band needs something to elevate it above other the fray. The secret weapon was often something we called a Stupid Human Trick, borrowing the idea from David Letterman. We knew that some people came to see us because Tariq was a virtuoso rhymer, and those people liked rhymes but might have been uncertain about the musicians onstage. And we knew that some people came to see us because Hub and I were virtuoso musicians, and some people liked the music but weren't sure about the whole hip-hop angle. But what was the wildcard for the rest of the people, the ones who were afflicted with cultural ADD? The Stupid Human Trick was something that would draw them in, an indisputably entertaining novelty. In this case, it was Rahzel, the great beatboxer. I had immense respect for beatboxing. At CAPA, I had performed the lunchroom version, but to hear Rich tell it, Rahzel took it to a theatrical level that none of us could imagine. Rich realized the appeal immediately. When the gospel tour ended—abruptly, and joyously, as the result of our signing our first record contract—we snatched Rahzel for the band.

Other changes were in store, too. Around that time I took on my new name. Tariq was already Black Thought, but I had something else in mind, a kind of Malcolm X meets Lamont Cranston move, and in those very first years I just used a question mark for my name. It's the ultimate form of ego gratification, anonymity. I wanted it to be a form of mystery, but then people started thinking that was my name, the question mark. On *Do You Want More?!!!??!* I ended up being credited as "B.R.O. the R.? (Beat Recycler of the Rhythm)," which is possibly the most unwieldy hip-hop name in history. That couldn't stand: I mean that literally, it couldn't stand under its own weight. And so I went to ?uestlove. I think the *Q*—or the absent *Q*, depending on your spelling, though I'm fine with either ?uest or Quest—had something to do with Q-Tip and A Tribe Called Quest. (Most of the things that we did were done in the shadow of the Native Tongues.) The rest was a mix of substance and style. I was questioning, I was on a quest, I was looking for approval, I was questioning my need for approval. All of that was tied up in the name. It was a calculated decision but also an arbitrary one, something that seemed fully invented but also something that was the result of a long evolution. I think that's the case with many hip-hop names: they're a combination of nicknames, self-mythologizing self-portraits, and cool artifacts. You need something that looks good in the liner notes.

Not too long after that, I was talking to someone about names and Philadelphia, about how I got mine and everyone else got theirs, and he told me that Philly was, for many years, the home to the man with the longest proper name in America. He was a German immigrant who had settled in Philadelphia named Hubert Blaine Wolfeschlegelsteinhausenbergerdorff, Sr.—or at least that was the short version of his name. His full name ran to something like seven hundred and fifty letters. He became a local celebrity in the late thirties, I think, because he kept getting into trouble with insurance companies and utilities and the voter registration office; they couldn't get his name right, and he kept insisting that they had to. It was his name. He was in the *Guinness Book of World Records* as the record-holder for longest name until they discontinued the category. I respected his choice, but I was happier with mine.

? ? ?

Quest Loves Records, Part III

"When you live your life through records, the records are a record of your life."™

1987: Prince, *Sign O the Times*

This was the most perfect year of music in my adult life. All the stars aligned. Hip-hop was in bloom and so were soul music and eighties funk. I had heard the title song when it was released as a single, and that created incredible anticipation. But black radio was very different then. They played album cuts. I remember when I first heard "Housequake," which was the last time that Prince made my world stop. I was doing the laundry at a local Laundromat, and when the song came on, with that needle-off-the-record sound and Prince's Camille voice saying "Shut up, already...damn!," I just freaked out. I went right home to get my hands on a cassette player so I could tape it. No, I didn't go home. I ran home, two long-ass city blocks, weaving in and out of people like "Flight of the Bumblebee" was playing behind me: *Hi, Miss Johnson, hi Miss Jones, can't stop now!* I made it home right in time to hear Prince say, "A groove this funky is on the run."

1988: Public Enemy, *It Takes a Nation of Millions to Hold Us Back*

I had my first real job in high school working at Big Al's, a fifties-themed restaurant where I made fries and milk shakes. I remember this cassette came out the second Tuesday in May, and I got it before I went to work. On my way there, I noticed that I was walking differently. My stroll was instantly and completely transformed. It was like John Travolta in *Saturday Night Fever*, with the Bee Gees playing in the background. Lord Jesus, it was powerful! By the time I got to work, I was up to "Caught, Can We Get a Witness?" and although I wasn't allowed to have my Walkman on when I cooked fries, I kept sneaking to the freezer to hear "Show 'em Whatcha Got." It filled my head. It enlarged me. And then there was a point where I couldn't take it anymore: not the album, but everything else. "I'm going on lunch break," I said. I bought eight Duracell batteries at a drugstore and went to the park and sat there listening to the album over and over again. I never formally quit, but I knew I was never going back. I couldn't tell my father, though, so every day the rest of the summer I got dressed and left like I was going to work and walked around and listened to music instead.

1989: The Beastie Boys, *Paul's Boutique*

I was going to pass on this record. I had heard *Licensed to Ill*. Who hadn't? But like the rest of fickle hip-hop America, I just knew that their fifteen minutes had run out. When I found out that the Dust Brothers, who had a hand in Young MC's "Bust a Move," were helming the project, I thought this would be at best a mediocre record. Then, the week after I graduated high school, I went to Cherry Hill Mall in New Jersey with my dad. Part of my graduation gift was a leather jacket—in the summer, of course, when it was cheaper. Next to that leather jacket store was a Waldenbooks, and I went to get the new *Rolling Stone*. Axl Rose was on the cover. I flipped to the Recordings section and saw the lead illustration: a three-headed figure on a skateboard. I read the review without looking at the rating, and the album David Handelman described actually sounded decent.

Then I checked the rating. *Four* stars? That seemed impossible. What were the chances of a novelty rap act being taken seriously by *Rolling Stone*? I bought three copies of the magazine and then I hightailed it and got the record. That got me through the rest of 1989. For starters, Tim Burton's *Batman* came out that summer, too, and the soundtrack was the first time that a Prince album had left me underwhelmed. I liked "The Future" and "Batdance," but I wasn't sure about the rest of it, and I had to come to terms with the fact that he wasn't going to provide the soundtrack for my year. A guy I worked with, Greg, told me the secret of *Paul's Boutique*—that the Beasties were sampling all this seventies music—and I realized that this was the remaining 30 percent of my father's record collection, the part that I never listened to. I remember having the Beatles' *Abbey Road* and the Eagles' *One of These Nights* and *Hotel California* in the house. I didn't take them so seriously. I didn't think I had to, especially since earlier hip-hop masterpieces, like *It Takes a Nation of Millions to Hold Us Back*, leaned more heavily on the soul and funk and jazz that my mother and Aunt Karen collected. But here was an album making art of my dad's soft rock and yacht rock and my sister's mainstream junior high school soft rock albums. That's when I realized I wanted to make records.

1990: Ice Cube, *AmeriKKKa's Most Wanted*

When I was young, we would often travel to Los Angeles as a family. At first we went via Trailways: three full days on the bus. After our first trip, in 1983, my legs were swollen for the entire trip and I spent half the time not being able to walk because I couldn't fit into my shoes. By 1990, we had graduated to the train, which was awesome. I loved the train. Somewhere along the way, there was a stop, and we had two hours to get off the train and walk around. There happened to be a record shop inside the station, and I bought the cassette of *AmeriKKKa's Most Wanted*. I hadn't been with Ice Cube from the very start. At first I wasn't sure about N.W.A. Their Jheri curls and Eight Ball jackets seemed kind of corny, especially since I had already found my flag-bearing fashion and philosophy heroes in De La Soul, who were the antithesis of N.W.A. It wasn't until Tariq made me listen to "Fuck the Police" that I realized how good they were. Ice Cube's first solo album upped the ante even more. It was like watching a movie with no screen; the lyrics were just incredible. Plus, here was a West Coast rapper with the premier East Coast production team, the Bomb Squad: still, to my mind, the most important summit meeting in hip-hop history. The title track is my favorite Bomb Squad moment ever, if only for how they used Funky George's hi-hat from Kool and the Gang's "Let the Music Take Your Mind." For starters, they sampled a solo. James Brown would give the drummer some as long as he didn't take a solo; this proved the error in that approach. And then they sampled this Bernard Purdie–style solo with the hi-hat! The intensity of that song is hard to believe. It's the most violent hi-hat I have ever heard. I have tried so many times to make that sound, and it's impossible.

1991: De La Soul, *De La Soul Is Dead*

I cut church to hear this in my boy Jason Brown's mother's car. We did Sunday school in the morning and then, after a break, started up real church again. For some reason I didn't have to drum that week, so I went outside to my friend's car. This was in February, and the real record wouldn't come out until May, but a bootleg was circulating. Out there in the car, listening, I believed that I was hearing the most perfectly sequenced album in history. It represented everything I loved about hip-hop and far exceeded my expectations. The only thing I can compare that moment to is the first time I heard Public Enemy's *It Takes a Nation*. Every song knocked me out, one by one: "Pease Porridge," "Let, Let Me In," "Ring Ring Ring (Ha Ha Hey)"... Sitting there at one twenty in the afternoon in a maroon Chrysler, I told myself that I had to cherish that magical moment, because there was no guarantee that I would never again know what it felt like to hear that for the first time. I begged my friend to make a copy. "No," he said. "I promised I wouldn't." I remember calling Tariq and telling him that the record was going to change his life. "No way," he said. "This can't be as good as *3 Feet High and Rising*." But it was. To me, that's the greatest year in hip-hop history. There are other candidates: 1988, 1994, 1998. But I vote for this year. Every other record was changing your life.

1992: The Pharcyde, *Bizarre Ride II the Pharcyde*

This was the year I really started to make music, so I started to listen a little differently. At that point it wasn't like other acts were competition, of course, but I was in the race. That Pharcyde album was a highly unexpected sucker punch. It was one of the greatest surprises I have ever had as a music consumer. I didn't like "Ya Mama," the single that came out before the album. But A.J. Shine, our comanager, who was a DJ at Drexel, told me that maybe I should reconsider my position. And I did, tremendously. The record just knocked me flat, especially "4 Better or 4 Worse." Back in the seventies, Parliament had animated commercials for their records, and on the one for *Motor Booty Affair*, there was a kind of watery effect that happened to the picture when the Fender Rhodes was playing. When I heard the tremolo effect on "4 Better or 4 Worse," that's when I knew that we needed a Fender Rhodes. That's kind of how Scott Storch got into the group. We wanted that sound, that possibility. Later on, when we made *The Tipping Point*, I tried to pay tribute. It wasn't easy: that was Tariq's record, more or less, and the feeling within the group was that you didn't meddle too much in records when the pendulum swung away from you. And so I tried to make "Star," the first cut on the record, as straight ahead as I could. But it was begging for my patented flip at the end, and that's when I decided to pay tribute to "4 Better or 4 Worse."

1993: A Tribe Called Quest, *Midnight Marauders* / Wu-Tang Clan, *Enter the Wu-Tang (36 Chambers)*

Classic hip-hop is a sentence. And if the beginning of the sentence is me purchasing Eric B. and Rakim's *Paid in Full* at Crazy Eddie's in 1987, then these two records are the end of the sentence. A year before them, Dr. Dre's *The Chronic* had changed everything. It had forced credible artists to consider commerce, which was then taken to an even higher altitude when Puffy and Biggie made *Ready to Die*. And something changed when commerce arrived. Good and bad stopped mattering; only effective and ineffective mattered. Whether a record worked on an audience became the standard, rather than whether or not it was any good. I consider these two albums the last pure, unadulterated moments in the genre. That's not to say that hip-hop hasn't offered anything of substance since, of course. There have been plenty of classic records. But these two were the end of innocence, and they came at such a great moment. Hub and I were freezing in that fifteen-passenger van with a gospel group that we didn't particularly like. Our minds were back in Philly and New York, wondering if we were going to ink a record deal or not. We had spent the greater part of 1993 chasing this record deal, which looked increasingly like a carrot on a stick. We did crazy amounts of auditions and showcases. People thought we were cute but they realized at the end of the day that they couldn't sell us. And that's how we found ourselves with that gospel band, in Oberlin, Kansas, staying in the basement of a pastor's house. Everyone was going stir-crazy. It was the whitest part of white America. The gospel guys would sneak out into the fields and smoke weed, the way that terrorists go out into the forest on *Homeland*. When we got word that the record deal was coming through, we just quit. We left them high and dry, no drummer, no bass player. I talked to Tariq on the phone, and he told me that the second I got off the plane I had to go to Tower and buy *Midnight Marauders* and *Enter the Wu-Tang*. I didn't make it to the store, but when the band picked me up in the van the next day to drive to New York and sign our record contract, they had both cassettes. It was the greatest day ever. We were just absolutely there—it was the last time we had that pure, old style hip-hop energy, the last time we were totally engaged. We had rewind moments trying to figure out whether it was a snare of a gunshot when RZA yells, "Don't do that shit!" We debated every song, analyzed every lyric. We picked through those things like they were academic texts.

TEN

Where were you when Kurt Cobain killed himself? I was a Nirvana fan from the time they broke out. I understood them, and not just because of the hits. I was a fan of their work and of the critical writing that surrounded them. I knew that Kurt Cobain was a significant songwriter and singer and that the group was turning things around on a big scale for the entire rock and roll genre, which had started to stagnate with the arena rock of the late eighties. But I never expected his death to affect me directly the way it did.

In April of 1994, my father had his second heart attack, and I was sticking close to home, helping my family work through it as he recuperated. It was a Tuesday night, I think, and I was sleeping in my father's bed, watching MTV on cable. I dozed off, and resurfaced to hear the announcer saying that Kurt Cobain was dead, that he had killed himself, shot himself in the head. I was stunned. I called Rich. "Did you hear?" I said.

"Terrible," he said. "Terrible for him, terrible for his fans, and terrible for us."

"For us?" I said. "Why?"

"We're fucked," he said. "Geffen's going to drop us."

"Slow down," I said. "I don't understand."

"All of their talent has dried up," he said. "Aerosmith went back to Sony. And you and I both know there's no new Guns 'N Roses album coming." GNR had released *Use Your Illusion* in 1991, which was a two-part album with two separate releases, and it was huge, and then they had put out *The Spaghetti Incident?*, an under-whelming collection of punk and hard-rock covers, in 1993. They seemed like they were coming apart at the seams with infighting, though no one at the time knew quite how apart they were com-ing. (The proper follow-up to *Use Your Illusion*, *Chinese Democracy*, wouldn't come out for another fifteen years, and that was with a com-pletely different lineup.) And then this had happened, with Cobain. The money machine priming the pump at Geffen had suddenly, vio-lently, vanished.

"You know what we're going to have to do?" Rich said. "We're going to have to pull another *Organix*."

"What do you mean?" I asked, but I knew what he meant.

We spent four days holed up in the studio finishing the record, shooting the cover photos, making a video. We needed to get our money from the label, because Rich had an idea of what we should do with it.

The way the Mercury contract had happened, or almost happened, we had gone pretty far in the process, and we had met lots of people who we imagined we would like working with. One of the most cru-cial sources of support within the Mercury family was a man named Gilles Peterson, a Swiss record collector and DJ. He was the man who got the ball rolling with the label in the first place. In fact, he was so in love with *Organix* that he took our CD and pressed it on wax, which was unheard of then, and used that private pressing to DJ the record in the clubs.

We had such a great relationship with Gilles that we hated to let it go when we switched over to Geffen. As it turns out, we didn't have to. He begged Wendy Goldstein to let him release an EP of our material. Even though we had spurned the American branch of Mercury, Geffen allowed Gilles to license a seven-song EP, *From the Ground Up*, and release it on his own label, Talking Loud, in Europe. It had "Mellow My Man," "Distortion to Static," and a number of other songs that were on *Do You Want More?!!!??!*

And so, in the wake of Kurt Cobain's suicide, with our record done, we took our cash, told everyone they'd see us at the end of June, and got ready to go to England.[5] Just like before, Rich had the idea that if we established ourselves elsewhere, we could return to the states triumphantly: hail the conquering heroes and so forth.

We had two last bits of business to conduct, one right after the other. We went on *Yo! MTV Raps* to host with Ed Lover and Dr. Dre, and then we went down to Washington, D.C. to do a show called *Rap City*—they wanted us to film it then for a later airdate. While we were in D.C., we were invited to pay tribute to Grandmaster Flash at an awards show sponsored by an organization called IAAAM, the International Association of African American Music. There were two honorees that night, Grandmaster Flash and Stevie Wonder, and after the ceremony Stevie invited us to come back to his hotel suite. It had a piano in it, of course, and he sat down and started to play. It was a very surreal moment. Natalie Cole was there with her husband André Fischer, who had been the drummer of the soul group Rufus and was an idol of mine. Recall that he is also the nephew of Clare

---

5. Let's not mince words: by the time we got to the end of making that record, we were broke. The record deal money was gone. The label gave us a rental car, and we were supposed to return it after a week but we kept that shit for four months. By the time we gave it back there had been blizzards and there was salt all over it, not to mention a dent from hitting a pole. We used to ask Geffen for free records. We would fill up duffel bags and take them back and sell them in Philly just to stay above water. We were selling-CDs-from-a-duffel-bag broke.

Fischer, the legendary string arranger who worked with hundreds of artists, including Prince—he was responsible for the string arrangements on the *Parade* record, for example. I talked about him earlier when I was going on about the Rufus album. Well, I was starstruck, and I'm sure André was eating it up. He wasn't the focal point of Rufus, but to me he was the most important player in the group. And he was telling some crazy story about being on the road with Chaka Khan and having to read her instructions about feminine hygiene products. It blew my mind. I was with André Fischer, who was sitting in front of his wife, Natalie Cole, telling a story about Chaka Khan and tampons. That happened. Oh, and the whole time, there's Stevie Wonder sitting in the background, playing the best songs in his catalog.

I have since learned that it's a tricky thing to meet your idols, and even trickier when the thing you want from them is the thing that they do in public but, for whatever reason, can't or won't do in private. If you met Michael Jackson and asked him to moonwalk in front of you, you'd be disappointed. If you meet Prince and you want him to do a kickass guitar solo in front of you, well, that's not going to happen. Most comedians I have met are quiet and depressed, the furthest thing imaginable from their stage personas. Stevie Wonder is the exception to this rule. He knows that you want him to sit down at the piano and launch into a brain-expanding version of "Ribbon in the Sky," and that's exactly what he does. It definitely has an effect on the ladies, too, but even if it's partly about women, if Stevie Wonder's deciding to sing his songs to help him pull women, I'm glad I'm in earshot. That was a rare, magical moment in my life.

———

We thought *From the Ground Up*, the EP Gilles Peterson was putting out, would be a staging effort for *Do You Want More?!!!??!*

We thought we'd have something in London: opportunity, money, something. We had nothing. We were staying in flophouses and then sometimes we were literally homeless, eating cheese and bread. Steve Coleman and Greg Osby used to tell me that when they went to play in Europe, they wouldn't even book hotels, that they just played their asses off and hoped they went home with a girl that night. We tried that existence for a little while. Then this acid-jazz group called Galliano saved us. They asked us to do a remix. We went from the brink of extinction to a loft in Queen's Crescent over a fish-and-chip shop.[6] It had a rusty stereo on the floor and all we did was listen to Method Man's *Tical* and Pete Rock and CL Smooth's *Main Ingredient*. If I hear those albums now, that's what I think of: the cheap fish and chips from downstairs, or drying my clothes by turning the oven on and putting my underwear in there, or our sexy-ass next-door neighbor who wouldn't give us none, or me walking through Trafalgar Square seeing Take That posters, or hanging with DJ Dego and hearing him invent drum and bass. He played "Sweet Love" by Anita Baker— who the hell plays that? But then it exploded into the drum and bass, and there were black kids moshing. I had never seen that.

London was fun, in a sense. We flipped a coin to see who slept on the bed and who slept on the floor. I explored the city as much as I wanted. Prince had just opened up a shop in Camden, and I went there as often as I could. But underneath the sense of adventure, it was kind of a dark time. For starters, Tariq and I had our very first real fight. It was a fistfight over a production faux pas. As it turned out, he was

---

6. We were in the fucking hotel on a credit card, and the manager didn't have the technology to check it to see if it was at its credit limit, which it was. Everyone pretended that everything was fine. We rode that no-good card as long as we could, and that shit ran out just as Galliano appeared. I don't know what we would have done otherwise.

not credited for producing the title cut, "Do You Want More?!!!??!" It was neglect on my part and Rich's part, just an oversight, nothing intentional, but he took it personally. He felt like maybe he was being squeezed out of the group. He confronted me and we went at it in the hallway, shoulder to shoulder. No one got hurt, really. It devolved into wrestling pretty fast. He got up and marched off in what looked like triumph.

"I'm not hurt," he said.

I didn't know until later that he went off down the hall and then snuck around a door so he could sit down on a chair and recover. I'd like to say that the wounds from that fight healed up right away, but the fact is that that was a fight so dark and so deep that I believe it affects us to this day. There's still an invisible wedge. That fight made me more insular and introverted, more careful around everyone.

London was also the first time that I remember dealing with Malik's impending drug problem. I guess it had been around for years, but I hadn't noticed. Back in Philly, he used to sell oils. Black men from Philly always had Muslim oils on them. Even now, people tell me that I smell like maple syrup. My father used to buy his oils from Malik, and one day he realized that Malik was cutting his product with baby oil, and that's when he figured out that there might be drugs somewhere in the picture. London was when I realized that Malik's behavior was more than just recreational, that he had a real problem. I'm not surprised that it took me that long to find out. I was naive about drugs, in part because my father put the fear of God in me. When I was five, there was a brand of cigarette called Belairs. The pack had clouds on it and I thought they looked nice. I told him I wanted to smoke, and his reaction was simple. If you said you wanted to smoke, you had to smoke, even if you were five years old. He made me smoke fourteen cigarettes. It was one of his most evil punishments.

Our time in London wasn't all dissension. In putting ourselves into temporary exile, we also gave ourselves the opportunity to see ourselves more clearly. Sometimes that led to fights, but just as often it led to important realizations. That stay in London was also the period where we met the first in a long line of female tour managers for the Roots. Someone had a theory that we needed female energy to offset the male-dominated personnel in the group, and as it turned out, whoever said that was right. Having a woman in that role ensured that more got done. Partly it was because we paid attention to her, and partly it was because the difference between a male tour manager and a sultry female tour manager might be half-off rates. Suddenly, we were using more honey than vinegar. Club owners would be like putty in their hands. We learned that lesson and it stuck for a long time: our first male tour manager didn't appear until almost twenty years later.

In general, though, that time wasn't traumatic. It was romantic. I still hang with starving artists now, friends in bands that aren't getting off the ground, or that aren't getting them where they want to go. I have talked people out of leaving behind their careers as artists or musicians, and in one or two cases I have even done my best to help talk people out of killing themselves—they were *that* frustrated and depressed with the game. It's a problem with the fundamental mentality of rap, maybe. Rap has a strong mentality of getting paid. And so if you have that romantic approach, the dedication to it as an art form, you preach the opposite. But is that naive? Imagine if there was a *Legend of Bagger Vance*–type figure who came to me when I was in London and told me that I wouldn't see my first big check—I mean a real big check, a check that could make me feel secure and safe—until I was twenty years into the industry. I don't know what I would have done. Back then, in London, I didn't know enough yet to be truly frustrated. It was all new. Later on, though, when lean times returned, a sense of panic surfaced, and in those times I didn't always react well. We were succeeding, or appeared to be succeeding, and I felt nothing but failure because my electricity got turned off or I had to go, hat in hand, to a friend to borrow some money. Whenever I would feel reckless, whenever I threatened to quit the band, Rich just told me to stay the course. He told me I was overthinking it. As it turns out he was right. Or was it just that he was wrong for a long time and then he stopped being wrong?

———

There are spiritual experiences that aren't necessarily religious experiences, even if they take place in a church. I know because I had a moment like that in London, and it changed my life forever. Early in our stay there, I fell in love with a South African girl. We spent lots of time together right off the bat, but after a little while, she was called away by the election in her home country. I was hurt, but what could you do? She felt it was her duty to go home and participate in the historic vote to end apartheid, and it was hard to make the case that hanging out with me the rest of the summer was more important. Before she left, she made me promise that I would go see a South African DJ named Aba Shanti. He performed at a place called House of Roots, which was a club that had previously been a church. The name seemed like a nice coincidence, maybe part of a divine plan, and so the whole band went to see him. I went with special interest, not just because of the girl but because I had been a DJ of one kind or another since I was eleven years old. But that one night changed everything I knew about DJing. Up to that moment, it was mainly about being a human iPod: you served up the best songs to people that they could imagine, and some that they couldn't imagine. After seeing Aba Shanti, I realized that a DJ could not only have a personality but *be* a personality, and that he could be a person with power over the emotions of others. He made me see that it was a psychological and even sacred responsibility, all in one night.

We went to the House of Roots and Aba Shanti was up at the pulpit, but with his back facing toward the audience. He was facing the cross, flanked by absolutely huge speakers. Unlike almost any other DJ I had ever seen, he only used one turntable, and though that seemed like a limitation at first, it turned out to be the greatest thing about him, because it was so integral to his sense of theater and control. When he finished one record, the suspense of what he was going to play next was almost too much to bear.

But Aba Shanti's greatest contribution to my life, and to my band, and to my music, was the way he handled sound. He did this trick before he played records where he went to the control board and turned everything way down: he took all the lows off, all the low mids off, all the highs off. Then he'd pick up the microphone with his right hand and extended his left arm. The closer the microphone got to his mouth the more the audience was screaming. His voice echoed deeply, and he sounded like a younger Lee "Scratch" Perry as he went through the basic roots reggae callouts, Jah Rastafari and so on. Then he'd reached down with his left arm into his box of 45s. It was a simple thing, bending his arm to pick up a record, but it drove the crowd wild. Think Michael Jackson: that's the level of showmanship he had. He picked a record, put the B side onto the turntable, cleaned the needle, and then let it drop onto the vinyl. Because of the way he had set the board, all you heard was the upper end, a tinny, ear-piercing version of the record clustered around the highs. The B-side was usually the instrumental version of the song, and he'd halt it midway, turn up the high mids and then the low mids, and finish playing it that way. Then he took the record off and flipped it. Now the A side, the real song, was ready to go, and that meant that he was ready for the payoff moment, which was when his arm went to the bass. He turned that up and boom: the bottom dropped into the room, and everyone was physically jolted. I had never experienced anything like it.

And I wasn't the only one. The next day I was talking to Rich, and he had a look on his face like a new convert. "That's what we have to do," he said. "We have to be that loud. I want people to have a colonic when you guys perform."[7] We tried it out at a place in Brighton. We were opening for Roy Ayers. Rich set all the levels and boom! That was the arrival of the Roots.

Since then, we've been every sound engineer's nightmare. Funk bands had dominated the seventies, but in the mid-nineties, the loudest bands were rock groups that operated mostly in the high end. They needed guitar screech. We were a low-end concern, almost entirely. I had a kick pedal. Hub played bass. Rahzel did beatboxing. And while most venues or even groups we were opening for capped our decibels at around 118, we preferred to do more like 135 or 140. It was dominating but it wasn't defeaning. The low end registers differently, somehow. It's a physical event.

––––––––

London was disappointment and tension and epiphany, but it was also prelude: we were about to become real recording artists. One day, in

––––––––

7. In the lounge area at the House of Roots, there were these little tealight candles in aluminum cups. We had to keep grabbing them because they were shaking off the table. It was an echo chamber of pure bass. I think part of that effect isn't even about the music. Some of that shit really is just physiology. There's a certain frequency that will definitely affect you. It's not imaginary or even cultural. It's physical. In the past, if humans felt something that deep, it was a stampede or an earthquake. These days, you feel it, and maybe it takes a second before you realize that you're not about to be killed, but you've been triggered, and off you go.

London, Rich came to us and told us that Geffen was about to release our first single, "Distortion to Static." The next week, he came back and updated the story. "Distortion to Static" had been released, along with two other singles cut: "Flava in Ya Ear" by Craig Mack and "Juicy" by the Notorious B.I.G. The way it works is that you're looking for adds: you see how many college stations add the song to their rotation, and then you see how many commercial stations add it. The first reports were back and, Rich told us, we were in first place, beating both Craig Mack and Biggie.

We were dancing. Break out the steak!

What we didn't know, though, was that the numbers were skewed. The real release date for those two other songs was a week after ours, but because they were so highly anticipated, they were being added early. So we were first only because our full week was slightly better than a single day of action for Craig Mack or Biggie.

Put the steak away. Break out the tissues.

As it turned out, they got something like 250 adds and we had around sixteen. We told Geffen to hold the record, that it wasn't ready, that we needed to do more promotion.

And that's when the hell began. We returned to the States to promote it. One of the first trips was to a mom-and-pop store in Florida. We couldn't all go, only Tariq and Malik and Rich. They arrived to find that no one knew who they were. No one from the label had done advance work and prepared the store. On the way back, they stopped at a club in North Carolina, and Rich slipped the club owner a copy of our single for the DJ. There were a hundred people on the floor, dancing, having fun, but the second "Distortion to Static" came on over the speakers, the whole place just cleared. There was only one girl left, out there on her own, trying, unsuccessfully, to dance to it. Tariq looked at Rich, panic in his eyes. "We're going to fucking fail!" he said. I only heard about it later, on the telephone (a dreadful conversation that

I recorded and would, fourteen years later, use as the opening of our *Rising Dawn* album), but to this day I can't play the Roots in one of my own DJ sets. The memory of that empty floor is too traumatic.

The second half of 1994, as we waited for our first album to drop and tried to calculate how much fame, if any, it might bring us, remains one of the most instructive periods of my entire career, though it wasn't always instructive in a good way. Thing was, we had expectations, and that was a problem. I took every failure personally and every imperfect experience as a failure, so every time another artist hit the big time with a magazine cover or a top video, it was like an arrow in my side. You hear so much about the tortoise and the hare, and the beauty of that story is that the hare is always going to come smoking out of the gate, but you know that eventually you're going to see his car set up on the side of the road as the tortoise moseys past on the way to the finish line. But what if you're the tortoise and you keep being passed by other tortoises? What if the band that was signed after you becomes huge? What if the band that opens for you becomes huge?

It took me a few years to come to terms with the notion that we were always going to be bridesmaids. Even now, I wonder what would have happened if it had gone differently. Rich and I have this idea about "The Bentley Moment," which is that beyond-your-wildest-dreams Hype-Williams-video-type experience, the ticker tape parade, the money raining down from the sky. Without that, have you made it as an artist? What is success? All I knew back then was that we weren't having it yet, and that I wanted it.[8]

---

8. I don't think early on you guys realized how little pop sense you had. Note to y'all: the Zeitgeist ain't a fuckin' bicycle built for two. I remember one time during an interview Tariq said, "This is a collective of people any one of which could have a platinum album." At that point I wanted to ask, "And do chickens got negroid lips?" Hubris is such a slippery slope. When I get a whiff I'm inclined to pull out

———

Just as my life as a recording artist was getting underway, my cushy home life exploded. When we signed to Geffen, we had a party to celebrate the deal. It was a celebration and then some. Everyone's mouths dropped when we came into the room. Tariq was wearing a $3,000 leather jacket. We played a great set. As a favor to my former employer, Ruffhouse, I promised that these young upstarts from New Jersey could play at our record release party in 1993. That group was the Fugees. Their approach at that time was more acoustic soul than hip-hop, exactly; they just had a guitar and some drums. That night, we recorded a triumphant live version of "Essaywhuman?!!!??!" that would appear on *Do You Want More?!!!??!* Also that night, just before I went on stage, my mother told me that she had made the decision to leave my father.

The news hit me like a sledgehammer. I grew up protected, privileged, whatever word you want to use. My home life had been so stable that it was the envy of most of the people I knew. But that doesn't mean that there weren't problems. At some point in my late teens, my father's personality began to change, triggered in part by financial disappointments, in part by creative frustrations, in part by fear of his own middle age, and then accelerated by a thousand other things I couldn't fathom at the time and that I probably still understand only vaguely. My father hadn't had an easy life. He wasn't encouraged to sing by his family; they saw music as an

---

Occam's Razor and hack my way through a nigga's loftiness. While you don't want to demoralize the artist or offhandedly denigrate their vision, it's simply irresponsible not to manage expectations. I was a Marxist during my college years (right??) and the dialectic approach stuck. As for wishful thinking, well, that's that shit I don't like. So, no pop sound scanning, just the long marched plop of one foot in front of the other.

instrument of the devil. He was one of eight kids, and the darkest, and since that generation was subject to the paper-bag test—if you're darker than a paper bag, you're treated badly—he was beaten the most, abused the most, punished the most. He dropped out of school early, and there was a real possibility that he could have been lost. But he had singing talent and drive and Denzellian matinee-idol good looks, and when he became a famous singer in Philadelphia, projecting that image became central to his personality. All he ever wore were suits. He felt such intense pressure to maintain that pose, to be handsome and debonair. But at the same time, he was starting to feel hollow inside. It wasn't clear to him that he deserved what he had, or if he'd be able to keep it. Take his relationship with my mother, for example. She was beautiful, and that made him angry and controlling, which in turn made her feel like she had to mask her beauty to keep him feeling okay about himself. It was a bad dynamic that got worse as he got older.

That insecurity spilled over to the way he treated his kids. My sister wanted to act, but she ended up in the family band instead, partly because my father controlled everyone with such a tight grip. I felt it firsthand. After I got my advance for *Do You Want More?!!!??!*, my father came to me and told me that I owed him. I was confused. "You owe me," he said, "for all those years in private school, all those lessons. I sacrificed for you. I want a cut." I gave him the money, but it broke my mom's heart to see me handing it over. She thought that a father was just supposed to do those things for a child without asking for something in return.

The beginning of the end happened in the mid-eighties, and it went slowly downhill. Then in 1993, the night of our party celebrating our Geffen signing, my mother told me that she had made the decision to stick up for herself. "If I don't," she said, "and if you see me take what I think is coming next, which might be hitting, then you're going to do the same thing with your wife, and that's not something I'm willing to let happen."

The week she escaped was like an espionage movie. It was a very slow, calculated process. She smuggled out one bag of clothes a day to my sister's house until the closet was empty, and then one morning a routine visit to the gym instead turned into a train trip to North Carolina, where she went to live with family. She left a note and I had to act all surprised when my father found it: "Ahmir! Your mother!"

I looked as shocked as I could.

At that point, it was just the two of us in the house, me and my father. Believe it or not, that was another revelation. When my father found my mother's note, I was ready for whatever was coming: blame, rage, shouting, a violent outburst. But it was the opposite. He became a shell of a man. He slumped down into a chair and made a noise like there was nothing left in him, and then he started to cry. I had never seen that happen before. In a strange way, it made me angry. I wouldn't say that my father was abusive, exactly, but he had a stage-father pathology and a stern personality. He was Joe Jackson, in some small sense. And then, all of a sudden, the curtain pulled back, and he was the Wizard of Oz. It became clear to me that he kept people under his control so he didn't have to admit to himself that he was scared. My mother left and it just all went out of him.

My reaction was related, maybe: I threw myself into my work. People always ask me how I have time to develop my sound. I set up one drum set and try it that way, then go to EQ buttons and try it a different way. When I describe the process, it sounds like a nineteen-hour commitment just to get the right settings for a single song, and it sounds that way because it is that way. It started that way after the first album, when I was avoiding home. The studio was an escape but also a necessary safe place for me.

———

We had turned in the finished tapes of our debut in April 1994, expecting to see the record by "the 28th of June," but we weren't ready, and then we thought the material wasn't ready. Finally, on January 17, 1995—the same day as the Great Hanshin earthquake in Kobe, Japan, and three days before my twenty-fourth birthday—*Do You Want More?!!!??!* was released. We went on *The Jon Stewart Show* to promote it, beginning a friendship with Jon that lasts to this day, even though we're now on a competing late-night show.

Mobb Deep came to our in-store signing at Tower Records in Philly to promote their new single, "Shook Ones Part I," and we said hello to them and they said hello to us, but that was the extent of our fame in that first week. It was a great time for hip-hop; unfortunately, the reason it was so great wasn't principally about us, or even our record. It was about one of the other new songs that came out at the same time, Ol' Dirty Bastard's "Brooklyn Zoo," which was a song that was so radical that it changed the way I thought about hip-hop. The way that song is structured, for starters, is bananas: just an intro, one extended verse, and then the chorus, which is repeated into infinity. And the vocals are spoken, or shouted, with amazing phrasing and total confidence in their own effects. It's like Screamin' Jay Hawkins somehow made the best hip-hop single in history.

———

As the weeks went on, the sense of anticlimax only deepened. In fact, the experience of having an album out was absolutely devastating. In my head, when I replayed our record next to other records that I loved, I was convinced that we were in the company of other classics. De La Soul's *3 Feet High and Rising* was such a creative record and the world ate it up. A Tribe Called Quest's *Low End Theory* was such a creative record and the world ate it up. But there was one thing both of those albums had that we lacked, and that was a hit single. If you were De La Soul, you could talk all you wanted about your commitment to artistry and pushing the boundaries of the genre, but the fact was that "Me Myself and I" was a gold single, and it moved the record along. It was the same thing with Tribe's "Scenario." The Roots didn't have that.

In fact, I wasn't sure what we had. Those first few months of being a recording artist were one disappointment after another. Even before it was released, half the band had visited the record store in Florida only to discover that Geffen's advance team had stranded us. Then there was the incident in North Carolina where the dance floor cleared.[9] That sense of failure continued on into 1995. We played shows in Europe where there was more waitstaff than fans. In Berlin, we drew only seven people. In Austria, we were harassed by the cops at the airport, even though we hadn't done anything wrong. There was a night where Hub got fed up with the sense of futility and lashed out at the audience—not in any Jim Morrison–type way, thankfully, but just enough for us to get a sense of his frustration. Many nights after a show I got back to the dressing room or hotel room and wondered what I thought I was doing. Even when we came back from Europe, it was a nightmare. We had been promised tour support and we got some, going out with the Beastie Boys and Jon Spencer Blues

---

9. I've said it before and I'll say it again: 1994 was a horrific fucking year. Still, we were happy with what we had. I remember doing fifty-dollar gigs and everyone getting a fiver and being cool with it. You went off and bought a T-shirt or someone scored some weed and tried to make it with a girl. It really was a simpler, even happier time, even though it sucked.

Explosion.[10] We played so loud that we demanded notice. But the commercial failure of that first record escalated the existing tensions in the band.

And yet there was no giving up. I had nowhere else to turn. I was too far gone from school, past high school graduation but unconvinced that I could find my way back to the right college experience. I had no specific skill that I could trade on. My father's dream of my becoming a professional session musician had grown faint to the point of invisibility. He used to tell me to get a "real" job—as if having a record deal wasn't enough—but I wasn't sure anymore what that really meant. The Roots *had* to work. It was all I had. Rich calmed me down, like he had before and like he would again. "Stay the course," he said. "Don't worry. It'll work out." He reminded me that Geffen had promised to support us through the first few albums, even when the going got rough. "We're in that period," he said. "Let them support us."

It was hard for me to believe that we would be taken care of, but I put my trust in Geffen because Rich put his trust in them, and I put my trust in Rich.

---

10. Remember that? Dude had a motorcycle jacket and a fucking *theremin*.

ELEVEN

From: Ben Greenman [cowriter]
To: Ben Greenberg [editor]
Re: The Circle Game

Did you get that note from Rich, the one where he talked about the Petrashevsky Circle and then went off on a tangent about how today's big artists are embarrassing the notion of Big Artists by only selling fifty thousand copies of their highly touted records, which surface one week only to slink out of sight the next? Started me thinking on some things to discuss with Ahmir. What is the purpose of making new art? Why does Ahmir keep doing it at this point? What ideas recharge him? And even if he manages to get recharged, where is he directing his energy? I was around, as a record buyer, as a fan, when hip-hop started. It was all so new and so much of it shone. But over the years, I have found myself less and less able to find that shine in new music. People say that it's the fault of that new music, that it's responding to different market factors, that there's not the same common language and community, and maybe that's true to some degree. But it's also my fault, and yours. At this point, I have a storehouse of records to go back to, and they sustain me. If I need another hit of *It Takes a Nation of Millions to Hold Us Back* or *Paid in Full* or *The Slim Shady LP*, all I need to do is get the CD out of the cabinet (or, more accurately and more disconcertingly, just search for the songs in my iTunes library). So what is the value, even the marginal value, of new music? I suppose you could ask this question about any form of art, but I have a vested interest in not asking it most of the time. When I write fiction, I don't worry about whether the novel I'm working on is similar to other existing novels or whether a reader would be just as well served going to a library archive as to the bookstore. I write things because I want to get to the point where I have written things. And yet, if I let my guard down, those other questions are quickly there, wolves at the door. How much does that haunt Ahmir as he moves forward as an artist? How does he get it up to make a new Roots record? And then add to that the fact that, as Rich likes to say, hip-hop carries water for all of black contemporary culture. Everything gets tagged with that adjective: fashion, food, even technology. So if the spark is dampened, if the powder can't get lit, where does that leave everyone? I'll talk to Ahmir about all that.

TWELVE

When was hip-hop's funeral? I know exactly when it was, because I attended it—the second *Source* awards, in May of 1995. I mark that as a definite turning point of my life. *Do You Want More?!!!??!* was four months old, and we were nominated for Best Live Act.

The ceremony was held at the Paramount Theater at Madison Square Garden. As you came in, you could see that there was a kind of aesthetic apartheid at work. They sat the artistic rappers, the have-nots of hip-hop, on the far right side: Nas, Mobb Deep, Wu-Tang, Busta Rhymes, and us. In the center of the place you had the Death Row crew and all the non–New York acts. On the far left of the place, you had the Bad Boy team. That room was like *Apocalypse Now: The Hip-Hop Version*. If you had sparked two rocks together the place would have exploded.

I saw Nas walk in, and he was wearing a Tommy Hilfiger shirt. I just stared at him. *What a strange shirt*, I thought. *He must have taken that from the outlet rack*. It was too big for his body. He later confirmed in an interview that he had had to borrow money from Steve Stout to buy it, but even without knowing that, I knew something was amiss.

And Nas was one of the two marquee names, potentially. That year was shaping up to be a battle between his *Illmatic* and *Ready to Die*, Biggie's current album. *Illmatic*, released in April 1994, had been crowned king by many critics and given five microphones by the *Source*, considered a gold standard. Right on its heels was Biggie's—another album that was a gold standard. But that's where the similarities end. One of those two records, *Illmatic*, was done in the naive old hip-hop style of just being a great album from start to finish, with great production, great MCing, a sharp perspective, and so on. The other album was done with an eye toward hit singles, and it succeeded beyond anyone's wildest dreams. So both albums were up for the same awards, and of course Biggie won them all. And for every award Biggie got I watched Nas just wilt in defeat, and that killed me inside. There was a look of shame and defeat. I remember turning to Tariq and saying, "He's never going to be the same. You just watch." That was the night Nas's Clark Kent turned into Superman, the night this mild-mannered observer realized he had to put on a suit and try to fly. But maybe he didn't have flying power in that way. When he released his next record, *It Was Written*, there was debate over whether he was following his own course or trying to be Biggie.

That was only the beginning that night. There was so much more divisiveness. Snoop Dogg and Dr. Dre cursed out the audience. OutKast was booed mercilessly. (They later put that on the end of "Chonkyfire" on *Aquemini*: "We just want y'all to know the South's got something to say.") And then, most famously, Suge Knight called out Puffy: in his acceptance speech, he told artists that if they wanted to succeed without having to put their egomaniacal executive producer in every video, they should come over to Death Row Records. That's the incident that people say lit the powder keg on the East Coast–West Coast beef, but there was bad blood all over that room.

It spread and thickened. As the night went on, I saw how Nas looked, how he was internalizing this crushing sense of defeat, how something that was supposed to be a community was being torn apart by infighting, ego, crosscurrents of jealousy. When Dre was announced as a nominee for producer of the year, people stood up in challenge, like they couldn't wait for him to win just so they could cause trouble. The room suddenly became even more menacing. At the moment John Singleton said "And the winner is..." I grabbed my date and ran. I heard them announce Dre as the winner, and there were thunderous boos, and Snoop said, "What, East Coast got no love for Dr. Dre?"

I was running out and at some point a man pressed a cassette into my hand. I looked and the name was familiar to me: it was a guy that a producer named Bob Power, who had worked with A Tribe Called Quest, had been talking about in the studio earlier that week: D'Angelo, with his debut album, *Brown Sugar*. I had heard of D'Angelo around this studio or that, but dismissed him as one of those generic R&B guys the world didn't need more of. But there was a symbolism to it, my running from that room, that I couldn't discount. I felt like we were Lot and his wife fleeing Sodom and Gomorrah, and I didn't turn around for that very reason. I felt like my life was in danger. I had been at the *Source* awards the first year, when Tupac unknowingly interrupted A Tribe Called Quest's acceptance speech for Best Album. While they were coming to accept, Tupac started his performance. I saw the seeds of Afrika Islam from the Zulu Nation threatening Tupac. I didn't know if I wanted to come back. But I did, and it was much worse. I sensed there was going to be a brawl, that someone might get shot. In my mind I felt like I had just escaped the war, and so when someone pressed that *Brown Sugar* cassette into my hand, even though my first instinct was to throw it away, something made me decide to play it.

I heard so much in that D'Angelo record. It was like music that A Tribe Called Quest would make, but he was singing over it. That was still revolutionary. (The day that Mary J. Blige's "My Life" came out in 1994, we all just sat in the van scratching our heads. We had never heard anyone sing over samples before, and here she was, with Roy

Ayers's "Everybody Loves the Sunshine" under her, making up a new vocal, new lyrics. We were so caught between rejecting it as untenable and accepting it as the vanguard.) Like any new development, there was lag time. It took a year for us to digest it and accept that R&B singers were trying to be hip-hop artists. There was nowhere left for them to go. I hated what contemporary R&B had become. It was trite. It was soulless. It had no authentic passion. It was doing very little for me. And then I heard D'Angelo and my head was turned. It changed my life. Here was a singer who connected with me as deeply as the best hip-hop. It was that first album, of course, but it was more than that: it was what I heard behind the album, the sensibility that powered the songs, the ability to locate the heart of the best soul music. It was out of step with the times but in a way that made it seem like he was stepping into uncharted territory.

What made it even better—or worse, depending on how you look at it—is that I had passed up a chance to work with him on the album. About a year earlier, Bob Power had asked me to play on "Shit, Damn, Motherfucker." He was setting up a session with the bassist Ron Carter and wanted me to join them. It would have happened if Ron had agreed, but he had concerns about the title and canceled, and when Bob called to see if I would play on another song, I begged off. I wasn't sure I was interested after all. It was R&B. It wasn't my thing. And I had even seen D'Angelo once when he had come by the studio to pick up a DAT (digital audio tape) from Bob while I was mixing "Mellow My Man." I sized him up and thought, eh, another corny R&B guy. I had no clue that he was going to be the second coming. When I finally heard the record I was kicking myself. I had the chance to make that connection and I passed on it. Here was fate, giving me a second chance, revealing itself to me as I fled hip-hop's Sodom and Gomorrah.

I didn't meet D'Angelo right away. I took my time. We started our second Roots record. We gigged for money.

Sometime around the end of 1995, we were offered a series of concert dates in Florida that we were going to have to pass on because travel and lodging were too expensive. If we played the dates, it would be at a loss. Rich came up with the idea that we should take the Land Cruiser, just me and him and Tariq and Rahzel, stack the drums in the back, and drive straight through to Florida. That didn't make sense to me, to go down with a skeleton crew like that, but Rich explained that Rahzel and I were enough music. He wanted to concentrate on areas where we rarely perform. (Even now, we only go to Miami once every other year. For the Roots map, it's hardly even part of the United States; it was outreach.) And so off we went, with Rich driving eighteen hours straight. I think he took one break for maybe an hour. Other than that, it was him at the wheel, and him only—none of the rest of us were licensed. He somehow managed to do a hundred miles an hour in that car. *Determination* isn't even the right word. He was like an arrow on the road. That kind of thing kept me focused on the goal. In fact, I would learn later that this kind of thing was part of Rich's philosophy. He always felt that we did our best shows under pressure. Side note: to this day, he stands by his belief that the best show the Roots ever did was without me. That one was on Mother's Day 1995, and I had to give my sister away for her first wedding. We had booked a show at the 9:30 Club, and when I couldn't make it, they went on with Rahzel instead. If you ask Rich to list the top five Roots shows of all time, he'll usually put that at number one.[11]

---

11. That was a fucking great show. It just had an unexpectedness to it that kept everyone focused. But you guys were always a special band live. The Rahzel

But that whole time, in my mind, I was cooking up a plan to meet D'Angelo. It took me exactly eleven months. I was obsessed with trying to find a way to be down with this guy. I knew that I could really get a movement going if I could pair up with him. Musically, he was expressing exactly what I wanted to express, and I knew that he could help me collect all the crazy ideas that weren't finding a home with the Roots.

I finally got an audience with him on April 1, 1996, in Los Angeles. We were on tour with Goodie Mob and the Fugees. Goodie Mob was the opening act, a relatively new artist, but already there was a strange dynamic between us and the Fugees. They had played our signing party back in 1993, when they were still mostly an acoustic act. About two years later, we did a show at Clark College where they were our opening act, and we invited Lauryn Hill on stage with us. I heard that two-thirds of The Fugees were none too happy about this summit meeting. On the bus our roadie later told us, "Man, you should have seen the look on Pras's face when Lauryn started rhyming with you guys. He was mad as shit." But they watched that show and they learned a lesson: They learned the power of live karaoke. Jonathan Shecter, the editor of *The Source*, had first suggested the possibility in a conversation. He had told me that audiences liked our jazz inflections, and our virtuosity, but that what they really wanted was recreations of their favorite songs. "Why don't you take all the great break beats in hip-hop history and just redo them?" he said. "Do 'Top Billin'," then do Big Daddy

---

show was one version of what was always the case: there was a karaoke element, you know? Much of your act was literally playing other people's hits, like a jukebox. And there were these amazing moments when you, Ahmir, would play these breaks. People were used to hip-hop as found sounds and recontextualized shit. There was no experience of seeing it that big, live. It was like an old-school Top 40 band on steroids.

Kane. Just do them. You'll notice a difference. You'll see." We did it, and there was a difference. People went crazy for it.

Soon enough, the Fugees were doing something similar. Actually, they took it a step further by playing on top of the records. We were the masters of live sonics, so we never had a DJ. We had to work hard to perfect our live sound. If you play on top of a record, you will fool people into thinking that you sound as good as that record. It's cheating.

When we went out on tour, there was a creative rivalry brewing. We got along with the group personally. I will always remember water fights with Lauryn Hill as a central part of my early touring experience. But creatively, we were maybe too close to them, or they were too close to us. They had watched us and learned certain tricks of the trade, and now they were doing them more slickly and more successfully than almost any other band. We were told we'd be co-headlining. We'd open some shows and they'd open others. We were about to agree to that. But then the radio started playing the shit out of "Killing Him Softly," and it was quickly obvious that they were the bigger group and they should be headlining. That was fine with me—in fact, I probably preferred it. I didn't want sloppy seconds. I wanted to go on first and establish the mood, make our point, and be done with it.

That strategy worked like a charm, and by the time we got to Los Angeles, we were a well-oiled machine. Somehow, I got word that D'Angelo was in the audience that night, and I realized that it was one of those make-or-break moments. I wanted him to know that he and I spoke the same musical language, that we could communicate telepathically via some African tribal shit. Back to the beginning, back to the drums. So that became the dilemma. Should I play to the band or play to a single person in the audience? I debated it before we went on, but by the time we hit the stage there was no choice. I was willing to throw our Los Angeles show for a loop. It was a calculated risk, but a big one nonetheless. It wasn't just an ordinary Los Angeles show. It was the weekend of the *Soul Train* Awards, a kind of unofficial coming-out party for the band. I faced the choice of sticking with what was tried and true or of venturing out into the unknown to try to capture the attention of one person. I chose the latter, much to the dismay of the rest of the band. Their eyebrows went up, like I was playing drunk or off rhythm or something. They weren't ready for me sounding like a skipped record. Then I would quote a Prince lick that wasn't in the song that I was playing, but that was in my head while I was thinking about the song I was playing. Again, it only confused the band. But it worked on D'Angelo. He came out of his seat and stood up for the rest of the show.

He came backstage and we started talking immediately. It was clear from the first minute that we were cut from the same cloth, that we were both obsessive fans of the same seventies soul, that we had both memorized every Prince arrangement, every Stevie Wonder outro, every twist and turn in every Curtis Mayfield and Bill Withers song. I saw it in him and he saw it in me. My plan had worked. I had hooked him. Within the month, we had started work on the last song for the second Roots record, *Illadelph Halflife*, "The Hypnotic," which flowed naturally into the first song of his next record, what would eventually become *Voodoo*. At the time, I didn't know that this dalliance would take up the next half-decade of my life, and that it would end up being one of the crowning achievements of my career. But I knew that it was a relationship that was different from my relationship with the Roots: not stronger, necessarily; not better; not more or less, but more intimate.

Meanwhile, we had our own record to make. *Illadelph Halflife* was considerably different than *Do You Want More?!!!??!*, partly because we had fully emerged onto the scene and now had an opportunity to reflect on what we saw. We didn't want to be as soft as we were on the earlier record, but we didn't want to surrender our thinking-man's perch either. We split the difference by making the music harder, and by making songs that sounded like they were based on samples, though in fact we were sampling ourselves. We kept a sense of jazz—Joshua Redman and Cassandra Wilson guested on "One Shine"—but also a sense of continuity. In fact, on some of the copies of the album, tracks were numbered beginning with seventeen, which was our way of saying that it was a continuation of the work we had started on *Organix* and *Do You Want More?!!!??!*. It was a small gesture, and possibly more annoying than effective, but we wanted to push back a bit against the idea that records were simply products, or isolated snapshots that weren't connected, spiritually and even physically, to the albums that came before and the albums, as yet unmade, that would come afterward. We finished up in the summer of 1996 and got ready for our close-up, again.

———

If I managed to pull off a calculated risk to meet D'Angelo, and to stay cool while I was doing it, I was a little less composed one night in New York, when Q-Tip asked me and a girl I was seeing if we'd be interested in going to a club called Life. We went downtown and then downstairs, and there in the club, standing right in the middle of the room, was Prince. I couldn't believe it. I was shaking like the shakiest leaf. "I want you to meet this guy," Q-Tip said to Prince, pointing to me. "He's the baddest..."

Prince interrupted. "I know who he is," he said. "I love that video. It's so funny." It hardly mattered that he complimented the "What They Do" video. Prince knew who I was.

It was my turn to speak. That's what you do in polite company—

when someone speaks to you, you speak back, right? But I was speechless. More to the point: I was making noise, but it wasn't exactly speech. It was a kind of gurgling noise, alternating with high-pitched squeals. Prince and Q-Tip were looking at each other. "I guess he's nervous," Tip said.

Words, finally, appeared in the gurgling. "Yeah," I said. "Just that... you are... knowing who I... be."

Q-Tip translated. "He's amazed that you know he's alive."

"Right," I said. "That you be knowing me. That I, I mean you, I mean. You know. That the thing is." At this point, Q-Tip shot me a glance. It was the look you give a guy in a plane when it's going down. Time to hit the silk. "I'm going to go," I said, and I went.

Out in the street, I was kicking myself in full view of my date. I kept telling her, "This is no good, no good at all. I blew it. It was a chance and I fumbled the ball. I need to run back. Should I run back? Tell me. Should I?" She was looking at me like I was crazy. About three blocks later I answered the question myself. I turned and ran back to the place and almost slid down the staircase. Prince and Q-Tip were still there with Lenny Kravitz, Kidada Jones, and a few other people. I burst in and all of them looked up. The bodyguards came off their stations for me. "No, wait," Prince said. "He's cool."

"Hey," I said. "I'm sorry about before. I didn't want to freak you out but it's really cool to meet my hero." The room got quieter. "And I just want to say..." Now the room was silent. I had the floor. I had my chance. What was I going to say in my first—and, for all I knew, only—opportunity to speak to the man I considered the most talented musician of his generation? As it turned out, it was this: "'Dinner with Dolores' has the greatest ending in postmodern black rock history."

Q-Tip put his hand up to his forehead. No one said anything. Exit Ahmir.

Illadelphi Halflife came out in September 1996, just two weeks after Tupac Shakur was shot and killed in Las Vegas. Our hometown paper, the *Philadelphia Inquirer*, noted this like it was some kind of passing of the torch: they called the record "The first major release of the post–Tupac Shakur era in rap," and said that we "reaffirm just how far-reaching (and how far removed from the gangsta stereotype) hip-hop can be." That's what we were trying to establish, though it was a little strange to see it linked to Tupac's killing, even as part of an argument about the options available to rap groups. Other reviews were equally positive: we got 3½ stars from *Rolling Stone* (this was ok, I guess) and 4½ mics from *The Source* (a personal bragging-right high for me). Selwyn Hinds gave us a nine out of ten in *Spin*, and said that it was an "artistic progression," and an "added confirmation of the Roots' place at hip-hop's vanguard" (near-perfect reviews were always the new black for me).

Within the group, there was excitement and pride, but there was also a reluctance to hope for too much to change. Given what had happened with the sales of *Do You Want More?!!!??!* I adjusted my expectations downward, and it's a good thing that I did. The second record repeated the performance of the first one—good critical reputation, modest commercial performance, nothing earth-shattering.

And there were reminders everywhere that we hadn't quite arrived, at least as celebrities. A few months after my embarrassing run-in with Prince, I was scheduled to play a show with D'Angelo. This was my first time drumming for him, and it was for the round of concerts to celebrate *Brown Sugar* going platinum. When I played with the Roots, I dressed fairly casually, thrift-store cool, boho hip, like I had always dressed, but as D'Angelo's drummer, I was supposed to wear a suit. And so I went to get one. I was in the store, shopping, and a man with a clipboard approached me and introduced himself as a segment producer for a talk show. "It's David Letterman's show," he said. "Would you mind appearing in a skit?"

"What do I need to do?" I asked.

"Just play natural," he said. "But I need to ask you one question to make sure this will work out. What are your plans for the weekend?"

"Well," I said. "I have a show in Virginia tonight and then a Fashion Week event on Monday."

"Perfect," he said. He made a mark on his clipboard.

"Perfect for what?" I was still a little confused.

"We want you to go as Dave's proxy to the Emmy Awards," the man said. Letterman had done his disastrous hosting gig at the Oscars the year before, and as a gambit, or out of genuine frustration with the awards establishment, he was boycotting the Emmys. The plan was to send a pair of "freaks" as his representatives, and his segment producers were out and about in New York looking for freaks. The producer didn't want me because I was in the Roots. He had no idea who the Roots were: if it was a band or a sports team or a marketing agency. He wanted me because I was a peculiar-looking six-foot-two walking afro. I told the producer that I was a musician, or at least I thought that I did. But maybe he just thought that I needed to be back because I was attending a concert.

At any rate, we shot the segment. They flew me to the Emmy Awards. I walked the red carpet for the segment along with Letterman regular Leonard Tepper. We made quite the odd couple. It would be easy, and maybe predictable to say that I resented the experience because it didn't have anything to do with my real achievements in the band, but the fact was that I loved it. I have always relished living in the space between being a big shot and being entirely anonymous. It's the pit and the pendulum.

Some years later, the band was invited on *The Late Show with David Letterman* to perform after the release of *Things Fall Apart*. When we showed up, Dave came over to me and said, "I see you still have the suit."

To this day, the video for "What They Do" remains most people's favorite Roots video, which strikes me as a little bit strange. Not that it's a bad video—far from it. It was directed by Charles Stone III, a Philly guy we've worked with over the course of our career, and who is probably better known as the "Whassup!" guy from the Bud Light commercials. He had directed a video for the heavy-metal band Tesla, our labelmates, that deconstructed the very idea of a video: every shot had a subtitle explaining exactly what it was within the context of the broader video, the glamour shot, the shot where the models turn away. We decided to take it all a step further. A civil war was brewing in hip-hop; the tension between the haves and have-nots that I had sensed at the *Source* Awards was now at a fever pitch. And people were trying to locate us on that matrix: "Why are you guys so accessible when you're on BET? Shouldn't you have a mansion?" We wanted to make a humorous video showing that hip-hop music was a career, that was hard work. At the same time, Charles Stone wanted to throw a thumb at the stuff Hype Williams was doing, all those rap-video clichés that were prevalent at the time.

I liked the idea, but I was also skeptical. I had a severe disdain for our previous videos. We did one for "Clones," and even though people loved it, I thought we looked motley. We weren't styled. We didn't have star quality. We were like a rap version of Christopher Cross, capable of delivering great music but totally lost in the image department. And image was starting to become central to the genre, thanks in large part to the way that Puffy had taken *The Chronic*'s vision and magnified it twentyfold for Biggie's *Ready to Die*. I didn't know our place in that world. I didn't mind representing true art but I would have liked it if we were a little more bipartisan, somehow representing both haves and have-nots. The "What They Do" video had a little glitz and glamour, although it was done satirically. Still, even when Charles screened the final cut, it didn't register to me that we were mocking Biggie's "One More Chance" video, as some people later charged.[12]

And yet, in retrospect, it seems obvious. There was no good way to isolate and critique the direction hip-hop was heading in without targeting the videos that Biggie was making with Puff and Hype Williams.

So there we were, in early March of 1997, in Paris for a show. The phone rang, and it was a reporter from *The Source* asking us if we would care to comment on these remarks that Biggie Smalls had just made about us. We weren't aware of any remarks, so he read them: "I had mad love for those guys. I'm the one who put them on to Brooklyn. My feelings were really hurt, man, because they were one of my favorite groups. I love Thought. He's one of my favorite MCs. Why'd he go and shit on me?" We didn't know what to do. We didn't want to act like a bitch and say we didn't mean it. What we were critiquing was obvious, and the satire was clear. But how could we communicate the nuance of the point, that although we didn't mean to personally offend Biggie, we were drawing battle lines that we thought were necessary—and, more than that—just?

Rich and I went into brain-trust mode and composed a manifesto where we tried to clearly articulate what was happening in hip-hop. We labored over it, tried to make every part of the argument do its job. It was long. It was righteous, maybe self-righteous in parts. It explained everything that anyone would ever want to know about

---

12. Before that, hip-hop had a sense of belonging. When Run DMC did "My Adidas," you could go out and get a pair of Adidas. You could put on jeans and a Kangol hat. You could be part of that club. When motherfuckers are talking about buying a jet or a speedboat, well, that's not inclusive. And think of where the videos are set. Early on there was lots of on-your-block shit, videos with regular locations: street corners, houses, empty lots. People could identify with that in ways they couldn't identify with mansions.

art and commerce, about the way that conspicuous consumption was a kind of acid that ate away at the souls of its listeners. It took no prisoners but tried to be respectful about it. And, finally, it was ready to go.

I called for the fax number of *The Source* offices. This would have been Sunday morning in Paris, which meant that it was still Saturday night in Los Angeles. "Fax?" the person at *The Source* said. His voice was bleary and sounded even further away than it was.

"Yeah," I said. "I'm writing in to respond to the comments Biggie made about our video."

"You didn't hear?"

"Hear what?" I said.

"He's dead."

I hung up the phone, my hand numb. I couldn't believe it. Dead? It was completely, 100 percent unreal to me. Hip-hop had deaths, just like any other part of the entertainment industry, just like any other part of society. Keith "Cowboy" Wiggins from the Furious Five had died in 1989 from drugs. MC Trouble had died in 1991 due to complications from a brain tumor. And, of course, there was Tupac's killing only six month before Biggie's. Were the two events connected? Had the tension I had seen at the *Source* Awards really become something this toxic and dangerous? The irony was that these events made the points in the manifesto even more relevant at the same time that it paralyzed me as to what I should do with it. It felt like the height of bad taste to send it to the magazine, and I felt personally horrible because the conflict with Biggie would now be unresolved forever. I decided to burn the manifesto. It was a ritualistic thing, a way of getting control and peace. Then I went walking through the Paris streets, trying to make sense of things.[13]

---

13. Dude, this doesn't have shit to do with Biggie, but I remember how the cops in Paris would come at you if they thought you were African and then, once they saw you

We finished out our tour and flew back toward the end of the month to do some dates in Jacksonville, Florida. That was the same time that Biggie's *Life After Death* came out, and that's all you heard anywhere. A few days after that, I went up to Richmond, Virginia, to do some work with D'Angelo. We went out one night, D and I, and we counted eleven cars all playing "Ten Crack Commandments." The verses weren't synched up, so it wasn't like the song was on the radio: it was eleven different drivers independently making the decision to play the song on their own CDs or cassettes.

I finally made it back up to New York. Biggie's death was still hanging over the entire hip-hop community. One night, Q-Tip told me that I had to see this kid named Mos Def at Lyricist Lounge. I knew of him a little bit through his first group, Urban Thermo Dynamics, and also from some of his acting roles: he had been in *The Cosby Mysteries* and also in Michael Jackson's *Ghosts* short.

Tip and I went to Wetlands to see him, and he was a new brand of MC. I had never seen such a charismatic, engaging, comfortable performer. He was like a veteran comedian who also had awesome hip-hop skills. The centerpiece of his act was an a cappella twist on Slick Rick's "Children's Story." Slick Rick's version is about a street crime; Mos's flipped the narrative so that it was about a record producer who jacked hits from the eighties, used them as the basis for new songs, and destroyed hip-hop in the process. It was clearly about

---

were American, let you go. That was routine. Once, maybe around 1999, 2000, I was walking down the street. The cops drove past on the sidewalk and then backed up and ran up to me. I pulled my passport out, but this motherfucker stuck his hand in my pocket. I had a teeny bit of weed in there, which he found, and then he handcuffed me and drove me down to the precinct. I had dreads and people were shouting at me as I went in: "Bob Mar-lee! Bob Mar-lee!"

Puffy and what he had done as producer for Biggie and others, and Mos was virtuosic with the narrative: the crime, the chase, the repercussions. I was standing there off to the side, amazed by the parody, his wit, how perfectly he had recast the song. There's a verse at the end—"This ain't funny, don't you dare laugh, just another case of the wrong path"—and with that, Mos just stopped and did a B-boy freeze. It's the exact moment that was captured on the cover image of his *Universal Magnetic* twelve-inch.

I was standing off to the side of the stage, and I went crazy. I did this over-exaggerated Arsenio Hall barking. I high-fived people I didn't even know, pounded knuckles with whoever was in sight. "Yo! He killed that shit! That was amazing!" I was laughing so hard I was snorting. Then, all of a sudden, out of the corner of my right eye, I see something and I shrink back. The only way I can describe it is that it was like the moment when Ola Ray backed herself into a corner and turned to see the ghoulish Michael Jackson in the "Thriller" video. Except that it wasn't ghoulish Michael Jackson. It was flesh-and-blood Puffy and eight of his goons. They were walking as a pack, dressed in the blackest of the black, like Run DMC on the cover of *Down with the King*. I was midway through another high-five or knuckle bump and I brought my hand down, slid to the side, and thought to myself, "Well, this is the moment I might die." I thought I was going to get a beatdown that would be talked about throughout hip-hop history. Even if that doesn't happen, I thought, I have officially, definitively, irreversibly ruined the Roots. There's no coming back from this moment. Puffy just stared at me. This was the first time he or any of his group were seeing me since the "What They Do" video. Biggie was no longer around, but his death was fresh, and one of the last things he had done was feel bad about the video we made. In my mind, I kissed my career good-bye.

But Puffy and his posse passed by me and walked to the dressing room. When I unfroze, I went to find out why they were there. As it turned out, Q-Tip had invited him to see if he would look at Mos as a possible signing. This made sense, though it made Mos's choice of song make less sense. I thought it was a little weird, frankly. You're going to do this "Children's Story" parody knowing that the guy it's about, the guy it takes direct aim at, has been invited to consider you for signing and possibly change your life?

I didn't have time to parse the finer points of Mos's motivation, or anything else for that matter. I needed to get out of there quick. There was only one problem: Tip was my ride. I waited nervously and eventually Tip appeared. "We need to have a meeting," he said.

"A meeting?" I tried to sound casual.

"You know," he said. "Just a discussion. Let's all sit down and talk."

I wasn't prepared to sit down and talk, but it didn't seem like I was going to get out of there, so I went into the back and we all had an impromptu summit: me, Mos, Puffy, and his goons. Puffy started off the meeting, and he let it all loose. For starters, he felt like Tip had set him up. But he was more angry for the string of comments, for his perception of how I had acted toward Biggie. "You shitted on my man," he said. "He had all of Brooklyn on your dick. He turned everyone on to you. And you treated him like dirt. You were his favorite."

I tried to explain myself as best as I could, and we came to a kind of understanding. When we parted that night, it was cordial, if not exactly friendly, and as we've both gotten older, we've mellowed considerably. Nowadays, it's nothing but love for Puff. He invited me to Marrakech for his birthday a few years ago but I wasn't able to go. When I think about that night, and that period in my life, I wonder how much of it was just young musicians talking shit and strutting their stuff. Everyone goes through those dumb rebellious phases, mainly because they're using music as a means of showing off their personality. They wear it as a badge. And it's a shame that people are so willing to hang their personality on their artistic tastes. If you're part of the segment of hip-hop that wants to be seen as thoughtful and progressive, then you don't readily admit that you like Jay-Z's *Blueprint*. If you're part of the segment that needs to keep its thug-life street cred, you don't readily admit that you like *Things Fall Apart*. What a shitty way to go through life, hiding your love for music so that people don't think the wrong things about you.

At the same time, though, I wrote that manifesto to fax over to the Source, which means that I thought that there was a principle at stake. It's still a principle, I think, and it's still at stake. Just recently, I was talking to a book editor about hip-hop. "Right," she said. "Is that the period where rappers were talking all about how they wanted to rape and beat women?" At first I bristled at the characterization. Then it hit me that I see hip-hop in much greater detail than most people. I've devoted at least half my life to it, so I'm a connoisseur even if I don't always think of myself that way. Pick any era and I can retrieve a vast array of awesome thought-provoking hip-hop artists who were genuine political thinkers, artists who were genuine comedians. A more casual observer will only see what's put in their face. That was the problem with hip-hop in the Biggie era, and it's the problem with what passes for hip-hop now.[14]

In general, I don't like to blame the creators. They are making work that appeals to them and the people in the room with them. They are making something that is, at some level, genuine. But the distributors, the networks that bring art to the population, they are

14. Listen, man. The other day I heard that new 2 Chainz record, and it's a fucking object lesson in thematic narrowness, one dumbass idea repeated over and over again. There's a song called "Crack" and then a song called "Dope Peddler," right next to each other. Then a little later there's a song called "I Luv Dem Strippers." I'm not knocking 2 Chainz. But what kind of market elevates a guy like that, to the exclusion of everything else? That's the thing these days: there's no diversity in winning.

the ones who ensure that there's a flattening and narrowing. The younger me may have sat up all night with bandmates raging against Puffy or DMX or whoever, but the fact is that they were never the problem. The problem was that someone in the corporate chain of command felt that there was a need to play those songs fourteen times a day and to eliminate alternatives.

———

My thoughts about Puffy and Biggie on the one hand, and about Mos Def and D'Angelo on the other, started to come into focus in those months after *Illadelph Halflife* came out. What was missing from much of the pop culture I saw—and not just hip-hop, by any means— was humanity. It made me realize that I had fallen into a kind of rigid inhumanity of my own. I had spent years learning to become a perfect meticulous drum machine, but now I wanted to go in the direction I thought music was going in, which was toward the woozy, fucked-up sounds I heard coming from artists like D'Angelo. There's an option on drum machines that lets you quantize them, program the drum sounds so that they sounds right, whether you're an eighty-year-old Japanese woman or the son of Bernard Purdie. Suddenly some artists were switching that off, and their drums would sound strange at first, but then warmer and better. Switching off perfection switched on the human quality. Real drummers slow down. They speed up. There are different dynamics at different times. Very few artists understood that. Prince definitely did, even though he didn't do it every time. D'Angelo was suddenly willing to be imperfect, and that was exciting to me. But there were so few artists who really embraced it. There was RZA, but he was an accidental tourist—he would loop something, it would sound exotic to him, and he would keep it. Maybe the only other producer who was hearing sounds the way I was hearing them was J Dilla. More on him later.

As I started to enter this alternate world of sound, where human error was perfection, where warmth and organic playing mattered more than precision, my relationship with D'Angelo became more and more central to my work. We had started work on his next album, which was now named *Voodoo*, and I knew I wanted to see that through to the end. The Roots were a dicier proposition, especially after *Illadelph Halflife* stalled, like its predecessor, after three hundred thousand copies. That's when Rich had a brainstorm. He decided that since we had a new label president—we had been transferred to MCA, still under the Geffen umbrella but a different part of the company—it was time to make some new demands. He told the label that we had simple needs: we wanted them to spring for a bunch of jam sessions at my house—I had my own house by now, a modest place on St. Albans in South Philadelphia—and two fifteen-passenger vans. We hired a chef to cook the best food, and that was the siren song that started bringing people in. Before I knew it, there was round-the-clock music: singers, musicians, MCs.

Some of the people there were from the Roots, but most weren't. Most were normal people who aspired to careers in entertainment. All were welcome. And so the next thing you know, the girl who worked at Jeans West wanted to sing. That was Jill Scott. The pizza delivery guy, Jamal, thought that maybe he'd take his turn on the microphone, too, because he had done some singing, and he thought he had something to contribute. That was Musiq Soulchild. The little teenager up past his bedtime, wailing jazz songs out of his mind, was Bilal. The stripper girl was Eve, who was still calling herself Eve of Destruction. A friend of mine visited from Atlanta and brought a girl with a guitar, and that was India.Arie. Jasmine Sullivan was there, ten years old but with the voice of a grown woman. Common was there. All of this unfolded in my living room in South Philadelpha in the late nineties.

It was a madhouse. People were milling around outside, waking up the neighbors, playing loud music until all hours. But it wasn't people playing loud music on boom boxes or stereos. They were actually playing it on guitars and singing with microphones. They were making loud music, putting it into a space where there had been no music before. By the seventh week, I was calling the police to say, "There's a disturbance at 2309 St. Albans." Just to get some sleep, I was calling the cops on myself! But when I think about that time, the most amazing thing is how many of those artists made it. There were at least eighteen record contracts in the room, and at least nine of the people who became recording artists ended up bigger than us. And yet, it was an indisputably magical time, a kind of rebirth. If hip-hop had died at the 1995 *Source* Awards, I felt like something new was being born on St. Albans.

THIRTEEN

A re there hip-hop creationists? I'm an evolutionist. In fact, I have a theory that hip-hop, being a living thing, evolves in five-year cycles. But I also have a theory that it's a little bit behind the beat, that the evolutionary moments occur not right on the decades and half-decades, but on the 2s and the 7s. The whole thing gets under way in 1977, the year of the big New York blackout and punk music and underground clubs beginning to spawn a new kind of DJ culture. In 1982, there's Afrika Bambaataa's "Planet Rock" and the rise of drum machines, and also Grandmaster Flash and the Furious Five's *The Message* ushering in a new kind of politically conscious hip-hop. In 1987, there's the absolute peak of mature early hip-hop, with records like Eric B. and Rakim's *Paid In Full* and Public Enemy's "Rebel without a Pause" single, which was the first glimmerings of the Bomb Squad sound that would produce *It Takes a Nation of Millions To Hold Us Back* the following year. And 1992 is all about Dr. Dre's *The Chronic*, which changed absolutely everything about hiphop: production, marketing, videos, chart success.

The fifth period of this cycle started in 1997, which was the end of the line for Biggie and Tupac and the start of what they wrought: a new era of conspicuous consumption and conspicuous charisma. In "Bad Boy for Life," P. Diddy rapped, "Don't worry if I write rhymes / I write checks," and that became more than just a clever aside, it was his style of hip-hop. Virtuosity disappeared and this other kind of skill—a ringmaster skill, something closer to what you'd find in a corporate manager—emerged. It was also a watershed year for Jay-Z, who had established himself with *Reasonable Doubt* in 1996, suffered through a terrible period following Biggie's death—they were very close, the twin pillars of the East Coast scene—and then had trouble getting commercial traction for *In My Life-time, Vol. 1*. At least, that is, until "Streets Is Watching" made him an icon. That same year brought a new minimalist phase in production, spe-cifically the work of Swizz Beatz on the one hand and Pharrell Williams and Chad Hugo as the Neptunes on the other.

So that's where we were, as a hip-hop nation. Puffy was tak-ing obvious sampling to its extreme. The Neptunes were stripping down songcraft to its skeleton and also riding the crest of a cult-of-personality wave. And where were we? Where was I? I was perched on the precipice of what would eventually be called neo soul. I was processing all the sounds around me, all the artists who were helping to make a new kind of music from those sounds, and I was feeling an energy I hadn't ever felt before. That house party that was running at all hours in my house in Philadelphia had migrated to New York, to Electric Lady Studios, where we were working on D'Angelo's *Voodoo* in one booth and Common's *Like Water for Chocolate* in another, and trying to find time in the middle to get the next Roots record together.

———

One day in the future, kids will turn to their parents and ask what life was like before Skype. Well, I can tell you one thing: it was more expensive. I probably could have had another ninety grand in my pocket if it wasn't for hotel phone bills. In the mid-nineties I must have poured $100,000 into hotel phones. The last time I got a gargantuan hotel bill, in fact, was at the end of 1996, or maybe the very beginning of 1997. I was on tour, and Q-Tip started calling my pager. I checked my messages, at the hotel's extortionate rates, and there was no message, exactly, only music: that third interlude from the Slum Village album. D'Angelo called soon after that and left a message of his own. "Whoo!" he said. "We've got some shit that I'll bet you haven't heard."

I called D'Angelo back. "The fuck was that?"

"It's Jay Dee's group," he said. "Slum Village."

I told him to put more of it on my answering machine. He called and put three snippets on it. I kept calling to listen to it over and over again. Three hours passed and the bills began to mount. But I knew that the record, *Fantastic Vol. 1*, was pushing us all toward something larger, toward a kind of music that many of us had dreamed about but did not possess the vision to turn it into something real.

Jay Dee, J Dilla, Dilla...call him what you will. I had met him for the first time, apparently, during one of the earliest moments of the Roots' national emergence. It was back in 1995, the week that *Do You Want More?!!!??!* came out, and we played a show at Irving Plaza in New York and then went west for shows in Los Angeles and San Francisco. Rich had told us for years that we were in our *Rocky* period, spending all our time in the gym so we could come out and win our first fight decisively. Finally we had reached the ring. The New York show, in particular, was my hip-hop dream: there were so many people in the audience whose work I had admired, like Grand Puba, the Pharcyde, the Wu-Tang Clan. Backstage, I was talking to the Pharcyde. "Why are you guys here in New York?" I said.

"We're getting more music from Q-Tip," Imani said.

"What?" I said. "You're not working with J-Swift anymore?" He had produced their first record, *Bizarre Ride II The Pharcyde*, but there were rumors that he was suffering from various personal problems, amplified by substance abuse issues.

"No," Imani said. "We're doing this next record with Tip and Diamond D." That was exciting for me: the Pharcyde and Q-Tip making music together. But as it turned out, Q-Tip didn't have anything for them, and he referred them to a guy he was working with named Jay Dee. I was disappointed because he was just a protégé. I wanted to see the real thing. And not for the first time and not for the last time, I didn't react well to my own disappointment. I shined Jay Dee off the same way I did D'Angelo the first time I met him, just literally ignored him. I looked the other way. I struck up a conversation with the people around him.

About a month later, the Roots were opening for the Pharcyde for a series of shows. After we finished playing one, we packed up our gear and went out to the parking lot, where I had a few minutes to kill before a kid from the local college came to pick me up for an interview at the college radio station. I headed back to the van to pick up my Triple Five Soul wool jacket, and as I went, I could hear vibrations coming from the back of the club. The Pharcyde had just taken the stage. I paused by the van, because the only thing I could really hear, amid all the rest of the noise and music, was a crazy discrepancy in the kick drum. It was almost like someone drunk was playing drums—or, more so, that a drunk, brilliant four-year-old had been allowed to program the kick pattern. I had to see what I was hearing. I left the van and ran to the front of the club to listen, and when I got there, the band was playing the first cut from *Labcabincalifornia*, "Bullshit," and Dilla was just going crazy on the kick pattern. At that moment, I had the same reaction I do to anything truly radical in hip-hop. I was paralyzed, uncertain how to feel. Usually, if I go over the top with my approval for an album or a band, it turns out to be a solid achievement: a four-star product, maybe even 4½. But like I said, if I'm brought up short by a piece of artwork, if I'm conflicted, confounded, and made uncomfortable, nine times out of ten that thing will change the course of history. That's the feeling I got when I heard Dilla's kick pattern on "Bullshit."

Then, a few years later, in my hotel room and lonely on the road, I heard the fruits of that experimentation, which was the Slum Village record that Dilla made. It was a messiah moment, in a way, for people like me and D'Angelo and Q-Tip. We had been looking for someone to lead us out of the darkness, to take us across the desert. Most of the time in those cases, you don't know who you're looking for until you see them. That's how people felt about Prince, or Jimi Hendrix before him, or about the Beatles, or about the Beach Boys. There wasn't a sound there and then, suddenly, there was one. It's a magic trick.

––––––

At first, to be honest, working on the new Roots album, *Things Fall Apart*, was a side dish for me. *Voodoo* was my main project. If someone had run into me in the street, I wouldn't have been able to stop talking about it: about the way that D'Angelo was going to revolutionize soul music and revitalize the very idea of soul, the way that it was going to permanently change the way that audiences experienced recorded sound. There was such excitement, such a strong sense that it was going to be a landmark. I was also working on Common's *Like Water for Chocolate*, an album that was also knee-deep in experimentation and excitement, and which also had the spark of the new. In my head at that time, the notion of a Roots album was a distant third. But maybe that just meant that it was kicking around in my subconscious absorbing everything I was learning with the other projects. Take production, for example. I've talked in the press about the way that an afternoon session listening to new material from DJ Premier, J Dilla, and D'Angelo made me recognize that I needed to work harder to be taken seriously as a songwriter and producer. Well, what I was starting to see was that I was already working harder; it was just a matter of opening my eyes to what was around me. For most of my time in the Roots, I had learned production from Bob Power, who had been an excellent mentor when it came to the basics of engineering and producing. Under him, I went from being mostly ignorant to being entirely competent.

But *Voodoo* was both a step to the side and a leap forward. That album was engineered by Russell Elevado, and everything he did on it—his philosophy about sound, his methods for producing it and capturing it—were revelatory. I went from having a strong command of primary colors to being suddenly aware that I could create any color I wanted. Growing up the way I had, with an appreciation for the warm sound of sixties and seventies records—remember, the band my father and mother created was one of the groups sampled on Dr. Dre's *The Chronic*—I had labored under the fear that I would never reach the level of the break-beat gods. The artists who made those original songs worked with different equipment in a different time. They got sounds that were fuller, hairier, at once more uneven and more complete than anything we could get. Or so I thought, until I worked with Russell. On *Voodoo*, there's one song, "Greatdayindamornin'," that has a second half to it called "Booty." For that interlude, Russell took my drums and fed them through a guitar amp, through a processor, and then back to the board. It gave them this unimaginable analog sound, like they were drums coming from 1950. Another day we'd come in and he would have everything set for a level of extreme compression, well beyond what I had been told was acceptable, or he would start recording vocals through these ribbon microphones that I'd never heard of before. New equipment, new techniques, a willingness to experiment: it was a profound awakening. If the color analogy doesn't work, here's a food analogy: If Bob Power taught me how to make a pizza, it was Russell who taught me endless ways to prepare it.

I spent so much time working with D'Angelo that it caused understandable resentment within the Roots sometimes. It wasn't that my loyalty was questioned, exactly, but my focus was. It was a concern, obviously, though *Voodoo* wasn't the only culprit. While finally focusing on

Things Fall Apart, I ran into Gerry Brown, Raphael Saadiq's engineer, who was working in the studio next door. Gerry is world famous for his all-year-round Christmas decorations during his sessions. Curious to see his elaborate arrangement, I burst into Studio B, and there she was. Gerry made introductions. I was smitten. I instantly ignored my album responsibilities for about two weeks, always finding an excuse to wind up in her sessions. We talked about music, I picked her brain, and I introduced her to my new favorite discovery of 1998: Krispy Kreme Doughnuts. Meanwhile, the album was slipping away from me. I didn't care. You couldn't tell me that things weren't accelerating with this girl, though progress was slow and I was—I always am—a nice guy. Then she mentioned a boyfriend. Our three-hour calls shrunk to "I'll call you back," and that either happened, or it didn't. That's the story of how I met Alicia Keys.

———

In the Roots, everyone had their role. I realized very early on that my role was to occupy the left, to add the sense of experiment and artistic risk. I was entrusted with that blue-state material. Tariq, on the other hand, defended the basic template. In his head, his audience was the guys in the barbershop, and so he was always wondering how far he could let me stray from that before he was embarrassed by my ideas. In my head, I was pleading my case before Reginald C. Dennis's Mind Squad and other examples of the hip-hop intelligentsia. Sometimes I thought of our records in terms of that scene in *Back to the Future* where Marty McFly, in the fifties, is failing to get his parents together, and as a result his image is starting to fade from the photograph he's carrying with him. I would listen to the music we were making and imagine if the review was fading from the front page and becoming somehow secondary. If we weren't breaking new ground, if we weren't raising the stakes aesthetically, then what were we doing? It was that kind of creative tension that kept the band vibrant.

As the sessions that would produce *Things Fall Apart* continued, as we started trying to capture this moment that people would soon start to call neo soul, I was determined to keep those left-of-center ideas in the music. Fairly soon, though, I ran up against my limit as a song-writer and a pop-music consumer. The Roots had long been the loudest and most powerful hip-hop group around, but we used to watch with a mix of confusion, frustration, and amazement as groups sped past us on the charts, acts that were playing the junior circuit to our senior circuit picked up steam and found themselves out in front. The two groups that were the most similar to us, in terms of sensibility, were OutKast and the Fugees; during that period stretching from 1997 to 2001, they were hip-hop's idea of what the left of the spectrum looked like. But as much as we may have felt a kinship with them, or even competition with them, we weren't them. At some point, I realized why. It was something I wasn't doing, something that maybe I couldn't do. I don't know how to put it diplomatically, but I didn't really know what pop songs were.

I had always been that way, even as a kid: as I said, I listened to the parts of the song that were in the background, or the secondary effects that were serving the main song. The main thing sometimes escaped me. When I started making my own records, I struggled with that same problem. My idea of making a catchy R&B-flavored song was limited to getting a certain texture in the instruments, or hiring someone to sing a hook. The rest of it, the real work of a pop song, eluded me.

There was one moment during the recording of *Voodoo* that really brought this home. We were recording DJ Premier's scratches for "Devil's Pie," and Q-Tip had just left the room to go work on something else, so there were four of us left there: Premier, Dilla, D'Angelo, and myself. During a break, Premier asked if anyone had any new shit to play for the group, and D'Angelo went for a cassette and played a bit of a new song, and the whole room just erupted in hooting. Then Dilla put on some new Slum Village shit and it was the same thing: an explosion of excitement. Then Premier, who had started the whole thing, played an M.O.P. song and some new Gang Starr material that he was working on for *The Ownerz*.

I was last at bat. All I had on me was a work tape for what would eventually become "Double Trouble" on *Things Fall Apart*.[15] It didn't have finished vocals yet, didn't have Mos Def's verse. It was just a skeleton. I played it, and I will never forget the feeling that came over the room, including me. It wasn't that they didn't hoot and holler like they had for the other songs. They did. But they didn't mean it. I know the move people resort to when they're not quite into a song: they keep a straight stare on their face and bob their head a bit, not saying anything, not making eye contact. That's the sign of death. That's what they all did to me, and I felt humiliated. I was like Glenn Close in *Fatal Attraction*: I will not be ignored! I went back into the studio that same night and gave that song a radical, extended facelift. I refused to sleep until I had that thing up and running.

I knew from then on that anything I did had to meet the standard of the room. It wasn't enough to appeal to some unseen critics. I needed the artists around me to react with more than the straight-ahead, quiet-as-the-grave head bob. It was a turning point in my under-standing of my own career. I knew that the other guys respected me as a drummer, as a player, but I also wanted them to respect me as a producer and a songwriter. I took a long look at myself after debuting "Double Trouble" for the room and realized that if I wanted to be in their fraternity, I had to pull it up a notch.

As a group, we were lucky to still have our relationship with Scott Storch, who had never lost sight of his great sense of melody. If I was

---

15. I love "Double Trouble." It's a masterpiece of sorts. But no one really gives a shit about that song, you know? There's lots of great weirdness on that album but most of its reputation rests on the few big singles.

putting in extra time and extra effort to get the rhythmic details right and Tariq was concentrating on the lyrics, Scott's right hand was always ready with a melody. Those three things combined to help us set course for *Things Fall Apart*. Plus, we had a theme. The Chinua Achebe novel of the same name is about a Nigerian man who returns to his village to find that the only constant was change, that Western ways were wiping out the traditions that made his culture distinctive. That resonated with me as an analogy for what had happened to hip-hop: we were part of a music that had, at least early on, been so new, so true to itself, but there had been a corruption from the outside, and what was once there was gone. That was the spatial dimension of the idea, inside threatened by outside, but there was a temporal dimension, too, tradition threatened by newcomers. That gave the whole thing a different kind of spin. We were on our third record. We weren't new kids anymore. But we weren't hoary old bluesmen either. Or were we? We were starting to write songs about our personal travails that didn't sound like ambitious whining. We were maturing, whether we liked it or not. And if blues is, as Ralph Ellison wrote, an "autobiographical chronicle of a personal catastrophe expressed lyrically," then that's what we were recording. Just listen to "The Return to Innocence Lost," the powerful poem by Ursula Rucker that closes the record. It's about violence in an interracial marriage, the tragedy of asking children to look up to a man who isn't prepared to be a father. It's about choices made in life, as wrong as often as they're right, and the fact that time extends past that, into a place where new choices have to be made. Is there anything more blues than that?

I don't know whether we felt at the time like *Things Fall Apart* was our make-or-break record. That may be the hindsight talking. But we certainly felt like a gap was opening up between us and a certain segment of our audience, namely the traditional hip-hop audience. After just two records, the second of which was fairly conservative by hip-hop standards, we were already feeling like we were on the margins: not strangers in a strange land, but strangers in our own land.

We tried to make sense of it on wax. For the start of the record we picked an excerpt of the dialogue from Spike Lee's 1990 film *Mo' Better Blues*. It's a scene when Bleek Gilliam, played by Denzel Washington, is lamenting the demographics of the crowds who come to see him play. Bleek is an aging trumpeter, a defeated purist, a little weary as he walks his road and more than a little disenchanted with the way that the black community has cooled to the jazz that he considers sacred. "If we had to depend upon black people to eat, we would starve to death," he says. "I mean, you've been out there, you're on the bandstand, you look out into the audience, what do you see? You see Japanese, you see—you see West Germans, you see—you know, Slavolic, anything except our people. It makes no sense. It incenses me that our own people don't realize our own heritage, our own culture. This is our music, man." Bleek's speech must have sounded familiar to our ears.

But the scene in *Mo' Better Blues* isn't a speech, it's a dialogue. Bleek is answered by Shadow Henderson, played by Wesley Snipes. Shadow's a hotshot young saxophonist, and he has a different idea about artists and audiences. "That's bullshit," he says. "Everything, everything you just said is bullshit. Out of all the people in the world, you never gave anybody else a chance to play their own music.... That's right, the people don't come because you grandiose motherfuckers don't play shit that they like. If you played the shit that they like, then people would come, simple as that."

And the scene isn't just a dialogue. It's a dialectic in the classic sense: a way of setting an idea against its negation in the hope of finding a ray of light. That problem—how to stay true to our idea of our music and also be appropriately inviting to audiences, how to court audiences without compromising the music we were making—was something that had plagued us since the beginning. We had been through at least two different versions of Roots-ness: the far left-of-center of *Do You Want More?!!!??!* and the tougher, more straightforward approach of *Illadelph Halflife*, and in both cases a certain size audience had come along for the ride, but when we turned to look at the backseat, saw empty spaces along with the smiling faces. Back in 1994, if you were a major label act selling three hundred thousand copies of a record, you were on the bubble. You were extending yourself into commercial space but not capturing the imagination of the mainstream. We were making music that mattered to us, but we needed to know that it mattered to anyone else—or, if it didn't, why not. The fact that we were somehow falling short was a source of consternation, not as bad as the scene that Ursula sketched out in "The Return to Innocence Lost," but a kind of suffering nonetheless. We had given most of our adult lives to that point to the band. What if success never came to us, or never came in the form we expected? Was there something we were doing wrong? Was it because we were too uncompromising? Was it because we weren't good at writing hits? Were we coming up short in the entertainment department or long in the substance department? Either one of those things could affect a record's sales.

The thing about dialectic, though, is that it's a process. You have the thesis (in this case, Bleek's argument that black people should support jazz, or is that hip-hop) and the antithesis (Shadow's argument that the artists who create that jazz, or is that hip-hop, need to be more mindful of the entertainment needs of their audience). Did we have a synthesis? It was 1999. The year before, OutKast had released *Aquemini*, which had a song called "Synthesizer." It was a slow burner, with George Clinton singing a filthy bridge part about cybersex and "psychosodomy." André 3000's verse got back to the title. He gives examples of the way that technology allows men (and women) to alter themselves so that they're not quite human anymore. There are riffs on plastic surgery and cloning, on virtual reality and virtual spirituality. Then, toward the end, there's a broader condemnation of the breakneck pace of modern life ("Hurry, hurry, rush, rush, world on the move") and the capricious nature of laws and rules ("marijuana illegal but cigarettes cool").

"Synthesizer" is about a culture in crisis, a modern America that's knee-deep in suffering. It's less direct than "The Return to Innocence Lost," but it's suffering nonetheless. How can society give us the tools to change ourselves but not, at the same time, treat the self-hatred that makes us run away from our true selves? Why are some things (cigarettes, say) labeled as permissible, even desirable in some ways, while other things (marijuana, say) are labeled as unacceptable or even illegal? And why has society been allowed to accelerate beyond the point where it makes sense to most of its citizens? That quick pace, without regard for the people caught up in it, risks destroying value, whether in food or art or music or human relationships. "Instant, quick grits, new, improved," André raps, not sounding convinced that they're an improvement at all. Progress pulls us along but it also holds us back.

So what to do? "Synthesizer" was a jester at the gallows. It laughed and left you hanging. Some people (most?) might think that the title is only about the process of becoming dehumanized, synthetic like the processed sounds of a synthesizer. Most people (some?) wouldn't see it as a call for the *other* kind of synthesis, the good-faith attempt to resolve opposing elements that is at the heart of the dialectic process. Unless that's exactly what it was. And if it was, if hip-hop was once again telling stories about the tearing of society's fabric, about well-intentioned people cast adrift, then wasn't it doing the good work that soul music had done before it, and blues before that? When Rich and I wrote the manifesto in Paris about Biggie and hip-hop materialism, about how the music was getting away from the people who listened to it, and the world that contained the people who were listening to it, those are the kinds of thoughts that were on our mind, and they remained there when we released *Things Fall Apart*. We wondered if they would continue to fall apart—and if not, who would keep them together, and how.

FOURTEEN

How did I know we had finally made it? My alarm was set for six one morning in 1999, and I woke to the radio, where the very identifiable voice of a young black woman was happily requesting a Roots song. *Things Fall Apart* was just about to come out, and she wanted to hear something from it. I didn't jump out of bed, but I thought about doing it. To me, that was a new world: black people loved the Roots? Black women? Maybe I could be Bleek and Shadow both.

I can't stress how strange it was to hear a black woman on the radio asking a DJ if he could find it in his heart to play the new Roots song. I had resigned myself to the fact that my life as a public figure would be confined to one kind of response: I'm at a movie theater or a mall, I walk by a young couple, and the guy just loses his shit. "Did you see that?" he says to his girlfriend. "Do you know who that is?" The girlfriend shrugs. She has no idea. She couldn't care less. Even when she's prompted, it elicits a shrug, or at best an anemic nod. It had happened so many times that I had been through a cycle with it: amusement, then confusion, then a little disappointment, then frustration, then amusement again. What are you gonna do?[16] But to be

---

16. Opinions in the band may differ. There were always enough girls for Tariq, that's for damn sure. But yeah, there weren't so many girls that you didn't have to be proactive.

in 1999, to be on the brink of *Things Fall Apart*, to hear that girl on the radio requesting our song, I felt like maybe we were moving into a new space.

It wasn't accidental. We had made a strong record, and the response to it suggested that the kind of music we liked, the kind of music that we were supporting in the artists around us, was coming to the fore in American culture. But there were also hard industry realities, and for once they were on our side.

Our life as major-label artists had continued to be a roller coaster as the record industry became stubbornly more corporate. We were in our third phase of life: DGC had defaulted into Geffen, which in turn had defaulted into MCA. This didn't seem like a bad thing from our perspective: MCA had absorbed Geffen's whole urban department, which had experience with the right radio stations and video channels and stores, and they had added a big positive in the form of Jay Boberg. Jay had founded IRS Records in 1979, and his main claim to fame was presiding over the growth of R.E.M. from college-rock stars to mainstream superstars, after which they decamped for Warner Bros. Jay believed in us. Maybe that's not fair—many label presidents believed in us. They all did, I'm sure. But Jay pledged to use his resources and his influence to get us to the level where he believed we should be. But it was a tradeoff: if he was going to the mat for us, he expected us to give him something to work with.

Back then, there was a fairly rigid system for releasing a new record. First you put out a street single that served as a kind of leak, the Paul Revere of the new record. For *Things Fall Apart*, that was "Don't See Us." Then you did a college single to get younger listeners and smaller radio stations interested: that was "Adrenaline!" Then when those two songs had prepared the market, you put out the so-called real first single, which was "You Got Me." For *Things Fall Apart*, for the first time, that three-part process worked like a charm. The first single attracted enough attention to create demand for the second single, and the second for the third, which meant that the product containing all those singles and more—the album—was already highly desired before it even existed.

We also benefited, I think, from being positioned as counterpro gramming to the dominant forces in hip-hop, which were perceived as moving toward the extremes of commercialism. By that time, the charts were filled with albums by artists like DMX, Snoop Dogg, the Hot Boyz, and Juvenile. Puffy's label, Bad Boy, was the leader as a production and cultural force, and Jay-Z was probably the second-most influential artist. In the broader music world, Disney had just broken big, and the pop landscape was dominated by highly calcu-lated acts like Britney Spears, Christina Aguilera, and so forth. We were embraced because of what we *weren't*. Add to that the fact that there was a void in conscious hip-hop—A Tribe Called Quest had imploded the previous year—and our elevation made sense. Authen-ticity was in short supply. We were perceived as something real. We filled a niche. (Just for historical context, our record came out the same day as the debut record by another artist who spun questions of authenticity in a completely different direction: Eminem. It was also the same day as Lauryn Hill's coronation at the Grammy Awards.)

And so there we were, embraced by critics as usual, but also by an unusually receptive public. And even then there were lessons in the way that *Things Fall Apart* was received and processed. Some were trivial in the global sense, but they were important to me at the time. For example, we finally got the lead-review spot in *Rolling Stone*: Touré was the reviewer, and he gave us a glowing four-star review, which was only a half-star less than the magazine had given Prince's *Dirty Mind* in 1980. The band was thrilled, and I was, too, except for one little heartbreak: somehow I got left out of the illustration that accompanied the piece. As the lifelong *Rolling Stone* review geek, it seemed like a particularly cruel irony. After all, when I papered my bedroom wall with reviews, I saved a spot at the end of the line for my own band's review, whenever that happened. Well, it happened, and I wasn't even in the drawing: they were using a reference photo from our *Illadelph Halflife* press kit, and even though I was one of the more recognizable figures in the picture, somehow I wasn't drawn.

That was a local injury. The larger hit came from the fact that some critics were starting to knock us for being too thoughtful or calculated, too brainy. That's when my eyes were opened yet again to the fact that a certain portion of our critical base felt more comfortable in a limited field. They wanted their same old U2 and their familiar Ice Cube, and never the twain shall meet.[17] And that wasn't the last time, by any means. It's part of a larger problem that springs from the way people—all people, but critics in particular—manage their identity through the music they champion. What I learned in the months following the release of *Things Fall Apart* was this: if you're going to be left-of-center, then you're going to have to win. What I mean by that is that most critics don't have room for two or three intellectually provocative, musically omnivorous hip-hop groups on their list. They have room for one. And so when they fill that slot in their list, they're going to be as conservative with that pick as is humanly possible. If the year's left-of-center release is Lauryn Hill, then the momentum builds for Lauryn Hill. If it's OutKast, then the momentum builds for OutKast. Years before, I had watched these issues play out at the

---

17. It's not just that, Ahmir. It's a question of how arty you're allowed to be when you're black. Take Dirty Projectors. I like that record. It's not like everybody in the world is talking about it, but they respect it and it sells 37,000 copies. I can't really think of black artists who sell so little and maintain a level of respect. For reasons that are part of history, the black middle class is not necessarily full of that kind of art-oriented thinking. They need for things to have concrete, readily apparent success.

Source Awards, seen the opposition between haves and have-nots, money rap and art rap, critical favorites and commercial powers. I saw it again with *Things Fall Apart*, and I've seen it with every album since.

But the problem goes even a little deeper than that, in the sense that it stops around skin deep. It's clear to me that there are certain critics who feel that they can't champion the Roots because it somehow exposes them—and here I'm talking mainly about middle-class black writers. It makes me sad to write this, but it also makes me sad to see it: some of them, I have noticed, will purposely bash us for what they perceive as a lack of street credibility—not *our* street credibility, mind you, but the street credibility that they get (or do not get) from endorsing us. It's too obvious, in a way, for them to come out firmly behind the Roots. To praise us would be redundant given the circumstances of their own life, the ideas they're interacting with, the pressures they're under. As I've gotten older, I have noticed this at record labels, in the TV business, and elsewhere: black people who are the only black people at their jobs will feel a need to overcompensate and show their blackness explicitly.[18]

I'm not immune to this. In fact, I'm so susceptible to it that I know where to look for it. I was at breakfast recently with a friend at a soul-food restaurant, and she was offered either grits or home fries as a side

18. I remember an interview with a writer who was in college during the Black Power movement, at an Ivy League school, I think. He said that the first time he heard the slogan "Black Is Beautiful," he felt completely empowered. Then an hour later he felt paranoid, wondering if he was black enough, if he was included in this new beautiful class. Hip-hop groups, even if they were smart, still wanted to have an air of black cool. Hip-hop was a simulacrum of black cool. And I don't really believe in black cool. I believe in it as a psychological device, as in having some emotional distance from things you can't control. From the outside that seems cool. And so I think middle-class blacks felt like these hip-hop motherfuckers were more authentically black than they were.

dish. She chose home fries. Instantly I got defensive. "Why didn't you get grits?" I said.

"I don't want them," she said. "I'd rather have the home fries."

"Right," I said. "But it's *grits*."

I felt like it was rude for her to reject the grits because it struck me as a way of rejecting her blackness. Then it hit me. Holy shit. Was that my version of being a middle-class black music writer? Maybe the grits were Mystikal or DMX and the home fries were the Roots, and the pressure was on to be blacker. Forget about the calories. Forget about what she might have actually liked or wanted. I became a grits peddler for all the wrong reasons. If we as a band make subpar material, then I can handle the lack of attention or the critical brush-off. But I don't want to be sold down the river because a writer wants to feel *blacker*.

Things Fall Apart was the first time that we heard whisperings of what we've heard more explicitly as our career has progressed—that we weren't black enough. What does that mean to say we're not black enough? I ask that straightforwardly more than rhetorically. What does it mean? This puts yet another wrinkle in the argument, by the way: in addition to middle-class black critics rejecting us, or at least embracing us reluctantly because we somehow signify "brainy" or "intellectual," we have had to rethink our own intellectual stance.

It's strange for me to admit this, not least because if you saw me you would find it absurd. I have a giant afro. I weigh over three hundred pounds. No one, upon first seeing me, thinks I'm not black enough. And yet, in interviews, I'm still going through that whole speaks-so-well syndrome. It happened with journalists early on, especially, both white journalists and black journalists. Rich taught me how to embrace it. You know that scene in *Good Will Hunting* where Matt Damon shows off his intellect to the guys in the bah? That's what it's like with Rich. Nothing pleases him more than for people to think that he's some kind of dreadlocked, dirty homeless man and then to hit them with that supernova intellect. He lives for that underestimation, baiting someone to think that he's less than he is. I have done it, too. I have used my own intellect to my advantage, as a kind of shock tactic. But there's still the same kind of classification. Where do you fall on the axis? How black are you? Whose cultural masters are you serving?

This problem spreads in all directions at once. These days, I'm frequently called upon to be a tastemaker. Say I'm asked to make my own year-end list of best records, and say I know that Grizzly Bear will be my top record, with PJ Harvey after that. Maybe Kanye West is on there, too. Filling in the rest is difficult, or gets increasingly difficult, because I'm both trying to list all the albums that mattered to me and trying to nuance my brand. If I want to impress people with my range, does that mean that I should put an alternative rock album on the list? It used to be that people would balk a little bit when I did that. They didn't know that I loved Brian Wilson, say, and that came as a shock somehow—hip-hop artist loves Beach Boys. Now that my love for classic rock is well known, now that the Roots have been a little clearer about our influences and our presence on Jimmy Fallon's show has demonstrated our connection to so many different kinds of music, the problem has almost reversed. Now if I embrace Big Sean or something obviously black, people find it strange. Recently, I did a DJ set that was chock-full of the most ignorant, retrograde rap I could find. Why? I don't know. To prove I'm still black? But isn't that just joining the long tradition of black guys wearing blackface? There's always the danger of minstrelsy.

In all of this, there are two currents: the personal and the cultural. And even though people like to furrow their brow like they suspect you're not being honest about yourself, the truth is that they worry that you're not serving their idea of you. The first time I ever heard the phrase "selling out," I heard it as Black Panther jargon—their idea that you shouldn't sell out to the man, to the system. But these days I hear it far more from white kids than from militant black kids. And when you hear that tossed around, particularly when it comes to cultural preferences, you can start to wonder if maybe there's something inauthentic about your own tastes. Am I embracing Radiohead based on a genuine love of it, or is it a survival tactic because the band carries a certain amount of critical cachet? This question has been on the table since *Things Fall Apart*, and it's not coming off the table. There are new rock records I love so much these days, but I'm gun-shy about saying so. Does that make sense? Is it all in my head? You'd think that at this point there'd be an understanding that I'm not faking, that I love music of all kinds. But there are so many signifiers whizzing around.[19]

For all the critical angst that it touched off, *Things Fall Apart* was also more or less an unqualified success. It put us significantly down the road to our goals. We were touring as headliners. We were on the radio more than ever before. We were selling more records. The album also made good on the promise of those Philly house-party jam sessions, and justified my sense that we had built a community of like-minded artists around us. Beanie Siegel, who was a presence

---

19. Listen, any critic has to do that, because what is at the heart of liking something? Say you like classical music. Or say you like classical music and traditional Chinese music and music from the Caribbean and black soul and hardcore punk and classic rock. Each of those genres has a certain history, so people feel it's not enough just to *like* them: they have to figure out who it appeals to, what are the active elements that spur on the people who listen to it. So white critics study the people who appreciate hip-hop, and they don't want to champion hip-hop that isn't respected. The same goes for a hip-hop artist trying to establish his bona fides as an indie-rock fan.

at the house, made his recording debut as a guest artist on "Adrenaline!" Eve made her debut on "You Got Me" and was nearly joined by Jill Scott on the same song. This was one of the cases of label intervention that we accepted, not always in the best spirits, but with the understanding that there were other factors at play. Jill had written the song with us, helped to develop it in those extended house-party sessions. But the label wanted a bigger name, so they asked that the part be re-recorded by Erykah Badu. Even so, when we took the song out on the road we took Jill with us, and she was able to reclaim the song somewhat. In either form, the song turned out to be a big part of the album's success. It caught on among mainstream radio stations and got us in rotation at video channels, and eventually it even won a Grammy.

Right around the same time as the Grammy Awards, *Voodoo* finally came out. I had lived with it, or lived within it, for years, but suddenly it was available to everyone else, and everyone else could hear what I heard, see what I saw, and draw their own conclusions about it. And yet, I had a privileged relationship with the record. D'Angelo liked to call me the "copilot" of the record, and now it was landing. Back then, and since, whenever people asked me about the nuts and bolts of the record, I was happy to oblige. I could spend hours talking about the way we arranged "Devil's Pie," or the way that the album took something from an early Eric B. and Rakim album and made it into something new, or the way that it out-Princed Prince in other stretches. Sometimes I did talk about it, and what I felt then is what I feel now: every single song is worthy of a chapter in a book. Maybe one day I'll write that book, a biography of those songs from the moment of their birth. But this is a different book, and where *Voodoo* is concerned, we only have the album—well, the album and the hundreds and thousands of words written about it. The release of *Voodoo* was, in some ways, stranger for me than the release of any Roots record: I was invented but not invested, central but not central, a participant and observer both. And so, when critics started to weigh in on the record, I took a special interest in what they said and how they said it. Most of them saw (or rather, heard) what was special about it immediately. They noticed that *Voodoo* was a different kind of proposition, creatively speaking. Prior to it, hip-hop had used the past in a certain way, stacking new sounds on top of old sounds and generating energy through that stacking, reveling in juxtapositions, unexpected collisions, and a treatment of existing classics that wasn't quite reverential but at once more analytical and more standoffish. It was brilliant bricklaying. *Voodoo* did something different; it connected to the past in a more organic way. D'Angelo may not have been Curtis Mayfield or Marvin Gaye, but he also wasn't a hip-hop producer intent on recontextualizing Curtis Mayfield or Marvin Gaye. But the individual reactions to it were only part of the story. Soon reviews were stacking up, one on top of the other, and it was a question not only of critical assessment but of a myth beginning to take root. When a few people believe something, it's science; when thousands believe it all at once, without conducting individual investigations, it's something more like religion. In this case, it was a kind of Protestantism: people believed, like I did, that D'Angelo was reacting against a kind of soul music that had grown too bloated and static for its own good, that had invested too much in production techniques (and singing technique) and not enough in the real grit and grain of the art. That's how the iconic status of the album began to grow. Was D a messenger who came bearing this Scripture? Was he himself a kind of savior? Or was it more like a *Life of Brian* situation, where the crowd was out in the town square waiting for their messiah and the next guy to come along got tapped for the job? When people heard "Left and Right" or "Devil's Pie," were they hearing some canny update on old soul music or new music grown in the same soil? And when many different people heard (or thought they heard) the same thing at the same time, when they looked at each other and completed that circuit of recognition, that's when *Voodoo* really started to pick up momentum. The music on the tracks wasn't different, but the people crowding around the tracks were. And that tipped down into a second part of the process: when you believe that something is special, how many people do you want on your bandwagon? Too few and you martyr yourself. Too many and the axle snaps and the whole thing breaks down.

It's important to remember, too, that not everyone agreed with my assessment. Not everyone anointed D'Angelo as their new soul king, and not everyone saw *Voodoo* as a divine document. When we were making the record, some other artists weren't sure about what was happening: they thought it was too abstract, too far into jam-band territory, not focused enough on the kind of songcraft that had distinguished his earlier recordings. They heard us saying that it was a step up from *Brown Sugar* but they worried that we were wrong. And some critics held that view, too: James Hunter, in *Rolling Stone*, saw it as an exercise in style over substance, and wrote that "long stretches of it are unfocused and unabsorbing." He was in the minority, and the degree to which he was in the minority only made the sense of the growing majority more impressive (and, in its own way, more worrisome).

In the wake of the album's release, there would be a tour. Of course there would be. How could there not be a *Voodoo* tour??? And I would be the drummer. How could I not be the drummer? This didn't sit well with the Roots, for obvious reasons. We had finally arrived. We were headliners. We had won a Grammy. Why was I interfering with our momentum? I wish I could say that I spent hours agonizing over the choice, but that would be a lie. Even though it wasn't an easy choice for me, it was a clear choice. As a drummer, as a musician, as a lover of music, I had experienced some of the most transformative days of my life working on *Voodoo*, and I couldn't imagine handing over the reins to someone else. We handpicked the backing group, which included James Poyser on keyboards, Pino Palladino on bass, and a number of other musicians who had played with us at Electric Lady as we made the record.

The tour kicked off at the House of Blues in Los Angeles on March 1, 2000. I could say it was exhilarating and exhausting, but that would be an understatement. It kept us out for eight months, and while we were out, the album just grew and grew. About midway through, the video for "Untitled (How Does It Feel)" was released. That was maybe the most traditional song on the record, the one that was closest to people's idea of neo soul. D'Angelo had cowritten it with Raphael Saadiq, and it felt like a perfect encapsulation of everything that modern soul music could do: it was smooth, like the best crooners, but also multilayered and complex in its arrangement, like Prince. It was abstract enough to be universal. But that was just how it functioned as a record. When the "How Does It Feel" video came out—call it famous or call it infamous, but everyone knows why you have to call it one or the other—the conversation shifted to D'Angelo and his body, to from the sensuality of the music to the straightforward sex-symbol pose of the video. That changed the complexion of everything: of the album, of his celebrity, of the tour. There were more and more girls screaming at him, trying to get backstage. It was a distraction—not an unpleasant one, really, but one that subtly, and then not so subtly, shifted attention away from the music we were making.

———

Back in 1994, when I saw the South African DJ Aba Shanti in London, I was transformed and transported by the way he used the turntable as something that was spiritual in addition to being musical. I wondered if I would ever have that chance. In Miami in March of 2001, at the Winter Music Conference, I did. I conceived of and executed the perfect DJ set.

Thanks to the success of *Things Fall Apart*, and then to the even larger success of *Voodoo*, neo soul and the hip-hop acts connected to it were at the absolute height of popularity, which meant that my star was in ascendance. That in turn meant that when I signed up for a DJ set, that the place was packed with like-minded artists. Dilla was in the house. Erykah, too. When I looked around the room, I felt a swell of pride. Our movement really was a movement. There was proof in every corner of the room. And it was like a personal history lesson for me as well: there figures from my Philadelphia past and people from London who had taken an interest in our career. Gilles Peterson was there, and Jazzy Jeff, and Louie Vega.

That night, I was able to shock them all. Part of it, I'm sure, was the result of lowered expectations. Most of the people there knew me primarily as a drummer, though maybe thanks to *Voodoo* they also had a sense that I was a bandleader or music director or coproducer. But most of them hadn't seen me DJ, even though I had been doing it since I was eleven.

My strength as a DJ lies in masterful segues. Even before I saw Aba Shanti, I knew that a DJ was a kind of crowd psychologist, an expert at observing the way the audience's minds work and how they respond. But developing a philosophy requires lots of trial and error. As a younger man, I had practice at Philadelphia clubs like Silk City and Fluid, where I learned that sometimes bad records are just as important as good records. In other words, if I want to get an orgasmic response out of playing the horn intro to Pete Rock and CL Smooth's "They Reminisce Over You," then maybe it's wiser if the two records just before it aren't as familiar or iconic. The mind adjusts to those other records. It relaxes. There's a refractory period. I've tried things the other way, with nothing but peaks, but it backfires. By the nineteenth record people are worn out. They're numb. When I figured out how to avoid the numbness and started to get a sense of how to thrust the best records into relief, I designed a kind of blueprint for the perfect set. By the time I got to the Winter Music Conference, I had it working like a well-oiled machine. I would play ten orgasmic records and then two cool-down records, then eight orgasmic records followed by three cool-down records, then seven orgasmic records and four cool-down records, and then repeat until the audience was satisfied. Bands do the same thing with their setlists. They pace themselves. And artists do the same thing when they build an album, which is something I know how to do well.

That night, in Miami, I worked the crowd like an instrument. Every time a new record started, people exhaled with pleasure, or their bodies moved automatically. I really started getting high off of the euphoric exclamations. Every record I put on I was like a baptism. I have read about legendary DJ moments, like the way Larry Levan wove the snippets from *The Wizard of Oz* into his set at Paradise Garage in New York, or the night he got fired from the World after playing the Jackson 5's "ABC" over and over again. It wasn't a Roots show. It wasn't a D'Angelo show. It was my show, and it wasn't even exactly that. It was music's show, with turntables as a conduit. Music can be a set of spiritual instructions; that was the level of control I felt like I had over the crowd.

With every high, though, comes a low. And sometimes, with every high comes another high that reveals itself over time to be a low. During the period where I was hard at work on *Voodoo* and *Like Water for Chocolate* and *Things Fall Apart*, *Vibe* wanted to do a story on me. I was uncomfortable with it at the time. It wasn't that I didn't have an ego, but I didn't want to be separated from the rest of the Roots. From the beginning, as in any band, there was always tension when one of us seemed to be taking on too much importance or hogging the spotlight. We dealt with it by enforcing an explicit all-for-one-and-one-for-all mentality. But by this point I was becoming more ubiquitous than the rest of the band. I was associated with more outside artists, starting to get a reputation as a producer. That's when *Vibe* called.

I didn't say no to the article, though, because I thought I might be able to use it for my own purposes, which was to highlight the community around me. I explained my idea to the magazine. "Down at Electric Lady," I said, "there's a group of us—me, D'Angelo, Jay Dee, James Poyser—and between the four of us we're creating some great music for a number of artists. It's like a kind of artist's colony and a factory and an independent record label all rolled into one. You should come and experience that."

One day, as most days, we all happened to be in the studio, and I discovered that Dilla was born in February, which was the same month that D'Angelo was born. James Poyser was born in late January, as was I. That put us all under the sign of Aquarius, and in the course of joking around someone invented the idea of the Soulquarians. Erykah missed the sign by about three days on the Pisces side, but we grandfathered her in, and we also made special dispensation for Common and Bilal and Mos and Talib Kweli. And Q-Tip: how could we leave him out? He was our hero. So in my head it was this utopian paradise I had always envisioned, the Native Tongues movement recreated. It was an extension of the Foreign Objects collective that we had created on South Street and the house jams on St. Albans. And while we didn't take the name so seriously, *Vibe* started coming around with reporters and photographers as their feature came together, and somehow the name got attached to us.

Now flash forward to when the feature came out, which was in September of 2000. I was in Chicago for a D'Angelo show, and we were in the middle of sound check. Someone came up and tapped me on the shoulder. "Ahmir, it's Mos. He wants to talk to you."

"Hey," I said. "What's up?"

"Yeah, man," he said. "I'm not an Aquarian."

"A what?"

"An Aquarian. Does that mean I'm not a real Soulquarian?"

"Well, I didn't name it."

"Yeah," he said. "But it looks like I work for you."

"I'm sorry," I said.

Later, Q-Tip called. "Yo," he said. "This article makes it look like I work for you." Then Erykah called, and she had a problem with the piece, too. By that point, I felt like I had to go see the story. When I did, I could see their point. I was the centerpiece of the photos, and I was prominently featured in the article. Mos and Q-Tip and the rest of them were artists, just like me, and they wanted to control the perception of their brand, just like I did. Not everyone in the group was mad. Common was fine with it. Dilla was fine with it. D'Angelo didn't care about that kind of thing. But it was at that moment that I realized that the paradise I had imagined wasn't headed in a good direction.

FIFTEEN

From: Ben Greenman [cowriter]
To: Ben Greenberg [editor]
Re: Choice of Voice

I'm not sure that's the problem. I mean, sure, it's part of it,
but I don't know that it could have been avoided. A memoir
is a pretty strange thing—a highly synthetic narrative
masquerading as something organic. For proof, you don't
have to look any further than the fact that sometimes Ahmir
will tell me the same story in two slightly different ways.
Maybe the first time it's set in spring and the second time
it's set in summer. When did it actually happen? It's hard
to say: since it happened for him in those seasons, does
it matter when it happened to him? He has earned the
authority to relate events of his own life.

Ahmir has, for the most part, always been surrounded by
other voices. You know how he said, in some conversation
with Rich, that the Roots were the last of a dying breed, not
just because they're older artists, but because they are an
actual group? These days, hip-hop is almost all solo acts,

and what's lost is the interaction of personalities and the richer artwork that produces. He's reiterated that several times: how Tariq represents the red-state constituency (street cred, the barbershop crowd) and he represents the blue-state constituency (art rock, record nerds, and the avant-garde). But he doesn't say it to privilege one over the other, at least explicitly. He says it to privilege the synthesis. I remember someone, maybe Junot Diaz, talking about footnotes in fiction, and how they're a flashpoint for questions of authority and history. But they can be playful in fiction in ways they can't be in fact, where they started as a kind of escape hatch for classical historians hamstrung by rhetorical convention in the body of their text. They couldn't acknowledge sources, integrate other viewpoints, or question their own conclusions in any efficient way, and that led to the rise of the modern footnote in the seventeenth century. It helped historians devise ways of dramatizing their own process.

Wait, I had a point: The other day Ahmir made a joke. "If Rich is shadowing me," he said, "can I shadow him? Or you?" I didn't know exactly what he meant, so I laughed. Today I think I know what he meant. He was wondering if he could, in theory, footnote Rich's footnotes, and maybe even our memos. He can't, of course. We don't want the book to go off the rails. Are there rails?

In Helsinki, Finland. This photo provides proof that we didn't always get to fly first class. *Credit: Ginny Suss*

Inglourious Basterds moment...playing "Celebrity" in a hotel room with our tour manager and some friends. Basically, you choose a Post-it with a celebrity name on it and stick it to your head. Your partner then has to describe that celebrity to you, without using their name, and you have to guess who you are. Kirsten Dunst taught me how to play this game. *Credit: Ginny Suss*

Group photo with our backs to some fifty-thousand-or-so Coachellians. This one was snapped sometime in 2003 on the *Phrenology* tour—going from left to right, we've still got Hub on bass, Martin Luther had joined us on vocals, Kamal, Black Thought, Frank Knuckles, me, and Cap'n Kirk on guitar. *Credit: Ginny Suss*

At the mixing boards on the first day of a long, three-year process of recording the Reverend Al Green's *Lay It Down*. I promised him that I would get him his first R&B Grammy. I lied. He got two. *Credit: Ginny Suss*

In the studio with Tunde Adebimpe and Kyp Malone from TV on the Radio. This was sometime in 2008 for *Soundtrack for a Revolution*, a Danny Glover–produced documentary that featured contemporary artists reworking Civil Rights Movement–themed protest songs. *Credit: Ginny Suss*

Yasiin Bey (formerly known as Mos Def) hops on vocals during my set. After months of campaigning, I DJed a celebration in NYC. Obama had just won. *Credit: Ginny Suss*

In Las Vegas, MDing a band I call the "Illadelphonics," comprising some Roots and some other incredible musicians who came out of Philly (including Adam Blackstone, Omar Edwards, and Jeff Bradshaw), for Jay-Z's pre–New Year's show in 2007, when he was still my boss at Def Jam. First photo is me and Jay in rehearsals. Second photo is backstage before the real show, with Jay-Z and Just Blaze, later that week. *Credit: Ginny Suss*

With Erykah Badu
on the first night of
the *New Amerykah*
tour in Boston,
Massachusetts.
She will soon be
my rival in DJing.
Credit: Ginny Suss

Indulging in overindulgence on the *Game Theory* tour. I let the Chili Peppers'
Chad Smith talk me into investing in a drum set that lit up every time you hit it. It
was the cost of a small condominium and I only got to use it for one month until it
broke. *Credit: Ginny Suss*

In my record room in Philly, right after the release of my Nike Air Questos, summer of '08. I finally have a shoe. *Credit: Ginny Suss*

With Tariq at the boards on the day we finished recording *Rising Down*. *Credit: Ginny Suss*

Christmas week at my new job on *Late Night with Jimmy Fallon*. *Credit: Dana Edelson*

Opening for Dave Matthews at Madison Square Garden. We literally ran off the Fallon set, jumped on the subway to MSG, and made it onstage just in time. *Credit: Ginny Suss*

In 2013, Los Angeles, with my best gal. *Credit: Maisha Stephens-Teacher*

SIXTEEN

How do you measure your own small life next to monumental historical events?

In early September of 2001, there was a Michael Jackson celebration at Madison Square Garden to commemorate his thirty years in show business. I wanted to go, just as a fan, as someone who loved his music and had been there for him as a record buyer since the beginning. But the Roots had been asked to serve as the musical director for a Levi's series. We were curating the show and backing up a number of the artists. My plan was to wrap it up by seven thirty and then get over to the Michael Jackson show. Easy.

But as the day went on, we got word that one of the artists, Meshell Ndegeocello, was running behind and that we'd have to delay her rehearsal. I was pissed. I really wanted to see Michael Jackson. Her delay stretched from an hour to two, and then to three, and we just ran out of time. The day was over. We had missed the Michael Jackson show and we hadn't even successfully sound-checked Meshell. Defeated and exhausted, we trudged over to our hotel room at the SoHo Grand. There, because of miscommunication, mismanagement, or possibly fate, all fourteen rooms being held for the Roots were no longer available. That was the last time, I think, that I threw a bona fide, full-scale, top-of-my-lungs, rock-star fit. It doesn't happen very often, but it happened then. I was angry about missing the Michael Jackson performance. I was frustrated about rehearsals. And I was in disbelief that we had ended the day hotel-less. I lost it. I flipped. There I was, yelling in the middle of the lobby as the hotel staff tried to figure out how to deal with the large group of angry black people in their ritzy establishment.

Nervous fingers flew over reservation keyboards, and soon enough they had secured us space at the Marriott right next to the World Trade Center. This was about one in the morning now, on September 11, 2001. But wait: one more twist. The computers were down. I got even madder, and the reservations staff got even more apologetic. They ended up dividing us up. Some of us had to draw straws and stay at a janky Howard Johnson's. Others went to the Sheraton up near 54th Street. Tariq and I were the lucky ones—we got placed in the Bryant Park Hotel. We got there, exhausted, demoralized, and went to bed.

My phone woke me up. My mom had called about nine times, which I ignored, naturally. But even with the vibrate function turned off, the light kept bothering me, and soon enough it was twelve missed calls, and then sixteen. I thought somebody had died, so I went to check my mom's messages. That's how I found out that the planes had crashed into the World Trade Center. I was as shocked as everyone else. It made no sense. The story was unfolding all around me but I couldn't understand; it was too enormous to process.

The second I found out that we were close to living in Armageddon, I knew exactly what I had to do. I ran to the front desk to make sure that I could stay there for the rest of the week. Then I ran outside. New York was as silent as *Vanilla Sky*'s first ten minutes, but I managed to find a taxi. I gave the cabbie a hundred bucks and told him that I only needed to make a short drive over to the Virgin Megastore. He dropped me on the corner just before, and I told him that there was an extra fifty in it if he waited for me. I loaded up on music. I can't remember all the records I got, but one of them was *The Blueprint* by Jay-Z, which became the soundtrack of that event, of that period, for me.

To say that I had mixed feelings about Jay-Z at that point in my career was an understatement. To me he represented much of what was wrong with hip-hop, although I couldn't have really made sense of my own theories: something to do with commercial success, or a lack of self-awareness in the lyrics, or a kind of concession to a certain gangster pose that didn't elevate the race or the genre. But I had an aversion. When I listened to *The Blueprint* in the wake of 9/11, though, and listened to it with a trancelike intensity, I started to feel such a deep connection to it, and not just in the Stockholm syndrome–type of way. I realized that Jay and I had plenty in common, including East Coast roots and a love for the music. We also had people in common, including the writer dream hampton, who was one of the pioneering female journalists for *The Source* and *Vibe* magazines and a central cultural figure in the lives of many rappers. I remember telling her that I really liked *The Blueprint*, and that it felt revolutionary for me to come down off my soapbox and admit it. That was a moment of distinct evolution, a kind of intelligent concession, like the moment in *Purple Rain* when Billy Sparks finally understands the Kid's music. As it turned out, dream passed the news along to Jay, and then told me how pleased he was that I had liked it. That was a secondary revelation: I didn't know that my opinion meant anything to him.

That fall was the beginning of an important relationship between Jay-Z and the Roots. When he got the offer to do *MTV Unplugged* he wanted us to be his backing band. I'm ashamed to admit that I panicked. Even though I liked his record, even though I was developing a tremendous respect for him as an artist, I still felt that he was the antichrist to a certain kind of hip-hop fan. Admiring him was one thing—but collaborating with him? That seemed like it could be a real train-wreck of critical signifiers: his big-money, above-the-title hip-hop, our legit indie reputation. It was like an aesthetic form of power clashing. He kept calling to try to entice us to work with him, and I kept avoiding his phone calls. Again, I think it was a conversation with dream that set me straight. "Look," she said, "he's a music nerd like you. Just talk to the man."

So I did. We ended up backing him on the *Unplugged* special, and then a bit later I was his musical director for the Madison Square Garden show that was the centerpiece of the *Fade to Black* documentary. And even later on, he ended up being our label president when we signed to Def Jam.[20]

The irony of ironies, of course, is that Jay ended up being one of the easiest people to work with I have ever encountered. Over the years, I have worked with hundreds of artists, and I have developed shortcuts, formulas, and psychological games to maximize motivation and minimize the strange ego collisions of collaboration. With some artists, you have to suggest the opposite of what they want, because they will come back contentiously and reverse your suggestion. With others, you have to plant the seeds of idea and let it flower in their own heads, where they can take credit for it. With Jay it was simple. He paid close attention to what everyone else in the room was saying, and when it was his turn he asked questions. He might say, "How would you make this better?" and when you told him, he'd take a little time to think about it, after which he'd either agree or tell you plainly why he wasn't comfortable with that approach.

---

20. I think Jay-Z's interest in the band came from the fact that he got to a point where he had to reinvent himself. He had been paying attention to the Grammy Awards and the critical acclaim, to this sense that you guys were some impressive shit as a live band, and he reached out as a way of nuancing his own brand. It was simpatico, game-recognize-game: it fit his overall vision of where he was going.

I had spent most of my life working with like-minded people, people from the left side of the artist-businessman spectrum. They prided themselves on their dedication to self-expression. The result, though, was often a tug-of-war about whose ideas got to win that was divorced from the larger goal of making successful art. Who would have ever thought that the easiest artist I have ever worked with is the one who seemed so different, not to mention the one who had the right to be a complete prick? Coming at the end of a year and a half of Soulquarian angst, this realization turned my head completely around. The people who were supposedly like me were the most mind-bogglingly frustrating people imaginable. The people who I thought were nothing like me were the smoothest sailing. People thwart your expectations every way you can imagine, and in many ways you can't.

———

When the Roots had taken their break after *Things Fall Apart*, while I was off touring with D'Angelo, Tariq had pursued a side career as an actor and started to ready what he thought would be his first solo album, *Masterpiece Theatre*. That album didn't come together the way he wanted it to, or maybe his vision for it kept shifting, and when he and I returned to the fold, it became clear that the schedule had moved out from under us. We were due for another group record, and it was going to have to absorb some of the material from *Masterpiece Theatre*. But what kind of Roots record was it going to be?

As usual, Tariq and I were the yin and the yang of the group, and since he was bringing in the lyrics and unfinished tracks, I started thinking, with Rich's help, about what the overall feel of the record should be. I was at Electric Lady Studios most days, working on Common's follow-up to *Like Water for Chocolate*, which was called *Electric Circus*, as well as the next album for Erykah Badu, *Mama's Gun*. Though I didn't know it for sure, I was pretty certain that it was the twilight of the Soulquarians, the last gasp of that utopia that had started to take root a few years earlier.

Because of my touring with D'Angelo, the Roots hadn't had a chance to truly cash in on the neo-soul movement. We were Moses and the movement was the Promised Land: We had led people to it, helped organize it, ushered people through the first awkward phases, made sure that there was an audience that understood and appreciated the music. And yet we didn't really benefit from it. There were artists who made big money and got a big hike in their status as a result, but by the time we were ready to come back, everyone was neo-souled out. More importantly, the principals were already planning their next moves. I remember having a conversation with D'Angelo at Electric Lady, during the time we were all making *Electric Circus*.

"Yo," he said. "We can't do this no more. I'm going to learn to play guitar."

"What do you mean?" I said.

"I'm going to go dirty. We should all go dirty." What he meant by "dirty" wasn't exactly clear, but it had something to do with pushing the boundaries of what was considered soul music, as well as challenging himself. He was going to master Eddie Hazel's mind-melting solo from *Maggot Brain*.

When I asked Dilla what he thought of that, his answer went off in yet another direction. He told me he was going Kraftwerk: no more Rhodes piano, no more crispy snares.

Common joined the chorus. "Yeah," he said. "We have to blow up everything and start something new." Common was so insistent on change, in fact, that I started to smell a backstory. At the time, he was engaged to Erykah, who was the mother of André 3000's child, and Erykah and André were still actively involved in each other's lives, at least creatively. When I would go to her house, she would play me tapes of what André and Big Boi were working on in OutKast. Common was showing such an appetite for experimentation that I wondered if he was hearing those work tapes and feeling like he needed to catch up. It was either that or the fact that he was falling under Erykah's spell. Raphael Saadiq and I had an affectionate joke about her: never look her in the eye for more than five seconds, because then your brain will be her brain. She'll take you over. Whatever the factors, the fact was that Common was pushing hard for *Electric Circus* to be a kitchen-sink record. He was interested in experimentation in a way I had never heard before, from him or from anyone.

In the midst of all these self-styled rebels, I was feeling a little bit lost. With *Things Fall Apart*, I had finally gotten the love and adoration I had wanted for doing my thing. And before I had a chance to enjoy it or figure out if I could extend it creatively, everyone else was jumping ship. We had newly minted guitar heroes. We had Kraftwerk. Suddenly I was the cultural conservative. I was also, frankly, still processing my guilt over the sense that I was the one who had stopped the Roots' momentum after *Things Fall Apart*. We would have had a victory lap, a whole year to be the Grammy-winning, neo-soul-a-riffic Roots. Maybe Dilla and D'Angelo and Common were ready to metamorphose again, but I wanted to be sure that I had my ideas properly sorted out before I changed my skis.

And there was still another factor, which was the sense that even though the Roots had come into our own with *Things Fall Apart*, we had unfinished business as a recording unit. When Robert Christgau reviewed *Things Fall Apart*, he gave it a B+, and wrote that listeners would be relieved when we finally let ourselves go and rocked out. That was something I heard from fans all the time, that the energy and sheer volume of a Roots show had never been adequately captured on record.

We added up all these factors and came up with a battle plan for *Phrenology*, which was that we were going to make the world's first anti-Roots Roots album. "We'll make every type of song that the Roots aren't supposed to do," someone said, and that became our template.[21]

When we started to collect material for the album, some of it came from unfinished tracks from Tariq's solo album, and for the rest, we relied on these extended jam sessions. Before we knew it we had a collection of songs that were as diverse and surprising as anything we had ever done. We had a cheesy R&B jam ("Break You Off"), a sexy strip song ("Pussy Galore"), a hardcore song ("!!!"), a twelve-minute antidrug screed ("Water"). We wanted to take the attention and goodwill we had generated with *Things Fall Apart* and present a catalog album of everything we were able to do. We wanted to shatter people's myths, not only about what rap groups could do, but also about what black groups could do. And we wanted to show everyone that our main reason for being was to change. *Do You Want More?!!!??!* was acid jazz, *Illadelph Halflife* was a kind of Wu-Tang–influenced hard hip-hop production, and *Things Fall Apart* was definitive neo soul. We were going into the cocoon again. I wasn't worried about our audience. They would follow us or they wouldn't—I was used to losing about half our audience each time and picking up new fans—but I was determined to extend our artistic winning streak.

---

21. Let's face it—*Phrenology* (by design, and mostly out of necessity) was a mishmash. It was a reification of your state-of-the-minute (post D-tour) musical leanings grafted onto Tariq's recalcitrant line in the sand *Masterpiece Theatre* (which, may I remind you, was itself a project he started because you went Michael Eugene Archering yellow-brick-road-style). It was a messy, circling-the-drain type of affair that ultimately revealed its own pretzel logic. But I guess good shit come to those who "weight," or maybe Cracker Jack–like prizes can be found after things fall apart.

We put down lots of different-sounding songs, and from fairly early on it sounded like the record I wanted to be making. But the song that most people know from *Phrenology*—certainly the one that got us the most crossover juice—came to us strangely and indirectly. When we were getting started, I was in Detroit for a show, probably the Smokin' Grooves tour, and I was driving with dream hampton, going to shop for records at a place called Melodies and Medleys in Grosse Pointe. On the way, she played me a CD that she had gotten from Ishmael Butler, a.k.a. Butterfly from Digable Planets, who had an off-again, on-again relationship with her. It was a demo with songs by a new artist that Ish was excited about, and he had sworn her to secrecy not to reveal who it was.

I liked the record, especially a song called "Bitch I'm Broke" and another one called "Boylife in America." I thought they were funny, with these unexpectedly blunt lyrics and DIY feel. When dream stopped to get gas, I snuck a look at the CD case and saw that the artist was a guy named Cody ChesnuTT. Twitter hadn't arrived yet, so I went on the online community I had created, OkayPlayer, and asked, "Does anyone know about this guy? It's one of the best demos I've heard since Jill Scott or Slum Village."

A few days later, I was at MCA, and I guy I knew there told me that one of his interns had seen the post. "You liked that record?" he said. "I didn't quite dig it myself." He went into the discard bin, all the way to the bottom like he was bobbing for apples, and he came up with two copies of the full Cody ChesnuTT album. I gave one to Rich thinking maybe this guy and I could work on a song together. Despite the Soulquarian backlash, I was still in the frame of mind of this communal utopia. As we went, someone had the idea that we should remake one of Cody's songs, and it became apparent fairly quickly that "The

Seed" was the prime candidate. It had a good groove and plenty of room to grow into a hip-hop version. Tariq liked it, too, though every time he brought us lyrics they were a little short of focused. Then at one point, he took it away, sat with it, and came back fully finished. We set up a session with Cody.

The day we recorded that track was one of the strangest, most hectic, and most productive days in Roots recording history. Normally, I did my real recording at night, going from around 10 p.m. to 5 a.m. Cody was scheduled to land in New York at 5 in the afternoon, and he was going to come right over. I figured we'd go all night. Rich had other ideas, though. He wanted me to get it done in the early evening, which was fine, except for the fact that I had a direct conflict. I had a date.

"Come on," I said. "This was the only time she could see a movie. I have to be out of the studio by seven forty-five, eight at the latest. Can't you wait until I'm back?"

"Fine," Rich said. "Maybe we'll just do it without you." This was one of his Jedi mind tricks. He knew I wouldn't let someone else do it.

Cody's flight landed a little late, and he got there at about 7:25. We did pounds: Mos was there, saying hello, and I think Ish came down, too. At around 7:40 I tried to apply the pressure, but by the time we finally sat down to play it was 7:50 and I was panicking. Next came formatting: we had to figure out whether or not we'd go through the melody straight, and where we'd start Tariq's rhyme. He was generally a twenty-four-bar person, as are many rappers, but this was clearly a pop song, which meant that it made sense to shorten him up to sixteen bars. Formatting was done at 7:52 or 7:53. Time was tight.

I was sitting behind the drums with my big-ass winter coat already on and my bag packed and ready to go on the floor next to me. Ben Kenney, who was playing guitar with us before he decamped for Incubus, was there with me, and Cody played guitar and sang in the control room. Tape started rolling at 7:54 or so. We got the song down once and then, because I lost count in my head, we had to stop and rewind the tape. As we started again, the breeze from the air conditioning unit blew my map to the floor. "Keep it rolling," I said. "Don't stop the tape." That's still on there. Now it was 7:57, and I figured that I could still make it to the Angelika Film Center a few blocks away by 8:15, which would have meant an angry girlfriend but not an ex-girlfriend. We went through the song again, straight, no pause, and on the last line of vocals, where Cody sings "I will name it rock and roll," I was drumming with one hand. The last three beats were done one-handed, my other hand on my bag, and then I left before Rich could stop me. The cymbal was still vibrating as I went out the door.[22]

As quick as it was, as hectic as it was, there was something about it. It had feel. I wasn't the only one who thought so. "The Seed (2.0)" was a hit and a big part of our crossover success. It was also Don Was's favorite record of that year. When he was making "A Bigger Bang" with the Rolling Stones, he played it for the band. "That's the kind of sound we want," he said. "This is what you need to be sounding like." About a year after that, he was producing the Italian rock star Zucchero, and he had me in to drum on five songs. At the beginning of the session, Don was hinting around, tiptoeing. I could tell that he was basically asking for "The Seed (2.0)" again. "Don," I said. "I know the game here. You don't have to sugarcoat it. If you just want five 'Seeds,' that's cool, just say so, man. You want that or not?"

He ducked his head a bit and came back up smiling. "Yeah," he said. "I love that energy."

---

22. Really? You remember being in New York for that? I remember it being in L.A., and I remember that you were the one who was late rather than Cody. Sometimes one universe can split into two alternate realities. Or maybe one of us is just wrong.

If "The Seed (2.0)" was spontaneous and fun, the other single from that record was the exact opposite. That was "Break You Off," our greasy R&B song. We had a great hook, and we wanted Musiq Soulchild to sing it, but he was signed to Def Jam and as such unavailable. We went to Alicia Keys next. She and I had become friends a few years earlier, and we got word that she'd be up for it. I went to the studio, waited, and then around two in the morning I felt someone shaking my shoulder. "Ahmir, Ahmir. Wake up."

"Did she come?"

"No. She didn't make it."

That happened again the second night. On the third night someone said she was called to Los Angeles for another project.

I started to the get the sense that Alicia wasn't going to do it, and so we moved on through what seemed like an endless series of artists: Jill, Bilal, nonsingers, people who wanted to give it a try. One of them opted in and then opted out and then opted in and then opted out, all on the same day. One of them tried, gamely, but couldn't manage to sound anywhere close to acceptable. One of them had their own record-company difficulties. The process of trying to secure a vocalist to sing the hook on "Break You Off" is almost too long and too tortured to be believed. I wrote about it in the Home Grown! series, in the liner notes, and even there it sounds like a comic novella, something out of John Kennedy Toole's *A Confederacy of Dunces*. In the end, as you'd expect from a comic saga, we ended up back right where we started, with Musiq singing the hook, and the song became the other hit off the record.

Powered in part by "Break You Off" and in part by "The Seed (2.0)," *Phrenology* was a big success. Critics loved it; *Rolling Stone* said that we were continuing the winning streak we started with *Things Fall Apart*, but with an even stronger sense of our versatility. Robert Christgau, who hadn't been totally convinced by *Things Fall Apart*, thought that we were making strides in pop songcraft; I think he called it "tune and structure." And record buyers responded, too: the album stayed on the charts for almost a year. The plan, which was to demonstrate our diversity, worked like a charm.[23]

Even then, there were reminders about the limits of our achievement. Celebrity is like a ladder whose top you can't see. One afternoon after the album came out, I did a panel discussion as part of a symposium in Philadelphia on the role of hip-hop in culture. We took questions at the end of the conversation, and one little hand went up in the back of the room. I called on the boy. "Do you know any famous people?" he demanded. Kids are so brutally honest. They don't mince words or even thoughts about what's happening in their world. As a result, part of me has always felt like kids are telling me the truth and that adults are bullshitting me. That moment was like a corrective for everything else: the two consecutive near-platinum records, the tide of critical acclaim, the videos, the television appearances, the famous friends. I don't remember how I answered the question, but I remember what I was thinking, which was that I feel like my cultural value comes from my role as a bridge. My job is to connect brilliant have-nots to the land of haves.

That mission continues to this day. I recently heard about a new

---

23. Like I said, *Phrenology* was collage, a cut-and-pasty thing that many previous fans found "discomfort" in. They were like, "What the fuck are you doing? You have this punk thing and this R&B thing. Who the fuck are you guys?" Our core fans were a center that would not hold, but critics seemed to favor the album's direction. So I figured that while our Teflon exterior was somewhat cracked it was still very much nonstick. Unfortunately for us, those cracks were fault lines, and we were headed for the *Tipping Point*.

Australian group called Kaiyote, an unsigned act with a really incredible debut song. I tweeted about it and within a few days that little ripple went outward in a way that was hard for me to imagine. Journalists started calling. Agents showed interest. I'm thrilled to be a connector like that. But at the same time, the bridge is spanning two different landmasses: one of them is called "Oh, it's so amazing to meet you—what an honor" and the other one is "You ain't shit." I never know for sure which one is my home and which one I am just visiting. Is that a tortured metaphor, or is it a metaphor about being tortured?

SEVENTEEN

How do things get their names? It's a strange process. My parents gave me my name, and then I replaced it with a question mark, partly because the labeling of a person with a few words didn't quite make sense to me. That question mark became a second name that today defines me even more than the first one did. The band started out as Radio Activity, then went Black to the Future, then Square Roots, each time pushed forward by our own internal creativity, by the certainty that something new and exciting would happen if we only kept trying. And yet the final shift to the Roots, the one that brought us into those new and exciting things, was motivated by something else entirely, by pressure from outside. Things are what you call them, but they're also not what you don't call them. I've learned that lesson over and over again.

One of the best examples is our album titles. Almost since the beginning, every Roots album had two titles during the period where it was a work in progress, and eventually one came to the fore. *Do You Want More?!!!??!* was also *Homegrown*. For *Things Fall Apart*, there was briefly talk of calling it *The Center Will Not Hold*, though our final choice referenced both the Yeats poem and also the Chinua Achebe novel. For *Phrenology*, it was either that or *Masterpiece Theatre*, the title of the solo record that Tariq had to scrap. For *The Tipping Point*, though, I think that we had the title fairly early in the process, and we didn't let it go. Rich had read Malcolm Gladwell's book and given it to me to read. He thought it would make a great title.

With most of the records, we wanted the titles to work on three levels: as a reflection of our own career, as a reflection of the hip-hop scene, and as a reflection of the world at large. Though I loved *The Tipping Point* as a title, I did have some concerns that it wouldn't resonate equally on all three levels. I didn't want people to think that we were talking only about our own music, that we were somehow hoping out loud that this would be a watershed moment for our success. In fact, we were coming off of two albums that had established us commercially: *Things Fall Apart* had "You Got Me" and sold almost a million copies. *Phrenology* had "The Seed 2.0" and sold eight hundred thousand. That put us in the stratosphere, as far as I was concerned. Five years earlier, there was no way you would have convinced me that we would sell a million records. A brainy hip-hop band that didn't really know how to make pop hits? What were our commercial prospects, really? We never had a "Who Let the Dogs Out?" or a "Gin and Juice." We had to make it as album artists. And suddenly, here we were, making it that way.

In fact, *The Tipping Point* appealed to us for broader political reasons. At the time, we were about a year into the second Iraq war, and there was both a weariness and a wariness regarding the way our leadership had behaved. I really didn't think that George W. Bush was going to win a second term, and I thought that a John Kerry presidency was going to mark the beginning of a new era where we were more careful about foreign entanglements, less aggressive on the international stage, more sensitive to the cost of those engagements for domestic health. I really thought that. I was certain. Most of my friends were certain. That's one of many reasons why it's probably good that I'm a musician rather than a political scientist.

And yet there was some truth to the title, at least from a business standpoint. The dominolike collapse of record labels had continued: we had gone from DGC to Geffen to MCA, and then, just as *Phrenology* was about to come out, we got word they were dissolving the label. Rich got right to it and managed to secure a promise that the record would come out about five weeks before the label disappeared for good, and that the staff would put full muscle behind it: that they would be in touch with radio the way they were supposed to, that they would work "The Seed (2.0)" properly. That happened, but just barely. To give you an idea of how rapidly it all unraveled, Common's *Electric Circus*, which came out only five weeks after ours, was essentially stillborn. Even though it was critically acclaimed, it arrived with no one to oversee it, promote it, or make sure that it reached its public.

Suddenly, we were on Interscope, which was a different kind of label than anything we had ever experienced. They had, at the time, a roster stuffed with hugely successful artists: multiplatinum acts like Sting, No Doubt, Dr. Dre, and Snoop Dogg. When MCA ceased to be, all its artists on the label fell to the floor like baseball cards, and Interscope shuffled through the cards to decide which ones they were going to pick up. They took Mary J. Blige without a second thought. She was more or less at the level of the major stars they were already working with at Interscope. One or two other acts got snatched up hungrily. But then there were the midlevel names, the singers and groups that had a strong following but weren't moving fast-food-franchise numbers of units. At that point, Dr. Dre intervened and told Jimmy Iovine, the head of Interscope, which acts he thought were cool and should be kept on. He pointed the fickle finger of fate at Talib Kweli, at Mos Def, at Common, and at us.

Call me naive, or lucky, but I had made it through more than a decade of being a major-label recording artist without encountering true corporate culture. We had a winning streak going where the art was paramount and the business concerns, though they were there in the background, didn't encroach to any great degree. Our tenure with Geffen/Interscope was the end of that winning streak. The second the Roots moved over to the label, we had to adjust the way we did business. For one thing, Jimmy was in Los Angeles, so we had no personal relationship with him. Rich usually flew out there to meet with him. There was some goodwill in the bank, though: Scott Storch, who was an early part of the Roots' success, had gone on to coproduce "Still D.R.E.," which, as the lead single for Dr. Dre's *2001*, was a massive hit for Interscope in 1999, and had also worked with Christina Aguilera. Scott found favor with Jimmy and some of that rubbed off on us.

Even so, it wasn't easy. The thing that struck us as troublesome, right off the bat, was Jimmy's reaction to *Phrenology*. He listened to "The Seed (2.0)," shrugged, and said, "Eh, sounds old." The song had been out maybe a year, at most, and it had been one of our biggest hits. How did it sound old, exactly? We felt like he didn't get what we were about as a band and wasn't really interested in learning.

I didn't want to underestimate Jimmy. I had great respect for him as a music-industry veteran. Still, I wasn't convinced that he was really putting his head into our music. He seemed like he was listening for a few seconds, deciding that it didn't move him like the most recent pop hits, and then making an executive decision that we needed to move in another direction. That didn't sit well with me. *Phrenology* was our most critically acclaimed record, a record we had designed to showcase all the facets of the band, and we wanted to build on it.

That was the tension: artistic expression on the one hand and serving a new corporate master on the other. And we served. That was the first time and the last time in our history as recording artists that we crafted something explicitly to suit the tastes of our label president. In a way, it was heartbreaking. Rich traveled across the country to explain the nature of the group: that we were an album-based enterprise and the result of momentum that had been painstakingly built over the years. Funding the movement—which is how we referred to those communal jam sessions in Philly or New York—was a central part of our story and our success. Jimmy didn't have much patience for that. He wanted us to come back with fresher material. And so Rich put us in with Scott for a weeklong crash course in everything Jimmy. We tried to absorb all the music that Scott had worked on with Interscope, all the music that was coming out of that scene. We marinated ourselves in 50 Cent, in Eminem, in Dr. Dre.

Then we went back to the Roots way of doing things, but with a twist. This time, Rich had the ingenious idea of turning our Philadelphia studio into a strip club. We took our advance money and got a stripper pole. We had free food, invited a bunch of musicians, ate, traded stories, played, and then at around one in the morning the strippers showed up. We responded to their energy, to the flashy, dark vibe. When I played on St. Albans Street, we were carried forward by the boho set, by Jill Scott and India.Arie. Now, it was Kamika and Heather and whoever else.[24]

---

24. It's been said that dudes celebrate the spirit of men and the bodies of women—and there we went, fact-checking the aphoristic. We were pastime patriarchs caught in a backsliding bildungsroman. It's like this: half the time, I think of myself as a feminist, and the other half is spent wondering, "What kind of fucking feminist does this shit?" Yeah, full disclosure: we're a conflicted bunch, selfprofessed "long dick niggas with real short fuses" who (like Jimmy Carter) "have lusted in our hearts" (to infinity and beyond). So, no the shit wasn't right, but it was fucking real. There was this specter of anachronism that ate at our sense of relevancy. The boho dance was played out and we missed the immediacy, the last-ditch-ness of the debauchery that we'd been talking ourselves out of for years. We were in this loop of life as art imitating life, at once us and this wanton wanting other. The center was not holding, our tipping point was an unraveling—not some Gladwellian singularity. That moment was about the sometimes-black saint and the sometimes-metaphoric sinner lady, and so creating this recording studio-cum-strip-club felt right, unprecedented even (although in retrospect it

From the beginning, it was a strange match. Some of the band members had wives or serious girlfriends, and they were devoted enough to their domestic lives that they felt they couldn't partake in the strip-club sessions. Even for those of us who stayed, there was a little bit of a disconnect. That kind of thing wasn't completely in character for the band. Because of my personality I have been relatively subdued on that front for most of my career—that's just the way it's been and the way it will always be. I'm beyond feeling strange about it, though part of me regrets that I'll never have a Led Zeppelin shark story. But facts are facts: we were a band of working musicians who were more concerned with the music we were making than with the extracurricular benefits of the rock-and-roll lifestyle. We had groupies who waited for us outside the dressing room, but the sad fact was that they tended to be twentysomething guys who wanted to know if I really used a Royer ribbon mic on that song, and if it was true that I tinkered with the tube to get that special effect on the outro.

And so, as we set off on that record, it was with a slight sense of distance. We didn't have misgivings, exactly. We knew that we were catering to what we thought Interscope would like and especially to what was hitting in the commercial marketplace at the time, and while we didn't want to dumb our music down, we also didn't want to delude ourselves into thinking that we were doing anything other than attempting to locate the lowest common denominator. We still wanted our personalities to shine through but we knew that there was a commercial frame around the entire enterprise. Ironically, it was probably the last Roots album where it was important to us that black people like our music.

---

was simply garden variety misogynistic or maybe just the cultural equivalent of an auto-erotic asphyxiation).

There in the studio/strip club we played a bunch of endless jams, as we had for *Illadelph Halflife* almost a decade before, and then we tried to mine songs out of the results. We would jam, then jam some more, then come back and listen and see if anything had sonic stickiness. If it did, we would isolate it and build it into a full-fledged song. But we were building with Jimmy's precepts in mind. He wanted us to dial back the analytical intelligence at the heart of the record, which was all I knew. I didn't know how to make pop music. I only knew how to make smart music. But our charter changed for a little while. We were trying to make sense of Jimmy's theory of the five-second read: if a song doesn't grab you within that short span, it's not going to grab you at all.

That's how the album came together, and it suffered accordingly. It wasn't disastrous by any means. I think "Star" is one of our best moments as a band. "Stay Cool" is on there, a song I love with a great Al Hirt sample. I love "Web" and "Boom." And I like the two covers that we added at the end: "Melting Pot," which was a Booker T. cover, and "Din Da Da," which was a cover of George Kranz's "Trommeltanz." And Dave Chappelle came by to contribute to "In Love with the Mic," which was a hidden track near the end of the record.

————

One of the commercial concessions we made is that we would be receptive to working with outside producers, and at some point in the session we went down to Virginia to do some work with the Neptunes. In Jimmy's eyes, it was a kind of Hail Mary pass: pair this band without a strong commercial sound, and maybe without a strong commercial sense, with the hot producers of the moment. They had sent us a demo of the song they wanted to do with us, with the understanding that we would replay it live in the studio. On the bus on the way down, we listened to it to prepare, and we didn't really like it.

Or rather, Rich didn't really like it—the way he put it, he wasn't getting goose bumps. And if Rich didn't like it, no one else really liked it either. He had a very unusual, domineering way of setting everyone's mood. If he's not sold, no one is sold.

He wasn't wrong, though. As a DJ, I knew what kind of Pharrell song I liked to spin, and the one they had sent wasn't that kind. Their work was frequently brilliant, but it was hit or miss, and what I was hearing wasn't the kind of hit that I thought we needed. The drums needed to be crispy. The whole thing needed to have energy leaping out of it.

By the time we arrived in Virginia, I had been nominated as ambassador to talk to Pharrell and communicate our uncertainty with the track we had been sent. He listened and nodded and went for another song, a track that turned out to be "Green Light" on Beyoncé's *B-Day* record, although it was more primitive at that time. That one didn't quite work for us either.

The rest of the band was down and a little impatient, but I was feeling a surge of Pollyanna optimism. We had four hours left and I had faith. "Look," I told the rest of the guys. "You're killing his vibe. Let me do this. You stay out in the van and I'll work with him. I'll get us a song."

I had an idea in my head; I wanted something that I could blend into N.O.R.E.'s "Nothin'," which was the definitive Pharrell beat of that year. I needed something to match that, a blast of exotic, minimalist rimshot funk, like what he had given Jay-Z on the "Excuse Me Miss" remix. All that had to happen was that my idea had to become reality. How hard was that? I remember going into the bathroom at the studio, staring at myself in the mirror, and talking to my own reflection. "You came here for something," I said. "You're going to get it. You're going to get a song that's ninety-six beats per minute that lets you play rimshot on the snare. You're going to match 'Nothin'' and then you're going to surpass it. You can do it. You are going to do it. You are going to do it now."

I came out of the bathroom and went into the studio and Pharrell was ready for me, already sitting at the piano. He played a chord. "Yeah," I said encouragingly, "that's it." I was still in this inspirational frame of mind. I knew that I had to motivational-speak the song out of him. I started drumming along with him, and soon enough we were making a whole song, more beat from me, more chords from him. Then he started singing, just a little bit at first, and at one point about four minutes into the track, he let out his patented "Whoo!" That's when I locked in even tighter. The piano was behind me, so he couldn't see the look on my face, but the engineer, who could see me, was probably freaked out, wondering what the hell was wrong with me. "This is what I'm talking about," he said. "This is it."

On we went. I played the beat like it was my own heartbeat, like my very life depended on it. We went like that for twenty minutes. My wrists were killing me. There were splinters on the floor from discarded drumsticks. I kept riding it hard, though, because it felt like a very special kind of connection, and you never know when you're going to get back to one of those moments.

Finally, he stopped playing and stepped away from the piano. He came over to me and gave a deep bow. "Yeah, man," he said. "We got magic there."

"We did," I said.

"This was a dream come true," he said.

"Likewise," I said. My brain was still tingling. I had done it. I had visualized what I wanted and then come out of the bathroom and created it. And now I could walk back to the van, triumphant, and tell the rest of the band that we had a top-drawer Neptunes track for our album. "I got my dream. We got our track."

Pharrell pulled up short. "What?" he said. He looked around, confused, a little deflated. "Oh," he said. "No. I can't give that to you. That's a song we already gave to Snoop Dogg."

Cut to us on the bus, headed back up to Philly with a song no one was thrilled about.

That was symptomatic of the *Tipping Point* experience. Overall, it's not a record I was happy with, exactly. It was the second time in the group's history that I was asked to take a backseat in the creative process. I was coming off *Phrenology*, an album where I felt like I was the central figure, and that had been immensely rewarding for me. *The Tipping Point*, for whatever reason, was a record dominated by Tariq. Maybe the way we were working opened up space for him. Maybe he was especially inspired. Band dynamics are hard to understand at the time, let alone recreate almost a decade later. But the further into the record we got, the more I felt it slipping away from me. It's a cliché, maybe, but one that turns out to be true: when you start making stuff for other people, that's when you lose yourself.

———

The lead single for the record was "Don't Say Nuthin'," which was risky for us in the sense that it was no risk at all: it closely resembled what was on the radio, albeit with a little bit of a twist, which meant that it deviated from our pattern of always changing our stripes. Our die-hard fans were used to being disappointed, in a sense. They were used to stepping up to the plate for each new album and being tossed a curve ball. "Don't Say Nuthin'" was a fastball right over the middle of the plate, and while it did okay for us—it stalled near the lower end of the Top 100—it didn't feel like a step forward or even an interesting step backward. It was a form of treading water, or responding to trends rather than doing anything new or interesting or even particularly real. Maybe I am exaggerating a bit. As I said, I love many of the songs on that album, and we put as much of ourselves into those sessions as we could, but at the time it felt retrograde and disappointing. And because it didn't sell as well as either *Phrenology* or *Things Fall Apart*, we felt like we had been deceived. Here we were, selling our souls for greater commercial success, except that it wasn't greater at all.[25]

The way we were treated by the critics, our unkindest reception yet, was also a tip-off that we were witnessing a sea change in the music-press establishment. We were now officially in the era of online critical sites, especially Pitchfork. Rich and I obsessively read every review of the album, and saw that many of the publications were using the same language as Nick Sylvester's review for the site. For the first time, alternative weeklies around the country didn't seem to be listening to the record themselves. They were mimicking Pitchfork's appraisal, which wasn't very positive at all. We had gone from high 8s and 9s for ratings for *Things Fall Apart* and *Phrenology* to a 5.4 for *The Tipping Point*. And other publications just went right along with that appraisal. There was consensus that the new record was a big shrug. I would rather have been absolutely destroyed by critics because they weren't on board with our concept for the record, but in fact what happened was much more sodden and tiring than that. They just didn't seem to care all that much about us anymore. The effect of all of that, of Jimmy's influence, of the feel of the sessions, of the response to the record, was devastating. That year, 2004, was probably the most disappointing year of my life, the first time I can remember actively feeling like a failure.

---

25. There was a black dude at the label who was sort of Jimmy's sidekick. When we got signed he went on and on: "If Jimmy pulls the trigger he can make anything happen...he just pulls the trigger, and everything changes for y'all...just wait until he pulls the trigger." As it turned out, we just got pounded like shit by the critics, and Jimmy disappeared on us, and that was that. So much for the fucking trigger.

Added to that was the sense that we were slipping again in the hip-hop hierarchy. Jay-Z had established himself as an icon by this point. And then there was Kanye West. After he released his first album, he grabbed Mos, Talib, and Common, and brought them into his orbit. Suddenly, they were satellites of Kanye's planet rather than ours.

I knew of Kanye's production work for Jay-Z's *Blueprint*, of course, and also the records he had made with Alicia Keys and Ludacris, and when his first solo record, *The College Dropout*, came out in 2004, I was elated. I loved it. He played the common man so well and had a real production aesthetic. There was no denying the charm of his record. When I heard "All Falls Down," I thought to myself that there was very little chance that it wouldn't be a hit. "Damn," I thought to myself. "I should have made that song." It was the first time I had thought that since OutKast's "SpottieOttieDopaliscious," from *Aquemini*, the first time that I had been blindsided by a production trick or technique.

And yet, I knew that Kanye's ascendancy was potentially a problem for us. "Are we old news?" I asked Rich. "Are we dead and I don't know it?"

In my mind, it was all about the mental space that different kinds of artists occupied, and he was moving into the space for the left-of-center messiah, which had been occupied by OutKast and by the Fugees before them. What was especially ironic about it was that his persona—the unashamedly materialistic artist, the trailblazer who was also happy to be a slave to fashion—was something that the Roots had toyed with a few years earlier. In 2001, Tariq cut his dreadlocks. "Damn," I said to Rich. "That's the end of the brand." We had both grown our hair out together, almost a decade before, and that's the image we presented to the world: the dreadlocked guy and the afro guy. But Tariq was fighting the band's boho side, hating the fact that our groupies were those five guys who wanted to smoke a blunt and talk about recording equipment. That creative tension worked brilliantly for the band, but it didn't always work well for Tariq, and I remember him basically doing everything he could to resist. Around the time he cut his hair, he did something else to shift his image: he started shopping at Barneys, for one. All of a sudden, he was spending thousands of dollars on a suit or $1,000 on shoes. He had a coat that was $5,000. I'm not knocking him—the way I was with records, that's how he was with fashion. And he looked sharp. He looked good. But it seemed a little like an affectation to me and to Rich, and in that sense it made us uncomfortable. Our audience had certain ideas about us. They counted on us to put ideas first, to resist materialism. This ran counter to all of that.

That's the thing that killed me about Kanye. He flaunted the very qualities that sometimes made me uncomfortable about Tariq. Right off the bat, Kanye came out and said, "I like Louis Vuitton and I'm a shopaholic, and also I'm underground." Tariq had done his best to distance himself from his boho side, even though it was just as authentic and legitimate as what Kanye was doing. And while Tariq hadn't really embraced interviews, Kanye seemed to live for them. He was never more himself than he was when explaining himself or contradicting himself, expounding or expanding. That's one of the central things about him, and the hip-hop world that he came to dominate, and it contrasts starkly with the world that Tariq and I had entered a decade before.

Kanye's rise also taught me something about our own band, about how Tariq fit into the broader hip-hop landscape—and how that broad landscape maybe wasn't so broad anymore. When Tariq started out, his virtuosity as an MC was his calling card: people loved the fact that he was brilliant and agile and seemingly able to rap about anything. His verbal dexterity was unquestioned and unmatched. What he wasn't, though, was a character.[26] Early on in hip-hop, characters were more comic: they were put-ons, whether it was the first incarnation of the Beastie Boys as snotty white teenagers, or Flavor Flav with his clock, or the way that Gregory Jacobs turned into Humpty Hump in Digital Underground. Oftentime the rappers were doing great work, but they adopted their character as a kind of costume. And there were plenty of rappers who weren't exactly characters, or who fought against that kind of thing: KRS-One had a kind of gangster pose, but he also fashioned himself as a teacher. Did Rakim have a character, really? But over the decade of hip-hop's evolution (or was it devolution?), characters became more and more central: not just personas, but actual characters that seemed sprung from the pages of comic books. Eminem was the apotheosis of that. He had the Slim Shady character and spent the better part of the first phase of his career reconstructing and deconstructing it. And Kanye was almost like a beat poet: he was a real-time character, completely immersed in his own development and entirely self-aware in ways that hip-hop had never seen. Look at the way he planned his album titles as a linked series of concepts, or the way that his songs dealt directly and overtly with spiritual crisis and conspicuous consumption. Nearly everything he did seemed like a cry for attention and at the same time a rejection of traditional forms of publicity. He worked his art tirelessly, and just as D'Angelo had

---

26. What Tariq was—what he is—is a long-breath singer, a nigga in the universe, a crack-era holocaust survivor whose loneliness won't leave him alone. As he said in "Act Too (The Love of My Life)," "Sometimes I wouldn'ta made it if it wasn't for you." Tariq grew up in some dark places and hip-hop was this great redeemer and his raison d'être . . . like it literally saved his life. He's always intuitively avoided the ersatz rapper character thing. I think he can appreciate that apparel on someone else but he ain't even going to attempt to try them duds on. I don't think it's even a conscious choice so much as some core aversion. Sorta like not eating food that smells like shit.

been in position to be a certain kind of savior in 2000, Kanye was in position to be a savior in 2005. Every micro-era passes the microphone to a different icon.

As hip-hop changed, it changed around us, around the Roots, without really changing the Roots. That isn't to say that we didn't change. We evolved with every album. We had more left turns than the Daytona 500. But we didn't seek to capitalize on the zeitgeist in quite the same way as other artists. Part of it had to do with the specific evolution of the MC. Tariq's brilliance and virtuosity, which had been one of our main propellers at first, started to feel out of step with the other forces bearing down upon us. And Tariq isn't the kind of person to create a character and submit himself to it. He was too intellectually restless in some ways, too proud of what we had accomplished in others. What he resisted, what he found possibly objectionable—that was exactly what Kanye capitalized on, and in a way that hip-hop had never seen. In some ways we were in awe of Kanye's pose. We had spent a decade seeing hip-hop as a division between the haves and have-nots, between artists who didn't play games with cars and fashion and acts that played games with cars and fashion but didn't aspire to making art. Kanye was an artist who took the audacious stance that he could do both, that there was no conflict between them, and audiences just went right along with him.

If there was a darkness closing in, there were at least some flashes of comedy. One night on tour, the band ran into Tracy Morgan at a hotel in Denver. He was out in town performing stand-up and we were booked for a show at the Fillmore. Late that night, after both of us had finished our shows and were back at the hotel, we went over to check out his room. I had heard through mutual friends that he liked to create Fellini-type situations, and this didn't disappoint: it was full of women and alcohol and strange props and a sense that anything could happen, and that when it did, it might happen fast.

"Hey," Tracy said. "The Roots. Come in." Not ten steps inside the room, I turned to talk to someone in the band and saw that Tracy had whipped off his shirt. When Tracy's shirt went, it was a signal for every shirt to go, at which point I knew I had to get out quick. I had a girlfriend at the time and I thought it would be in my best interest to act in a respectful manner toward our relationship.[27]

I didn't get out quick enough. There were a bunch of wide-eyed Roots watching a bunch of girls in the process of going wild, and one Buddha-bellied lunatic ringmastering the whole situation while looking for Bobby Brown's "Tenderoni" on his iPod.

I waited a minute there in the Satyricon, and then another minute. A mental picture of my girlfriend hovered in my head. "Man," I said. "I am taking off. See you later."

Back in my room, I was protected by a wall, but it was only one wall. I heard sounds, music among them, though what a motley set of music it was: "Billie Jean," "Night Fever," "Sister Christian." If there's a karaoke hell, it's located in Denver. I eventually dozed off to sleep, probably to the Thompson Twins or something.

The next day, in the van heading to the airport, I asked the other cats in the band what went on in Casa de Morgan. I got looks of shame and a conspiracy of silence. "Come on," I said. "Tell me what happened." I forget who spilled the first bean, but after that the details started to come fast and furious.

"Yeah, it was so weird cause he started yelling at us: 'Okay, Roots, we're going to have a toe-licking contest. Y'all better not have fungus on your feet. I know you bitches play it natural. I know you walk in the wilderness.'"

---

27. And to keep your shirt on.

"Really?" I said. "Who was sucking the toes?"

Someone else interrupted. "Then he pointed at the girls in his room and told us that we could have them. 'I like my white girls like Ball Park franks, plump 'em when you cook 'em. It's a waste for a white girl to be that skinny unless she's in junior high. I suck underarms and inner elbows.'"

"That's lots of sucking," I said.

Tracy kept his rant rolling. It was hilarious. "I want to leave my legacy in Colorado! Your fathers and great-great-granddads would roll in their grave if they saw this scenario. I wanna impregnate four of you girls, minimum. Oh, and will someone play 'Billie Jean'?"

The next four days were nothing but Tracy Morgan impressions. We worked his one-liners into stage patter. We called each other and asked about Ball Park franks. As road stories go, he was crazier than any rock band we had ever encountered.

For a while, I assumed that we had caught him on a particularly altered day, but it turns out that he's like that all the time. Whenever I get hungry in the middle of the night and head out to an all-night food spot, Tracy is always there, and always in Trace mode.

———

Comedy may have saved me that year in more ways than one. About a year before, I met Dave Chappelle, who was in the process of starting his sketch-comedy show on Comedy Central. He had run into Talib Kweli and his manager at a restaurant down the street from where we were recording, and they had invited him to come hang out. Almost from the start, I was drawn to him. He was one of the rare celebrities who didn't just jump on the bandwagon and tell you that his favorite hip-hop act was whoever was popular at the moment. And when he dropped by to watch us record, he would entertain us and then some. One of the first times he came by, he gave Q-Tip a script. It was the first draft of *Half Baked*, and he wanted Tip to play the role that Snoop eventually got. Compared to the finished movie, that first draft was a masterpiece. To this day, it remains one of the funniest things I have ever read; one of my dreams is that it will get made the way Dave intended. I started visiting comedy clubs when he played, and along the way he introduced me to Neal Brennan, his cowriter and coproducer on *Chappelle's Show*. One day, Neal called me up and told me that they were about to start work on season two of the show. "Want to be the musical director?" he asked.

I couldn't say yes fast enough. I was there for all the magic of season two, all the skits that have since become classics. That fall night in 2003 that I was onstage with Jay-Z at Madison Square Garden, Dave was shooting the legendary Rick James skit across the street. Working for Chappelle was just fantastic. I'd be in the studio awaiting instructions and the phone would ring. "Yeah?" I'd say. "What do you need?"

Sometimes they needed regular music. Sometimes it was something intentionally cheesy, like for a fake sitcom. Sometimes it was something very specific, like a *Thriller* soundalike for a skit about a "Beat It"–style knife fight between Vincent Price and Michael Jackson. Watching Rich's wife trying to sing the theme from "The Niggar Family," an intentionally old-fashioned faux sitcom about a white family named Niggar, was one of the best things ever. That experience, mixing music and entertainment, using all my accumulated knowledge to execute these precise little orders, was the best preparation imaginable for my Fallon job, though I didn't know it yet.

———

Chappelle was also instrumental in one of the most moving musical chapters in our history. A few months after *The Tipping Point* came out, Dave met the director Michel Gondry and started to bring him around. He had an idea for a kind of city party, something similar to Wattstax, and he wanted Dave to be the MC the way that Richard Pryor had been. He was starting to assemble musical talent: Kanye had agreed to participate, and Erykah, and the Roots jumped right on.

The movie, *Dave Chappelle's Block Party*, was shot in September of 2004, at the corner of Quincy and Downing in Clinton Hill, Brooklyn. It was just a few short weeks before the election that I was sure would sweep George W. Bush out of office. I remember one moment so clearly that it's like it happened yesterday—more than that, it's like it's happening right now, and will continue to happen. We were shooting a performance of "Jesus Walks," and Kanye wanted to come in with a marching band. I remember a welter of political and artistic thoughts crowding my mind. I thought about how presidential he looked and how the black kids were responding to him, something I had never really focused on in our own audience. I remember having a kind of out-of-body experience and investigation of the thought of my own artistic death. "Am I dead already?" I wondered.

It was a metaphor, but it wasn't just a metaphor. A few years earlier, my mother had been driving on a mountain road in Pennsylvania when she lost control of the car. She rolled over six times, and for whatever reason—fate, God, luck—her body went out the window, perfectly, like a letter being delivered, just before the car crashed down into the woods. It was one of those near-death experiences when death was way too near. She told me that as she went down the embankment, her only thought was, "Oh, this is how it's going to end." She wasn't panicked. She wasn't even sad. It was more a mix of resignation and realistic observation. I remember experiencing that same feeling the day of "Jesus Walks," of thinking to myself, "Oh, I see. This is where I get off." I saw the rest of the plot stretched out before me. Kanye was going to be the new leader, and I was fine with that. I was acting like I knew it was my last day. I took lots of photographs. I said lots of good-byes. I told myself, "You're not going to get all these people together again," at the same time that I concealed from myself the fact that I hadn't even gotten them all together that time. It took Michel Gondry making calls and Dave Chappelle putting up capital to get them together. That kind of experience, with everyone all around me and music in the air, was nostalgia at short range, a perfect snapshot of life as I had known it from 1996 to 2001. We had been doing it for years but we just hadn't been filming it.

EIGHTEEN

What's the right way to react when your failure becomes a success?

Even though *The Tipping Point* was a frustrating album to make, even though it exposed some fault lines in the band and made me question some of my most basic assumptions about what we were doing, it still got nominated for a number of Grammy Awards. The Grammys were a blast, as usual. My girlfriend at the time went with me to all the shows, many of which were shows by friends of ours. On the Monday after the awards, Jill Scott was playing, and Raphael Saadiq opened for her. His set was great, as usual, and her set was, too. Halfway through Jill's set, I got a text from Prince's assistant. That's how things go in the Prince universe: you get a pre-message saying that a phone message is coming later. But this time, the message said something different. It said that there was going to be a roller-skating party that night, for Valentine's Day, and that I should bring some cool people.

I was puzzled. What did Prince mean by "cool," exactly? I wasn't sure if he was trusting me with the word or with the concept. I texted back: "Cool?" It turned out they meant the people who were already with me: Mos, Talib, Jill, Erykah, Common. I started to line people up in my mind and called them to give them the news. I thought they would do backflips: a party with Prince? To my amazement, most of them weren't up for it. Jill came backstage and told me that she was tired. Talib said that he needed to be in bed before midnight. I ran into Alan Leeds, who led me to Raphael's dressing room, where Chris Rock and Eddie Murphy were sitting and talking. I went to my same pitch: "Hey, guys, want to go roller-skating with Prince?"

"Right," Alan said. "I'll be in the grave before I'm in skates."

"Right," Chris said. "Like I'm skating with these knees."

"Right," Raphael said. "I'm too old for that shit."

I was confused and a little depressed. How good were these people's lives that they could pass on Prince's roller-skating party? Only one man was brave enough—visionary enough—to see what lay before us, and that was Eddie Murphy. "This is historical," he said. "For starters, I need to see if Prince can roller-skate. I'm a comedian, and honestly, what's funnier than that?"

Prince's assistant texted me directions to a rink in Glenside, way out in the middle of nowhere. It was around one in the morning by the time we drove out there, and the place was empty, a bare rink, and I started to worry that I had the wrong place, or that I had been punked. Maybe Alan and Chris were in on the joke. Maybe they were all somewhere laughing. Then I saw DJ Rasheeda and some of her friends skating. "Hey," I said.

"Hey there," she said. They were so happy to see us that I started to feel bad that I hadn't brought more people. "No," she said. "Don't worry about it. Prince likes to keep things intimate. A dozen people is a big crowd to him." That may have been true, but it was crazy for her to say, as a DJ, and just as crazy for me, as a DJ, to hear. Do you know how hard it is to entertain a crowd that small?

The rink staff was professional, if a little nonplussed. "He's paying for us to stay open," one guy told me. "Let's make the best of it. What's your shoe size?"

My girlfriend and I skated for about an hour. No Prince, no nothing, and the longer we went, the stranger it seemed. Was he coming? Was he up in the rafters, laughing? It was a strange setup, to say the least. Someone was putting down cash to keep the kid behind the snack bar there, watching the pizza bake under the heat lamp. He should have been home studying for his spelling test.

Around two in the morning we were ready to go. Still no Prince, and the anthropological benefit of watching this strange half-attended all-skate was wearing off. Suddenly, Eddie came in. "Hey," he said. "I have an idea. Maybe don't take those skates off just yet."

And there he came, Prince, followed by a Princely entourage: his wife, Manuela; Larry Graham; some kids. I didn't recognize the kids but they were a familiar type—show-biz small-fry, like I was all those years ago, when my father took me down to the green room to meet KISS.

Prince was carrying a big briefcase in his hand, and he was acting all mysterious, like it contained the glowing substance from *Pulp Fiction* or something. He made like he was going to open it, then stopped, then started again. Then he walked toward me.

"Where's your phone?"

"What?" I said.

"Yeah, right, what?" he said. "I know you have it, Ahmir. Where is it?"

I thought maybe he wanted to make a phone call. I admit now that's not a plausible reading of the situation, but it was all so surreal. "It's here," I said.

He took it from me and turned it over in his hand. "Your coat is in coat check?"

"Yeah."

"Put this with it."

"Why? You think I'm going to record something?"

"Check the phone."

"What about him?" I pointed at Eddie. "You're not going to take his phone? He'll tell everyone."

Eddie put up his hands. "Hey, man, I don't know what you're talking about. My phone's in the car."

I put the phone in coat check. Prince was asking me. I was being asked by Prince. It was *Prince* who was asking *me*. And fine, maybe I didn't understand any part of what was happening, but sometimes you just have to launch yourself out into the river of an evening.

When I got back, Prince had the briefcase out on the floor. He clicked the lock and opened it, and took out the strangest, most singular pair of roller skates I had ever seen. They were clear skates that lit up, and the wheels sent a multicolored spark trail into your path.

He took them out and did a big lap around the rink. Man. He could skate like he could sing. I watched him go, so transfixed that I didn't even notice Eddie Murphy appearing at my arm. "I'm going to go get your phone for you," he said.

———

Roller-skating at Prince's party was cool. Watching Prince roller-skate was cooler. But then it was back east, to a life and a career that suddenly felt like they were in crisis. Rich took that year in stride. His attitude was that we were hardened veterans: we had recorded a number of albums, some of which had done better than others, and we would record a number more. I wasn't so sure. Kanye's ascendancy and the relative failure of *The Tipping Point*—or at the very least, the sense that it happened apart from us, wasn't as intimately connected to our creative process—sent me into a bit of a tailspin. I had lost my confidence and also my community. In the wake of *Voodoo*, and especially the mind-bending transition to sex symbol and soul savior that occurred during the second half of the tour, D'Angelo had withdrawn to his place in Virginia and was now semiretired from the music business. Every once in a while he would call me and we would put some music down, but I could hear depression in his voice. And it wasn't just my subjective read. He started to take his spiral out into the real world. In 2005, he was arrested in Richmond for drunk driving; the cops also found weed and coke on him and charged him. He and I had been talking on the telephone mostly, so I was shocked to see the mug shot: the Adonis from "Untitled (How Does It Feel)" looked like he had been on a yearlong bender. He was puffy and had put on at least thirty pounds. I called him up but he didn't really want to talk about it. When he said he was taking a break from the way things had been, he wasn't kidding. In September, he cracked up his car and broke his ribs, and the album that he was making—that, at times, we were making—as the follow-up to *Voodoo* just got further and further away.

———

D'Angelo was the most conspicuous absence from my life at that time, but he was by no means the only one. Zach de la Rocha, the vocalist from Rage Against the Machine, who had been a good friend and a collaborator, also took a step back. And for every artist who receded, there was one who proceeded up the chart. Jill Scott became an established platinum recording star. Common finally went platinum with Kanye. Mos Def graduated to movies. And there were geographic realities, too. Tariq fell in love and moved out to Los Angeles. Common moved, too, and Dilla also: they even roomed together. I felt displaced even though I was staying in the same place. I felt lost even though I wasn't going anywhere. The world I had built, which had started to show cracks in its foundation in 2001 or so, was now definitively dismantled.

I didn't know what I would do. I didn't know if the Roots had a future. I thought that I would go on and do some movie scoring, or focus on my hobby as a DJ, which had moved up and became a nice piece of change. Even beyond that, it was time to see what was up with plan B. For the first time since South Street in Philadelphia, I thought I might not make it to the finish line if I held on to music. I looked into teaching; Princeton had offered me a part-time position. I looked into magazines; periodicals were still a going concern, so I got a few offers to guest-edit or write a regular column. I may not have looked lost, but I was.

———

In January of 2006, James Poyser and I were in Los Angeles. We had been asked to do some music cues for Will Smith, and it was also Grammy week, which meant more parties and more concerts. The meeting with Will went well enough that James and I decided to drop by and see Dilla. We wanted to share the news with him. Dilla and I had been talking by phone over the last year and a half, and we continued to collaborate in small ways: he helped out with music cues on *Chappelle's Show* and contributed some production to every Roots album.

Since Dilla had moved to California, I had been hearing stuff on and off about health problems. Common had told me that he had been in the hospital once or twice, though he wasn't specific about why, and Dilla himself never really talked about it. When I stepped into his house in California, I was totally unprepared for what I saw. It was just Dilla and his mother, and it wasn't really Dilla at all. In his place was a frail, eighty-pound man in a wheelchair. He couldn't communicate at all. He was mumbling and gesturing weakly. I found out later, along with everyone else, that he was suffering from a rare blood disease, thrombotic thrombocytopenic purpura, and possibly lupus. But all I knew at the time was what I saw, which was that he was dying. His mortality hit me square in the face. I made a mental imprint of his setup, which was nothing like his setup in Detroit, where he had the best gear and a sophisticated rig. In Los Angeles, he had a small drum machine and a small keyboard. It was simple, makeshift, and frail. There was a Rotary Connection album on his turntable. I'll never forget that album, how out of place it looked, how everything suddenly seemed like it was tending toward some inevitable end. James and I left the house in a state of shock, not entirely certain what we had just seen, or what, if anything, we could do to change it.

———

That year, which was 2006, Prince didn't have a skating party. Instead, he had a party at his house, and the reunited Time was providing the entertainment. I went with Dave Chappelle and Erykah Badu, and while Dave sat outside, a group of us—me, Erykah, Wendy and Susannah Melvoin, Nikka Costa and her then-husband, Doyle Bramhall II—sat in Prince's home performance space to watch the show. The band started with "Girl," and then Jerome Benton did a bit where he moved around the room, pointing every celeb out to Morris Day and putting them on the spot. "Morris, look who we've got in the house tonight, yeah, yeah, who do I see? I see Gabrielle Union with her fine self! And who else? I see Lindsay Lohan."

He went right around the room like that, pointing at each of us, poking fun. He saw Christina Aguilera. He saw Verne Troyer. He saw Jamie Foxx. The closer he got to my section, the less comfortable I felt. I had always been shy about that kind of thing, and I wasn't sure what he was going to say about me. "Morris," he said. "Look here. We've got Naomi Campbell. And there, right there next to her, we've got Shelia E. And we've got Alicia Keys."

Alicia was next to me. That meant that it was my turn. I froze... and Jerome skipped right over me. "We've got Nikka Costa. We've got John Leguizamo. We've got George Benson."

I tried to play it off like I was cool, but Susannah later told me that my body language had defeat written all over it. Then Morris called Erykah to come up with them and sing "Girl," and my embarrassment dissipated. (Luckily, she knew the song. At a concert a few months before, it hadn't gone so well when he had asked Alicia to sing "777-9311" and she blanked out.) I went out to the tennis courts, talked to Dave for a little while, watched Om'Mas, from the L.A. hip-hop group Sa-Ra, defiantly smoking weed. I kind of admired that: Prince was strictly antidrug, and if he had seen that, he would have probably kicked him right out.

Just before I left, I went over to give Jimmy Jam a pound. Out of the blue, Morris was there. "My goodness gracious," he said. "If this ain't the baddest, funkiest cat ever. Give me some dap." I didn't know who he thought he was talking to. He obviously didn't know who I was. Then he did: "Quest," he said, "show me some love." I was flabbergasted. We had a long conversation, and he was surprised I knew about his training as a drummer. We talked about his earliest bands, Flyte Tyme and Enterprise, and how he worked with Prince when they were in junior high school. It confirmed one of my pet theories about very famous people. If you want to get to know them, don't bother talking to them; instead, talk to the five people who know them the best. That way, you get a picture of them without having to deal with their overdeveloped defenses.

———

The very next day, I got a call from Common. Dilla had passed. He was thirty-two years old. At his funeral, I told my girlfriend that I wanted to sit in the back in a pew. Tariq and Common were up in front, but I didn't want to sit with them, because I didn't want Tariq to see me crying. I have always had issues showing my feelings. I was raised by a Joe Jackson type: "You want to cry? Well, okay, I'll give you something to cry about." I have spent a lifetime hardening myself emotionally.

We went from California to Hawaii for a Roots show, and the morning after we arrived, I fled my hotel room and went for a run on the beach. I had never done anything like that in my life, but at that point I was crying uncontrollably and I didn't want anyone to see me that way.

It's been more than half a decade since Dilla passed, and I still don't really know what to think about it. He had been there at the beginning of neo soul, though we didn't call it that then, and his music will be around long after people don't call it that anymore. An album like *Donuts*—thirty-one short snippets, manipulated samples, overlaid dialogue, no real songs except that everything there is so endlessly tuneful and rhythmic—made people rethink some of their basic assumptions about music, and not just hip-hop, but all recorded music—made them go back to the beginning, to the drum, to a unit of measurement, and wonder what constitutes a full work, what's a partial work, what's original, what's borrowed, whether you could take the Jackson 5's "All I Do Is Think of You," rearrange it so that the intro is located closer to the chorus, and call it a new song. There's a chef's aesthetic at work, if a chef diced, pureed, and served while he was walking on the wing of a biplane. There's a daredevil's aesthetic, if a daredevil never left his house. There's a postmodern critic in there, too, pinning pictures up on the wall but so that they're facing the wall. There's a love for the past but also an awareness that the past is destroyed every second by the present, and that the future's laying in wait to wreak more havoc. And then there's a radical rethinking of the relationship between artist and work: the album's credited to Dilla, but what does that even really mean, given how he builds his house from other people's bricks while at the same time decoupling the snippets of song, the bits of music, the loops, from their original source? There's a guessing game and a veiling game and a process of slow disclosure: in traditional music, you see (or at least imagine) the source of the sound. If it's Aretha Franklin, you see her holding the microphone at the Fillmore or sitting at the piano pounding out "Spirit in the Dark," and even if you don't see her, you see her, if you know what I mean. If it's Wilson Pickett, you see him even if you don't see him. If it's Chuck D, you see him even if you don't see him. Here, there's something more profoundly acousmatic—that's music whose source you can't see. Where are these sounds coming from? Where are they going? Are they working in concert with each other, by design? Are they strangers being herded into the same elevator? And once they meet, what conversations crop up? These were central questions in hip-hop from the beginning, and they go back far before that. They go back to jazz, where traditional melodies were remade through improvisation. They go back to the beginning of recorded music, where the first break was made between performer and performed. They go back to the thing that's at the root of both Dilla and the Roots and every other inspired composition in any and every genre: it's the music in your head. That's the seed at the beginning of every artwork. How do you take what you hear and translate it to something that can be heard?

Dilla didn't answer all those questions definitively, but he asked them, and he stayed true to that quest, and I love him for it. I have the last beat he ever made, which was built on a sample from Funkadelic's "America Eats Its Young," a dark, morbid piece of music. He must have created that knowing where he was going. Everything he did had hidden messages. He made personal music even when he worked on productions for others. That's the kind of artist he was. *Block Party*, the movie we had made with Dave Chappelle and Michel Gondry, had been shot in 2004 but delayed due to various Dave-related wrangling. When it was finally released in the spring of 2006, it was dedicated to Dilla.

His death came at a time when the Roots were in flux. We were considering our own mortality as a band. None of us knew how to deal with a midlife crisis; we were guys in their midthirties who had started when we were nineteen. And while we knew that something had gone wrong with *The Tipping Point*, that we hadn't really found ourselves in the right place at the right time, we didn't exactly know what to do about it.[28]

For my part, the crisis cut deeper. When I searched my soul, I found that I didn't want to make music anymore. After *Things Fall Apart*, fans thought they had a bead on our sound. They thought they knew who we were as a band, finally; we had jumped from style to style but finally settled in something that felt comfortable to them— because, I think, it felt comfortable to us. The truth, though, is that much of that record's success was due to the fact that it was the finest record that Slum Village never got to make. Their demo was our food and fuel during that period. And the same is true of *Voodoo* and

28. Jimmy Iovine really believed in this project. He went as far as to call me personally when the album was done and tell me that it was a high-water mark in popular culture. Look, I'm a natural-born contrarian. Doubt is etched into my being like it's part of my DNA or synaptic wiring or sumthin'. So, the whole idea and experience of the near-mythological Jimmy "Fuckin'" Iovine, Mr. No Doubt himself, counting the ways in which he loved us, right on the other side of the transceiver... well, it seemed more than just a bit surreal. It seemed big (and ersatz elevator-like). So, I thought about how it truly didn't matter what I thought about the shit and about how rarely good has much to do with anything. All the world's a stage, and all its actors are on the grift. And, contrary to Gladwell's thinking, it was the big things that seemed to make the big difference. But herein lies the rub. For all Jimmy's puff-n-stuff, niggas did not warm to the record. And, on top of that, we had lost our most beloved critical swag. After *The Tipping Point*'s release I remember an influential editor telling a close friend that the Roots were "so 2002." It was August 2004.

Mama's Gun and *Like Water for Chocolate*: we succeeded because we managed to beat them to their own game. We upped the ante with *Phrenology*, which felt like a different kind of earned success, a way for us to spread our wings, and then we found ourselves earthbound again for *The Tipping Point*. But after Dilla's passing I couldn't imagine going back to the sound of *Things Fall Apart*. It was too fraught, too sad, too connected to the admiration I had for him. He was my idol, and I didn't want to make my mark in his shadow, or in his absence.

There were also changes on the label front. After the less-than-ideal experience with *The Tipping Point*, I wrote a letter to Jimmy Iovine explaining humbly that we felt like we needed to be on a label in New York so we had access to the people we were working with. He didn't disagree and, just like that, we were cut loose again.

———

Homeless, rudderless, without motivation or direction: that's how the band was feeling in the summer of 2005. Luckily, Rich had a plan, as always, which was to put us on a steady diet of drill-sergeant motivation and some psychological prodding. When we were in New Orleans playing a show, we went out one night and saw a group called the To Be Continued Brass Band. They had started at G. W. Carver Senior High; a bunch of teenagers from the Seventh and Ninth Wards who didn't want to die from drugs and crime decided that they would rather play music. "See this," he'd say, pointing at them. "This was you back in Philadelphia, when Tariq was freestyling and you were playing on the bucket. This is what you were and what you need to become again."

We planned to collaborate with them on an album that used New Orleans music the way that Paul Simon had used South African or Brazilian music. That was in June. Because we had two months to spare, we decided to hop over to Europe to make some quick cash before returning to New Orleans at the beginning of August. On our last day in Portugal we played a concert that's infamous in Roots circles; Tariq lost his temper and cursed out the crowd. That same day Hurricane Katrina made landfall. The TDC Brass Band was literally washed away. One of them died, and the rest were relocated: to Portland, to Houston, to the Northeast. We did a few benefits and got HBO involved in helping to reunite the band, but our idea of working with the kids was swept away along with the rest of the city, and we were left with this empty feeling.

NINETEEN

From: Ben Greenman [cowriter]

To: Ben Greenberg [editor]

Re: You think there's time?

I think Ahmir's doing a great job balancing them, yes.
No question. But your subject line made me laugh.
Do I think there's time? What is this book except proof
that there's always time, and that we're always moving
through it? There's this show on HBO called "Witness," a
documentary series about photojournalists in the world's
trouble spots. We just ran a short review of it in the *New
Yorker*, and in her piece, Emily Nussbaum made a point
of how deeply strange the setup really is: a TV camera
crew trailing a photographer, taking footage of him, also
taking moving pictures of the same things that he's taking
still pictures of, the whole thing packaged for viewers
to consume as a single product, experienced within the
confines of their home screen. Well, Ahmir's looking back
on his life as I'm looking at him looking back on his life, and
everyone else is looking at that process in its finished form,
fixed in time.

By the way, I'm also finding that there's a Doppler effect
in personal memory. The normal Doppler effect, the
one we all learn about in high school, happens when an
ambulance comes toward you on the street. Because
the distance the sound needs to travel is shrinking as it
approaches you, the frequency of the sound waves is
compressed, so it sounds higher-pitched than it actually is.
I think the same thing happens with autobiography. When
Ahmir talks about his childhood, the years are receding
from him, and so they have a lower pitch. It's not just that
he has processed them, or that he's resigned to them.
He actually hears them differently. A few times, we have
started talking about the future. That's time that's still
coming on, and so there's more urgency, a higher pitch. It's
not as comfortable. It reminds me of Ahmir's story about
Aba Shanti, and how lower frequencies, even when they're
very loud, aren't destructive or grating in the same way.

I mention this because we're at the point in the book where
Ahmir is dealing more with the recent past, and while
that's not pitched quite as high as the future, it's not as
low as the distant past either. There's less perspective and
sometimes more of an almost physical discomfort. Losses
are felt more painfully, failures still sting, confusion may not
have cleared quite yet. Just thought you should know.

TWENTY

How do you plan a rebirth? I'm not sure you do. You just stand in the darkness until you can't endure it any longer, and then you move forward until you're standing in the light. Around the time we cut ties with Interscope, I was feeling as low as I had in years. My emotional life was in a shambles: I had lost Dilla and felt the chill of his absence on my music. Also, I had broken up with a girl I dated for three years. All my friends were getting married and starting families, and I was being left behind. Relationships among the Roots were not what they had been early on, either; by that point, Tariq and I had started riding in separate tour buses. Mine was Gryffindor and his was Slytherin. It wasn't open hostility by any means, just a kind of exhaustion and uncertainty if any of us wanted to go on.

It was in that environment that Rich started to shop us around to new labels. One of the first ones he tried was Def Jam. It had always seemed like a natural fit, maybe even more so now, given that Jay-Z was running the label. When we went to talk to him, though, he was skeptical. He pledged to support us, but he also was candid about his reluctance to expect too much from us commercially. "Man," he said, "I don't want to look like the guy who killed the Roots." Instead, he sat us down and told us that he wanted us to follow our instincts.

"Make an art record," he said. "Do an album you'll be proud of. You're not going to get on Hot 97. Funkmaster Flex isn't going to drop twenty bombs when he plays your single. He's not even going to play your single."

Game Theory, the album that grew out of that directive, out of the rubble of Katrina and the confusion of the band's middle age, was also a pained love letter to Philadelphia, which had become a virtual war zone, with twelve to fourteen murders per week. We were sick to see our home city this way, and hopeful that we could bring attention to the situation, even if we couldn't directly affect it. All of those factors made *Game Theory* a very determined record, a very serious record. We were looking back to early hip-hop masterpieces like Public Enemy's *It Takes a Nation*, both generally (the album has a coherent feel and plays straight through like a manifesto) and specifically (our song "False Media," for example, references "Don't Believe the Hype"). In that sense, *Game Theory* reached back toward albums that were, in their own way, blues records.

A quick lesson. When people think about blues, they think of personal music: a man reflecting on his hard luck with women or his disappointment at his own moral limits. They think of Skip James singing "Devil Got My Woman" or Robert Johnson worrying about the hellhounds on his trail. But that's not all it is. With apologies to Brother West, blues looked outward, too. The *Titanic* sank in 1912. Eighteen years later, Blind Willie Johnson wrote "God Moves on the Water" about the tragedy, and to him it was the deepest blues imaginable— because of the hubris it represented, because of the imperialist, Tower of Babel–like push behind the idea of making the world's largest cruise ship. There's a chilling, if not exactly accurate line in there about the ship's captain, Edward Smith, who went down with it: "E.J. Smith, mighty man / Built a ship that he didn't understand." That song is a monumental work, a nearly perfect example of how a song can extract a fearsome sermon from history. And then there's a woman named Minnie Wallace who's a kind of shadowy figure in the blues, not very prolific, not a major artist, but she wrote a song called "The Cockeyed World" about the 1935 Italian invasion of Ethiopia. Many black people in America were proud of the way the Ethiopians and their emperor, Haile Selassie, tried to repel the invaders, and some of them even tried to go fight in the resistance. Wallace's song is a kind of strange reverse view of that Afrocentric moment: it's from the perspective of a woman who is lamenting the way that the situation in Ethiopia is taking her husband or boyfriend away from her, or at the very least directing his attention elsewhere. "This old cockeyed world will make a good man treat you mean," she sings. "He'll treat you just like a poor girl he's never seen." Blind Willie Johnson's *Titanic* song was written nearly two decades after the ship sank, but Minnie Wallace's song was a quicker reaction: The invasion took place on October 3, and she recorded her song only nine days later. She was reflecting on events before they even had a reflection. (That's about as fast as Neil Young did with the Kent State shootings and "Ohio," or as Tom Petty, with "Peace in L.A." following the Rodney King beating—now that's from-the-headlines songwriting.) I don't remember if either Blind Willie Johnson or Minnie Wallace ever came up while we were making *Game Theory*, but those were the kinds of songs we had in mind: outward blues. The world had just gone wrong, was continuing to go wrong, whether it was the breached levees in New Orleans or the murder rate in Philadelphia, and we wanted to say so, in no uncertain terms. It was our right as artists but also our responsibility. Did I say a lesson? Sorry. I meant a lecture.

And yet we didn't close our personal window onto the world, either. The album opened up with a tribute to Dilla, "Dilltastic Vol Won(derful)," which sampled Slum Village. If *The Tipping Point* was a chronicle of compromise, the sound of the Roots back on their heels, *Game Theory* was an illustration of what happened when we planted our feet again. The tour that followed was augmented with a miniature brass band, a reminder of the collaboration with the TBC Brass Band we had envisioned and a kind of memorial to the fact that it was no longer possible.

————

What's a late-career renaissance? Maybe it's just what happens when you clear your ears and clear your head. We had set aside some of the distractions of *The Tipping Point*, as well as and some of the unreasonable expectations that stretched back as far as *Things Fall Apart* and *Phrenology*. For the first time in a while, it made complete sense again to be in the Roots, to be a Root, to be making the things we were making.

I was also doing more production work. One day, James Poyser and I got a call asking if we'd be interested in producing the new Al Green record for Blue Note. We jumped at the chance. Al Green was more than just another soul vocalist. He was a legend, or maybe even more than a legend. It seemed like a perfect opportunity to reenter that neo soul space and bring his sound into the present. James and I lined up musicians. We lined up guest vocalists like Anthony Hamilton and John Legend and Corrine Bailey Rae. We called in a bunch of songs and got ready to go.

What we learned pretty early on is that working with Al Green isn't exactly like working with other singers. For starters, he showed up the first day all ready to sing, and without much interest in meeting the rest of us or even learning our names. We were just supposed to run tape and let him do his magic—which, by the way, was an approach that worked much of the time. The problems arose when it didn't work, or when Al and the rest of us didn't exactly see eye to eye. There's a song on *Lay It Down* that Al was oversinging: we wanted him to go subtle, and he was going rough and intense. We didn't like the way he was doing it. But breaking the news to him was another matter entirely. We decided to let Rich be the bad guy and broach the subject with him. It didn't go well. Al insisted that this was his voice and that he could only sing it one way. "I'm not going to do it any other way no matter how many times you ask," he said.

"Okay," I said, and the rest of us started packing up.

Al didn't like that. He wanted us to beg him to stay, but we had been practicing reverse psychology, and even *reverse* reverse psychology, for years—in the band, with friends and collaborators. You couldn't run that kind of game on us without getting it run right back on you. "Where are you going?" he said.

"We thought you didn't want to sing anymore."

He was mad. "Right," he said. "If you motherfuckers put your computers away, and concentrate on your job, and stop worrying about my job, then you might see how things fit. If you think it's so easy to sing that part, you sing that part."

We agreed. "You're right, Al. We're wrong, Al."

The more we tried to placate him, the madder he got. He was mad at us, mad at the computers, mad at technology and the passage of time and the nerve of young producers who dared ask him to do something that he, Al Green, didn't feel in his bones. But after he boiled over, he calmed down, and he sang beautifully. Replay that ad infinitum, and that will start to give you some sense of how *Lay It Down* got done.

———

Game Theory had recharged us somewhat, especially since we felt that we were making our music for a label that unconditionally supported our vision. As we started to collect material, it became apparent that we were headed in an explicitly political direction. It would have been hard to avoid it, frankly. It was the end of 2007, and we were shooting for a mid-2008 release date, which meant that we had a responsibility to at least think about the presidential election. And it wasn't just any presidential election. It was an election where the Democratic field had been fairly quickly narrowed down to Barack Obama, Hilary Clinton, and John Edwards. In November, Oprah Winfrey got into the game, announcing that she was going to actively campaign for Obama, and that changed everything. The Iowa caucus went by, then the New Hampshire primary, then Nevada, then South Carolina, all Obama victories, and all of a sudden it was plausible that the Democratic party might have an African American nominee. It's hard to overstate how important that was within the hip-hop community. Around that time, John Legend came to us and presented us with an idea for an uplifting record that would sum up all of the promise of America, and how an Obama presidency might crystallize that promise. We thought that was a great idea, to make music from the optimistic feeling sweeping the country. We eventually put that record out in 2010, as *Wake Up*, and it was a beautiful, affirming collection of songs by Harold Melvin and the Blue Notes, Ernie Hines, Baby Huey, and others. It was a labor of love and also a labor of light, a way of acknowledging the power of the yang surrounding the Obama candidacy and what followed.

But there was also a flip side: the growing backlash. It may be all too obvious now, after five years and one more election clotted with birther insinuations and "food-stamp president" slurs and Paul Ryan worrying out loud what effect Obama's reelection might have on Judeo-Christian values, but the racially tinged ugliness was just getting into gear. *Rising Down* was our response to the response to Obama's rise, even though it came out before he was actually elected. For cover art, we used an 1896 propaganda poster called "Negro Rule." It shows a black devil taking over a plantation, a terrifying black figure plucking innocent, hapless whites from the earth. We

wanted to think about what would happen once the magic wand wasn't
working quickly enough for America, once Obama was an actual
president facing actual crises rather than primarily a symbol. Would
the people sit back patiently and give him time to work through the
country's problems? Would Obama's detractors block him the way
that other presidents had been opposed? Or would there be a special dimension to it (a dark side, so to speak)? All these thoughts, all
these ideas, coalesced into what may have been our most consistent
record since *Things Fall Apart*. It was so unified in its message, in fact,
that one of the songs we thought would be the lead single, a track
called "Birthday Girl" with Patrick Stump as a guest vocalist, had to
be taken off the record. It was a topical song, a story-song about the
perils of men dating younger women. But it was also a pop song, and
it just didn't feel right with the rest of the material. The production
was dense and menacing, louder and harsher than any record we had
made, and so were the lyrics. The album took on prescription drug
addiction, the way the media distorts the news, the risks of technology, and the financial crisis. And that's just on the title track. There's
another song, "75 Bars (Black's Reconstruction)," where Tariq says
the word *nigga* three dozen times, and not one of them is gratuitous:
the whole thing is a fearless look at the tricky business of black male
identity. We made sure that the whole enterprise was sent off with a
sense of community. On *The Tipping Point*, we had hardly any other
rappers joining us; here, we had nearly a dozen. We were speaking
for other acts, and letting other acts speak along with us.

We knew that there weren't many records like *Rising Down*, not in
our own catalog, and certainly not in the music world at large. Hip-
hop in general was in crisis, with a sense that maybe the only way to
succeed was through a kind of minstrel-show behavior, act a certain
thuggish or clownish way to satisfy society's sense of what a hip-hop
star should be. Hip-hop sometimes felt like it was over, which had

been a common refrain ever since De La Soul declared they were dead and put flowers on their own grave back in 1991.[29] But here we were, with the increasingly likely prospect of a black president. Wasn't it about time that everyone else stepped up, too?

When the record came out, we held our breath a bit. There's a scene in the movie *Set It Off* where Cleo, played by Queen Latifah, gets surrounded by the police and goes out in a blaze of glory. That's how we felt a little bit after *Phrenology*, and even more pointedly after our experience with *The Tipping Point*. We had said our piece and found our hill to die on. We weren't going to compromise for anyone. We had the attitude that every record we were making might be our last and that we were well within our rights to give the finger to naysayers on our way out. That's why those albums are so angry in comparison to some of our earlier work. If you're going to kill us off, we're going to give it to you on the way out.

Critics understood the record in the spirit we intended it. They praised it almost uniformly. Harry Allen, writing in the *Village Voice*, compared us to Samuel R. Delaney. The *New York Times* called it our "best album since *Things Fall Apart*"; the *Daily Telegraph*, in London, said it was our best album ever. And even though Robert Christgau

---

29. Hip-hop ain't dead, but it has become a winner-take-all affair, and its winningest artists consistently portray the patriarchal swag of lives that "ain't nothing but bitches and money." To quote the noted scholar and cultural critic Tricia Rose, "commercial mainstream American Hip Hop has become the cultural arm of predatory capitalism." Is the genre "technically" better on some beats-and-rhymes-shit level? Yes, but "technical better" isn't really what it's about. A true better is about being able to empathize with the artists who are doing it and being able to build a sense of self on that empathetic platform. Hip-hop these days is a reductive thing. When people respond to Jay-Z, are they empathizing with him, or are they just admiring his altitude—the things and people he's acquired—and losing part of themselves in the process?

gave the record an A, for the first time I didn't feel like were earning good grades. I felt like we were teaching the class.

———

I had heard rumors from Neal Brennan that Jimmy Fallon was starting a late-night talk show, and that he might want to open a discussion with us about being his house band. I took it with a grain of salt. We had just graduated to the point where we were making good money on the concert circuit—not as much as real rock stars, but the top of the mountain for us. After swimming in purgatory for fifteen years, we were making a steady living, and I didn't think I could turn my back on that.[30]

At the same time, I was looking to buy a new house in Los Angeles. I had a number of residences, though I wasn't really using them. I had bought Jazzy Jeff's condo in Philadelphia and set my mom up there. I had a place for my dad. I lived in a small apartment that I didn't see very much, at least not while we were recording. At some point along the way, maybe 2007 or so, I decided that it made sense to buy a place in L.A. also. I was there so much anyway, and every trip I took ended up costing me at least $4,000 by the time I got done with airfare and hotel and food. If I had a house, I figured, it would pay for itself. I was being responsible with my money. I was always responsible. It's not like I'm a spendthrift. When you become a hip-hop luminary, you're supposed to go to Jacob the Jeweler and get yourself a $65,000 chain. I went there exactly once in my life, and got the cheap-

———

30. But even at that level, we were limited in what we could do. Unless your shit is mega poppy, you're not going to play Wisconsin regularly. You can do New York, D.C., Boston, Philly. You used to do Detroit before it became untenable. Definitely Los Angeles and San Francisco, maybe Portland. But you can't really do a gangbuster tour as a black act because that shit just isn't popping in the middle of America.

est item on the list: a very simple tennis bracelet for the girl I was dating. Jacob took me out of the store to a coffee shop across the street. He didn't want anyone to see that he was letting me off so easy. And it wasn't about the jewelry. The stuff I wanted was small time. I might drop five grand total on a record collection, which is something that I could easily afford, but even that seemed to send my business manager, Shawn, and Rich into fits. They were like high-school bullies with me when it came to my finances. And keep in mind that these are the same guys who managed other artists who were considerably less conservative with their money—guys who might at the very same time be buying a new Porsche for a porn star, say. So I felt that asking for a house was fair. It was a solid investment, a way of saving money. I was proud of myself for thinking of it. I did the math, prepared a presentation, and went to Shawn, who promptly said no.

The begging lasted for three years, and finally he relented. I bought myself a place in Silverlake, but nearly a year went by, and I still hadn't really moved in. That's when Shawn started to put the heat on me. "See," he said. "You said that you needed this place, but it's just sitting there empty, eating up your mortgage payments." When I finally got around to moving into the house, it was a big deal. And then, my second day out there, on my way to a Roots show at UCLA, I ran into Jimmy Fallon.

"Hey," he said. "What are you doing out here?"

"Moving into a place I got."

"Nice," he said. "Hey, listen: I have something to ask you."

I knew where he was headed. "Your show? Yeah, Neal mentioned it to me."

"Oh," he said. "You think you'd be interested in something like that?"

I knew the answer was no. I just couldn't see giving up the tour money we were making. "Maybe," I said.

"Great."

"Why don't you come by the show tonight?" I said. Jimmy said he would.

I headed home, figuring that I would deal with the idea of Fallon the same way that I dealt with the meeting at Geffen back in the early nineties: not going to happen, but nice to think about anyway. Back then we took the meeting for a free glass of orange juice. Now I was indulging the idea because it felt nice to have a prominent fan. Having him come to our show wasn't hurting anyone.

He came to the show, hung out with us backstage. And then, about ten minutes in, I saw something I thought I would never see in my life. I was in an interview and when I got out I saw Jimmy with almost the whole band—Tariq, Tuba, Owen, Frank, Kamal, and others— making a huge human pyramid. Everyone was laughing. By that point, the band had taken a lighter turn, personality-wise. Owen really made the most of the fun factor that Tuba brought to the group, and Kirk came alive in ways I hadn't seen before. Jimmy brought all of that to a boil, in the best sense, and I couldn't help but laugh at how silly they all looked. Oh, shit, I thought to myself. We're stuck with this guy, aren't we?

I can't say that I really knew what it meant. I just knew that we fit with Jimmy like hand in glove. It hadn't even been ten minutes and he was already able to get everyone loose and joking—no small feat, since we were a fairly guarded band. Relationships, while never exactly toxic, were not always as open as they could have been. But from that first meeting Jimmy had the ability to turn us all into thirteen-year-olds. The spirit of J. M. Barrie is in him. He's a very childlike presence. And it worked like a charm.

That night, at our after party, Tariq came up to me and gestured over to the corner, where Jimmy was joking with some guys. "I think I can see this happening," Tariq said. And I could, too.

————

Jimmy was sold on us and we were sold on him, but Lorne Michaels was skeptical. He was honest about why: he felt that the Roots, already established as artists, would distract Jimmy, who would be struggling with the pressures of a new show. No talk show comes out of the gate winning, he said. There's no honeymoon period; instead there's a period of being kicked and beaten, a trial by fire. The only person who really had it good from the start was Arsenio Hall, and his show was as much a social experiment as it was a comedy show. But once we made it clear that we understood those risks and that we were willing to work to Jimmy's benefit, Lorne agreed. We were in Korea playing a show the day of Obama's inauguration, which also happened to be my birthday. We flew back to New York and reported to work at NBC on Wednesday.

I laugh so hard at those shows now. I have told Jimmy a million times that when we get to our thousandth show, we should air the first practice episode. Now we have such a perfect rhythm, almost telepathic, but back then everything was awkward in the extreme. Plus, Jimmy was dealing with pressures from the other side; I remember watching the way Lorne walked around the set pointing at things, and thinking how anal retentive he was about every little detail. He didn't like the cuts of the intro montage. He hated the curtains. He wanted certain lights to point in a different direction. At the time, he seemed like a fussy uncle; it didn't really occur to me that he was a guy who had run a late-night empire for almost forty years. As it turns out, those fixes weren't just minor details. They were major improvements. The difference between what the show is now and what it was in practice is vast, and more than a little was due to his initial detail mongering. Lorne used to say that the average late-night show didn't really catch on for about for four years. It took us about a year.

———

Justin Timberlake and Robert De Niro were the guests on our first real show. Once again, this was a stroke of brilliance from Lorne: he booked De Niro because he wanted a very difficult guest interview for Jimmy. He knew that the press would be relentless regardless, so he figured that he might as well give them a reason.

We introduced De Niro with the theme from the TV show *Taxi*, because he had starred in *Taxi Driver*, and we used the Bee Gees' "Nights on Broadway" for Justin because of the fake Brothers Gibb talk-show skit that he and Jimmy had done on *Saturday Night Live*.

The first show was rocky, though less so than the practice one. The second show was less rocky than the first. But I still wasn't convinced that we belonged on a late-night TV show. When you're in a new situation, there's always a flash of recognition. Sometimes it's the flash that you can't handle it. Sometimes it's the flash that you can. And sometimes it's the flash that illuminates you for everyone else, that shows that you've been able to handle it all along. For us, that came the second week of taping. One of the writers had come up with an idea for a bit called "Freestylin' with the Roots." Jimmy would go out into the audience and talk to them about their lives, their jobs, whatever, and we would take their answers and turn them into a song. This required Tariq to freestyle and for me to give him a beat, which had been happening since high school. But Jimmy upped the ante by asking us to play the answer song not just as hip-hop, but as surf music, or heavy metal, or country.

We killed it. We were right there with the audience. We took everything that was thrown at us and spun it into gold. For me, that was the turning point. I started to see that there was a new way to live, and that this might be it: a day job with a steady stream of new challenges. It wasn't easy, especially at the beginning. We practiced six hours a day six days a week. We refused to fail—not because we needed the job, necessarily—but because we needed to refuse to fail. If that's a little abstract, so be it.

Fallon's show was also a musical education, or maybe it makes more sense to say that it was a reeducation. There I was at the age of forty, exposed to a whole new world of music, and at first I wasn't sure how to handle myself. I freely admit that I initially dismissed Dirty Projectors when they first came on the show, probably about five months into our run. Even at that point, I was starting to see a pattern among Brooklyn groups—broken-down drums, rickety keyboard setups, rock bands that copped a certain attitude—and I mentally put Dirty Projectors into that category. I was pretty sure that I'd be getting more of what had already, for the most part, failed to impress me. But the second they started performing, there was this incredible vocal complexity: the three female singers doing this syncopated thing that sounded like a keyboard program, then all of them shifting into these intricate, choirlike vocals. Kirk and I looked at each other with our jaws on the ground. "Holy shit," he said. I could see every syllable falling out of his mouth like he was on *Electric Company*. Back in the dressing room, we were like little kids. "Can you fucking believe what we just saw?" I said.

"Was that ProTools or real?" he said.

I just shrugged, still a little bit in shock. It just so happened that Amber Coffman, one of the singers, was in the hallway. Kirk went out there, still in his underwear. "Hey," he said. "Can you come here a sec? Would you mind doing that one more time?"

She got the whole band and brought them in, and they duplicated the performance exactly. If I had been in disbelief before, now I was numb with amazement. At the time I was reading Malcolm Gladwell's *Outliers*, and I was obsessed with this whole theory that expertise was the result of 10,000 hours of concentrated practice. But that didn't make sense here. Who *does* those kinds of vocals? Who could conceive of them, let alone execute them to perfection?

I posted that dressing-room re-creation online and it turned out to be my first super-viral video. Every blog picked it up. It made me look cool and forward thinking because Dirty Projectors were cool and forward thinking, and that set me back on my heels a bit. I had heard the band's name, seen little articles about them on Pitchfork, but I wouldn't have given them a chance if I didn't have the best seat in the house. Ever since then, I have vigilantly researched every band that gets booked on the show. It has turned into a modern-day equivalent of digging in the crates. The second I find out that a band has been booked, I go to Metacritic and read their reviews. I go to Rdio or Spotify and listen to their albums. I look for their interviews on YouTube. I want to make sure I'm well versed by the time they arrive—not just so I feel I can understand them when we back them on the show, but also to see if it's worth investigating a future collaboration.

TWENTY-ONE

Where were you when Michael Jackson died? I was in the commercial break of the second segment of the Fallon show. We were about to introduce Tiger Woods, when my road manager, Keith, ran on stage. He had a look on his face. He came right up to me and said, "Yo, Michael Jackson just died." It was a shock to the system. It was still the first year of the show, and once you drop a bomb like that, there is no going back to the silliness and lightheartedness that is Jimmy Fallon. That's over. You're in another space. At first, I wasn't sure whether to believe Keith. Who believes something like that the first time they hear it? Because my computer was next to me I went on CNN. (The rule with black people is that it's not legit news until a legit white news source confirms it.) I was probably looking at the GlobalGrind website, and they were reporting it, but I thought no, that can't be true. But CNN was saying the same thing and that eliminated any doubt. I was so overcome with misery that we just stopped playing the song. My face went numb. It was as if I had been told that both my parents had died in a fire. People in the audience, some of whom hadn't heard what Keith said, didn't understand.

I had heard the news earlier that day that Michael Jackson was headed to the hospital, but it was murky at best. And I had a theory about it that I was telling people all afternoon. When Michael

announced his run of fifty shows, I had made a plan with a girl to go
see one of them. We were trying to decide which one. Did we want
to see a performance in the first half of the run? The finale? As a performer, I knew that other performers really get in their zone in the
exact middle. Catch them too early, and they're still working out the
kinks. Catch them in the second half of the run, and you might get a
bored superstar. But then it occurred to me that maybe the whole thing
was more tenuous than that. The Jacksons had a history of scheduling
shows and tours and not quite making good on them—I had never
heard the word *exhaustion* until the Jacksons came along. I had seen
some Janet shows on a tour that was later canceled due to exhaustion,
and it turned out the presales were too small. Michael had pulled the
exhaustion trick at the Beacon Theater in 1995; he was supposed to do
an intimate HBO special, and at the last minute—exhaustion. When
he entered the hospital this time, I figured he was trying to find a way
out of the grueling fifty-show commitment because he just wasn't
ready. I took a hard-line, disappointed-fan stance: "Come on, Mike, I
knew you were going to pull this shit. Exhaustion, here we go."

But then it wasn't exhaustion at all. He was dead. I went home
that night to Philadelphia. At that time my trainer and my engineer,
Steve, were in my house, and I sensed something coming on, something inside me, a welling up of grief. I knew that it was only a matter of time before I had a loud, screaming breakdown. And so I went
and got in my car. I didn't have tinted windows, so I didn't stay out
on the street. I drove around until I found a parking lot that spiraled
all the way to the basement. I parked there and wept uncontrollably
for ten or twelve minutes. I remembered first encounter with *Off the
Wall* at the Carlton House in Pittsburgh, in the winter of 1979, when
I was wearing a worn-out *Fish That Saved Pittsburgh* T-shirt that I
got for free and spent my evenings recording TV shows on a Real-

istic tape recorder so I could play them back and memorize them. I remembered first encountering *Thriller* in Puerto Rico in 1982, where my parents did a four-month residency, where there was summery, tropical weather in the winter and posters of these young guys named Menudo, whom I had never heard of but who drove the girls crazy, and where my dad made me go to the outside bar and sit by the drummer to learn samba and bossa nova rhythms. I didn't have a record player there so I just spent a month studying the *Thriller* disc and wondering why "Human Nature" had all these weird ridges in the groove—the shaker parts. It was psychic tunneling, a way of going back in time, a way of reliving my own childhood through those songs and those records. And you know in *Goodfellas*, how Robert De Niro beats the phone in the phone booth? I beat the shit out of the back of the front seat. I cried until I had a massive headache.

We went back to work the next day. We asked permission not to wear our suits, to wear Michael Jackson-related stuff instead. I got my T-shirt company to make me a quickie shirt, what I call Helvetica in Harlem, that had the six names of all the brothers. Other members of the band wore leather jackets and studs. Erykah Badu joined us in New York to sit in with us and we spent the day making sandwiches and trying to come to terms with Michael's death. And we played his songs on the air. Usually, they would be too expensive to use, but there is a special stipulation, a death memorandum, that grants a 48-hour grace period where songs can be used for a standard rate for news purposes. I don't know if the full weight of the loss hit me then, or later, or if it has hit me yet. It wasn't that I expected him to make more great music, necessarily. I figure that with everyone who's designated a genius, especially people of color, has an expiration date. But Michael was so woven into the fabric of my life that it was painful and also unthinkable to have him suddenly gone.

There was no thought of tabling the Roots' own music when we went to work for Jimmy. But we knew we'd be making the record in a different environment, with different framing questions. How does a hip-hop band mature into middle age? There was no precedent. There was no blueprint. As we went into *How I Got Over*, which was our ninth studio album and eleventh overall, it wasn't clear to me at all what we were supposed to be. When I sat down to think about it, I could only think about what we weren't supposed to be, what we couldn't be any longer. There's no *throw your hands in the air, wave 'em like you just don't care.* There's no psst, hey baby. So where were we again? We were at the edge, at risk, aesthetically. The risk was in the very fact of the album, and answering the question of how we moved forward. I remembered when we first signed with Geffen, and they had said something to us about releasing our ninth album, or our tenth, and I had stopped them cold. "That just doesn't happen," I said. "Hip-hop bands don't do that kind of thing. They're usually three and out." I wasn't trying to be disingenuous. It was just that back in 1994 it was hard to imagine being a hip-hop recording act across the span of two decades, or three. I'm sure that the Rolling Stones had the same confusion when they finished up with *Let It Bleed* and looked back over the sixties. Ten albums? Maybe that was supposed to be the whole story. I'm almost certain that neither Mick nor Keith thought that they were only one-quarter of the way through their career. And yet, we had arrived at *How I Got Over*. We couldn't reverse time. We had to take time as time took us. That's the theme that you hear all over that album.

It started with the song I still consider the centerpiece, "Dear God," which was a song originally recorded by the Monsters of Folk, the supergroup with Jim James, Conor Oberst, M. Ward, and Mike

Mogis. The Monsters were guests on the show, and we backed them up on that song. When they sang it in rehearsal, it just blew me away. It had been a long time since a song floored me as much as that song did—I'd have to go back to Cody ChesnuTT, at least. I thought it was the best gospel song I had heard in what seemed like forever, but it also sounded like an emo song that was crying out for a Ghostface Killah rhyme. I walked right up to Jim and told him that I loved it and wanted to find some way for the Roots to record it.

Then I called Rich, told him that I had found the touchstone that would help us set the mood of the new record, and sent him the song. I was accustomed to Rich rejecting my epiphanies—usually strategically, so I'd have to redouble my efforts and make a stronger case—but this time I felt it in my bones, and he agreed.[31] For me it wasn't an existential lyric. It wasn't questioning the existence of God. It was more about social justice and how any divine being with an interest in his human creation could allow certain circumstances to persist. It reminded me of what KRS-One said on *Edutainment* twenty years before: "If the Christians really heard Christ / The black man never would've lived this life." The song felt sincere, earnest without being naive. It made Tariq human to people and not just a virtuoso rhyming machine. That mood spread throughout the entire album. We found a way to be mature within the context of hip-hop, and to reach out to the people in our audience who were trying to find a way to grow old gracefully. For all those teenagers who grew up on *Paid in Full* and *People's Instinctive Travels* and *Fear of a Black Planet*, we were offering a dignified path into middle age. And it was a spiritual awakening for

---

31. It wasn't often that simple, but that time it really was that simple. You called me, played the record, and we agreed it was a great direction. The funny thing was how fucking long it took for anything to happen after that. We kept waiting for Jim James to come and sing with us again.

us, as well. I wasn't always happy with the results of our career. There were albums where I got frustrated, or let myself be envious of other artists. We still hadn't had our Bentley moment. *How I Got Over* made me think, for the first time in a while, that maybe I was doing things the wrong way, that maybe my perspective was crooked. I don't want to be too grandiose about it, but I had a sort of spiritual awakening, at forty, on our eleventh record.

Part of it, too, was that we made that album under different circumstances. Tariq had become the guy who needed the certain room in California, a particular engineer, a special atmosphere that allowed him to write lyrics. I always felt that I worked best when I was uncomfortable as hell. The worse the conditions in the studio got, the harder I worked. We recorded that album in the little room at Fallon, and it was a reset for me, a bracing return to working the way I needed to work.

That album has lots of guest stars on it: not just Jim James singing "Dear God," but also Joanna Newsom, John Legend, and the Philly rapper Peedi Peedi. Some of those artists we had already known, but some of them came from the new job. Joanna, for example, came to our attention because we were in the loop at NBC, going to *Saturday Night Live* after parties, and Joanna, Andy Samberg's girlfriend, was always around.

It's a short album, our shortest. It's a soft album in some ways, not in the sense of lacking resolve, but soft in the sense that it's clearheaded, sometimes jazzy, less bunkered than *Rising Down*. It's an album that's about itself, in a way, about how you go on as you're getting on. The *New York Times* called it "a serious deliberation on perseverance," and other reviewers noticed that there's an undercurrent of self-help in the lyrics, or at least a consideration of what kinds of things—platitudes, philosophies, magical thinking, realism, religion—might provide the necessary lift in a time of doubt. The financial crisis was in full swing, and plenty of reviewers viewed the album as a response to it, which was a satisfying way to look at it. That's the old Roots adage, to make sure that every album works on three levels: as a personal statement, as a statement about hip-hop, and as a statement about the world.

My first car was a Scion, and I got it by accident. When they first released it to the market back in 2004 they wanted me to do a commercial for them. I agreed in principle, but as we went along they discovered that I didn't have a driver's license. I grew up in a two-van household, and when we went on the road, as the youngest son, I had two very specific jobs: navigator and DJ. On the one hand, I knew all the maps and all the routes; on the other I was responsible for making mixes to keep the driver company—and to make sure that he or she was concentrating on the task at hand. Maybe in the middle of the night there would be a little bit of soul and then Rahsaan Roland Kirk shrieking away on the tenor sax to make sure everyone stayed awake. When I was too old for my parents to drive me around, friends drove me around—Josh, who was in the Philadelphia street-musician incarnation of the Roots, had a station wagon. And then we were the Roots, and we had a Land Cruiser that Rich drove. I tried to explain that to Scion, but they weren't having any of it. "You think we're going to let you get behind the wheel of this vehicle without a license?" they said. They regrouped and came back two weeks later with a new idea: they were going to build a spot around sending me to driving school; they would pay for it and document the experience. Right around that time, I met a girl who lived out of town—she was a designer at HBO—and I figured that at least with a car I could drive from Philly to New York to see her.

So that was my one and only car. I had a ritual that when we finished a record I would take the finished mix and listen to it as I drove around. This is a common practice in the record industry. In the basement at one of the studios we recorded in, they had a full-size van that engineers used to sit in when they were working on a record. Jimmy Iovine told us that back in the seventies, he used to have a half-car set into the wall so that people could listen to albums in their natural environment. When we wrapped *How I Got Over*, I put it in my jacket pocket and went out to the Scion, Portable Studio A, to take it around Philadelphia and see if it held up. It was late Saturday night, early Sunday morning. No one was around except for the cops, and after about fifteen minutes one of them pulled me over. The first officer checked my license, gave it back to me, let me go. About fifteen minutes later, I was pulled over again, same thing: license, please; thank you, sir; you can go.

The album was working for me—I liked what I heard—but after a little while I was hungry, so I got myself a fish sandwich on Broad Street and pulled over to eat it. That's when the third police cruiser pulled up alongside of me. The officer got out, walked up to the car, shined his flashlight through the window. "Evening," he said.

"Hi," I said. "I'm Questlove."

He stared at me for a second, eyes narrowed in confusion, and then his face uncreased. "Oh, yeah," he said. "Hi." He came closer to the car, friendly now.

I was happy that he wasn't giving me any trouble, but now my curiosity was aroused. "Tell me something," I said. "What's the matter? Why am I a magnet for you guys tonight?"

"Oh," he said. "That's easy. We're in the Temple University neighborhood."

"Right," I said.

"And you're in this car."

"And me in this car what?" I loved my Scion. It was part of my identity. I thought anything more lavish was the kind of thing a drug dealer would drive. This was the car of a thoughtful artist, a man who didn't live through his material possessions.

"It's the wrong car for you," he said. "It just doesn't look right. If you were driving an SUV, you'd look like a professional football player. But this little thing sets off alarms. It looks like you took it from a college student."

———

One of the best things about the Fallon show—maybe the best thing—is that it's a test of ingenuity every single day. It sent me back to the days of working with Dave Chappelle. But that show was brilliant guerrilla comedy; it happened on the fly and then some. The Fallon show is a day job in the best sense. We're in by noon and gone by seven, and in between we make a show. It's highly structured, and as a result, the opportunities we have for creativity are really distilled: not reduced at all, but disciplined, forced into existing forms and packages. "Freestylin' with the Roots" is one of the highlights for us. One of the others is the walkover.

The walkover, or walk-on, for those who don't speak backstage, is the song that the band plays as a guest comes out from behind the curtain and walks over to the host's desk. Once upon a time, maybe, it was straightforward, a little musical cue or a song associated with the artist. But then came Paul Shaffer's work on Letterman, and the walkover became its own little art form—an obscure musical reference that the audience (and sometimes even the guest) had to decode.

From the beginning, I wanted the Fallon walk-ons to be classics of the genre, the talk-show equivalent of video game Easter eggs. When we had Salma Hayek on the show, rather than play "Mexican Radio" or even "Salmon Falls," we did some Internet research and unearthed the theme song from the first Mexican soap opera she ever starred on, *Theresa*. She knew it faintly at first, or at least knew that it was something she should know, and her eyes went wide when she figured out what it was. When Edward Norton was on promoting *The Bourne Legacy*, we played Patrick Hernandez's 1979 disco hit "Born to be Alive." And we thought we had a great left-field pick when we played the Dave Matthews Band's "The Space Between" for football player Michael Strahan, but somehow he knew it immediately. Howard Stern once came up to me during a bathroom break, confused, to ask me why we played this disco song by Bell and James for his wife, Beth Ostrovsky. "She's from Pittsburgh, right?" I asked. He nodded. I explained that everyone from Pittsburgh gets that treatment—it's a band in-joke that refers back to the late-seventies basketball comedy *The Fish That Saved Pittsburgh*. I'm not sure he was satisfied by the answer. The Fallon walkovers, as trivial as they may seem, have been the culmination of everything I've cared about my whole life: making strange musical connections, reveling in the way that something obscure can illuminate something obvious.

Because the songs we select are a kind of code, some of the guys in the band use them to slyly flirt with female guests. I let Kirk talk me into playing The Lonely Island's "Lazy Sunday" for Christina Ricci because he had heard she has a *Chronicles of Narnia* tattoo on her back. I did it but got no reaction at all. I put him on six-month probation for that suggestion; he was forbidden to send any more secret messages to anyone. And I can remember one case where I totally fumbled the ball. We had a famous actress on—I won't say who, to protect both her and myself—and I thought she had been in a particular movie, and I built the walk-on around that title. After the show, her publicist came up to me. "Hey," she said, "what was that walkover song? I'm not sure I understood the reference." I started to explain, but the blankness in her face stopped me. I realized I had made the wrong reference completely. I had confused her with someone else. I was so embarrassed.

But even in the walk-on world, there are limits. Chuck Berry may be the inventor of rock and roll, but he still thinks he needs a payout of $2.5 million anytime anyone plays "Johnny B. Goode" on TV. That seemed to scotch our plan to play it when Michael J. Fox came on the show; we wanted to recreate the whole prom scene from *Back to the Future*—you know, where Marty McFly plays the "Johnny B. Goode" solo and one of the guys in the band, Marvin Berry, calls his cousin Chuck? Rather than give up, though, we found a workaround. We played "The Clock," by my father, which is basically a B-flat blues ripoff of the Berry classic, and that gave us the solo we needed. I played the role of Marvin Berry in the skit.

Most of the time, the walk-on is harmless fun, a way to flex our musical and pop-culture muscles. But there are times when it gave us a chance to practice a bit of commentary. When Ashlee Simpson was on, we played a Milli Vanilli song to tweak her a little bit for her lip-synching scandal on *Saturday Night Live*. (Viewers with sharp ears may have noticed that we didn't even do the original song, but the version from VH1's *Behind the Music*, where Fab and Rob were stuck singing the title phrase because of a computer glitch.)

And then, in late 2011—November 21, to be exact, at the height of the Republican primary season—we found out that Michele Bachmann, representative from Minnesota, was coming onto the show. Bachmann had been offending people left and right with her comments about gay rights and Muslims in America, and she also seemed to have a casual relationship to the truth. I learned that at one point, fact-checkers had set a limit for themselves on how many of her evasions and misrepresentations they were going to catch. That was my starting point, and I set out on a mission to find the best song about politics and evasion and untruth. I considered "Lies," either the En Vogue one or the McFly one, but we don't generally sing any lyrics, so I ended up picking Fishbone's "Lyin' Ass Bitch," a ska number from their 1985 debut. It had a good little melody and lots of energy. It seemed funny to me. I figured it would be another exhibit in Ahmir's Hall of Snark, and not much more than that.

So, that's what happened. Michele Bachmann came out on to the show and spoke to Jimmy. She didn't know what song we were playing. I'm sure almost no one knew what song we were playing. That was part of the fun of it. I felt satisfied to the point of smugness. We had pulled one over on the man.

Then, the next day, satisfaction and smugness turned to ego. I was sitting around at home thinking that I had done something historical, something political. I had struck a blow for truth. I wanted credit. When you want credit for something and you don't want to operate via traditional channels, where do you go? In this day and age, you go to Twitter. That's where I went. Someone tweeted me a question: "Was that 'Lyin' Ass Bitch'?" I answered like someone in the grip of ego, which is exactly what I was: "Sho' nuf." That was it. The fuse was lit. The news began to spread. Then a conservative blogger got hold of it and it spread some more. I went to sleep, and woke to a reverse tooth fairy situation. Instead of finding money under my pillow, I found my phone flashing with six missed calls, all from Rich.[32] I had a sense, maybe, what it was about, so I looked on Twitter and saw that I had more than seven hundred mentions. Then I called Rich back.

"You know this is a problem," he said.

"How much of a problem?"

"Looks like this could be a big problem."

"How big?"

Rich paused. I didn't like the pause or what was in it. "I don't

---

32. More than six calls. I'm guessing it was close to a dozen. The pin was out of the grenade, and I was trying to get that shit a safe distance away before it blew.

know," he said. "This could be a wrap for you. This could be a wrap for us." My heart sank. Had I taken the band down with me?

By the time I got to work, the fire of outrage was blazing. Fans online were cursing Jimmy. People were calling the NBC switchboard. The conservative blogger Michelle Malkin re-tweeted something that included my name in it, and all of a sudden I had three thousand more responses. I had benefited from things going viral, but now I was suffering from the same thing. At one point I passed Jimmy in the hallway and tried to play it all off as a joke, and he nodded, trying to keep a good face on it, but I could see how exhausted he was.

By two o'clock, it wasn't just a conservative firestorm, but a feminist one. Women were posting letters of support for Michele Bachmann, lining up against me for saying "bitch." Even Sara Gilbert, on *The Talk*, came out to say that even though she found Bachmann's politics reprehensible, she was left with no choice but to be an ally in this particular case. That's when things shifted into a whole new dimension of horrible. I had picked the song so that I didn't have to sing it, but the fact that it could be seen as misogynistic just escaped me. The word is so commonly used in certain music, and means something slightly different: it has as much to do with cowardice and slipperiness and unreliability as with gender. It wasn't that I wasn't thinking clearly. It was that I wasn't thinking at all. At least, not about that. I just wanted to hit a home run in the game.

We had a meeting in Jimmy's office, Team Fallon and I, and they told me that things were looking bleak, but that we would try to ride it out. Jimmy made a formal apology to Bachmann on Twitter, which put me squarely in the crosshairs (which, to be fair, was exactly where I belonged). In the end, we got lucky. That Tuesday night there was a Republican debate, and Bachmann went out and made a blunder. She was a member of the House Intelligence Committee, and she said that six of Pakistan's fifteen nuclear sites had come under jihadist attack.

Almost immediately, people were up in arms. (Is that a pun? If so, it's not a good one.) They claimed that she had disclosed classified information. Her staff had to get busy putting out that fire, fast. Plus, it was the week of Thanksgiving, which disrupted the normal news cycle. We were saved by the skin of our teeth.

Things could have gone differently. They almost did. I had some friends at Fox News, and on that Tuesday, I asked them for the damage report. As it turned out, people over there had combed through every last lyric of every single Roots album, looking for a smoking gun—something violent, something misogynistic—and found nothing. There was no story there. Finally, the politically correct, mindful hip-hop that we had been practicing from the beginning—the same thing that had maybe kept us off the chart or kept our posters off the walls of teenagers' bedrooms—had worked to our advantage.

I have replayed that episode in my head hundreds of times, like Kennedy obsessives do with the Zapruder film. My drum set is up on a grassy knoll. Jimmy's desk is the book depository. The whole thing happens in terrible slow motion, though there's clearly only one shooter: me. In retrospect, I would have chosen Sam Cooke's "What a Wonderful World," with its "Don't know much about history" line.

A few days later, I heard from Fishbone. Their management loved me for it: they were wondering why all of a sudden people were cheering so loudly for the song in concert. Unfortunately, Angelo Moore was scheduled to be on the show to promote *Everyday Sunshine*, a documentary about the band, but we had to disinvite him: Jimmy figured that a year should pass before anyone associated with the band came on as a guest. But we still used other Fishbone songs. For instance, we did "Bonin' in the Boneyard," from *Truth and Soul*, when Jennifer Lawrence came on to talk about *Winter's Bone*. The best thing to come of it happened a year later, on David Letterman's show; after a Top Ten about Bachmann, Paul Shaffer played a few seconds of "Lyin' Ass Bitch." It was almost like I was dreaming, but I'm sure I heard it. Thank you, Paul.

And then there was Steve Martin's reaction. When he appeared on the show as a guest in December of 2011, he found a way to turn the controversy into a bit. He wanted us to do a number of different songs, each of which annoyed him in a different way: he wanted the first one to be offensive, the second one to be too boring, the third one to be too generic, the fourth one to be our revenge for him objecting to every previous selection, and so on. Eventually, we'd try Carly Simon's "Nobody Does It Better," and that would satisfy him. We did Steve's bit, and that was the moment where I finally felt that the heat was officially off.

———

You'd think that the Bachmann debacle would have taught me all I needed to know about tact, but you'd be wrong. Some time after that, I was on Andy Cohen's Bravo show, *Watch What Happens Live*, and he asked me which guest I most dread coming on Fallon. I said Tina Fey, and then I tried to explain why. Since early in my career, I always felt a kinship with Philadelphia artists, every actor and singer and author. We had met Tina Fey on Letterman when we were both guests, and we tried to make small talk with her and failed. It was painfully awkward. Then we were at another function and it was painfully awkward again. Even though she was from the Philly area, even though she was from the same NBC family, she felt distant to me. I'm not saying it was her any more that it was me. She just felt distant.

There was also an issue with her appearances on Fallon. In the history of the show, there were only a handful of guests who came out to talk to Jimmy without waving to the band. We had a little ritual where we marked that kind of thing down. Tiger Woods did it, twice, and Tina Fey, at various points, had done it five times. Maybe it was shyness or reserve. I understood that; I often felt the same way. But after a while it wore on me. All those things were on my mind when I was asked the question on Andy Cohen's show, and I said something that I thought was a tongue-in-cheek, faux-wounded remark: "Tina Fey, you are never nice to the Roots. We're from Philadelphia. Be nice to the Roots!" But of course, because the media is a game that people play, they took that one sentence out of context and found a freeze-frame of my face, looking angry, and all of a sudden there I was on the front page of the Huffington Post, having trouble yet again with a powerful woman.

This time, Lorne had a fit. "I want him out of here," he said. "He's gone." I thought that he was a little angrier than the incident deserved, but it was only about seven months after Bachmann, and things had been building. In fact, I think that I was fired for about an hour, until Jimmy begged for my job back.

––––––––

And now it's now, which means more shifts and more settling. The past tries to cozy up to the present while the future cowers. But now isn't only now. It's the recent now. Toward the end of 2011, the Roots finished a record, *undun*, which was one of the most rewarding works we had ever made. It's a play in sound about a character named Redford Stevens, and it's also an attempt to integrate more indie-rock and even classical elements along with the neo soul and jazz (we took the name of the character from a Sufjan Stevens song, which we put on the album, and part of the last movement is a free jazz piano-and-drums duet with me and D.D. Jackson that floats off into strings), and it's also an iPhone app with pictures and videos (we wanted to show this character's life, which was short and sometimes violent, like the album, and like the confused and thwarted and frustrating and joyous lives of many other young men, black or white or any other color), and it's also a return to *Game Theory* in the sense that it's explicitly political, and a return to *Things Fall Apart* in the sense that it's elegiac and mournful and personal (the character, Redford, is a composite, but he's a composite of people we knew, of people from Philly, of people in Tariq's family, of the life that Tariq or any of us might have lived if the Roots hadn't happened), and a return to many other moments in music history, from the late nineties, when high-concept hip-hop records were all the rage (I specifically had Prince Paul's *A Prince Among Thieves* in mind) to classic rock (the title of the record is lifted from a song by the Guess Who, the great Canadian band featuring Burton Cummings and Randy Bachman—no relation to Michele—although their song is a gentle, sad portrait of a woman unraveling because she's been deceived, not a young man being unraveled by society). But *undun* was also a record very much of its moment, a record only made possible by the changes in our life, and the fact that the Fallon job afforded us a place to work in tight quarters, a daily space where ideas could reverberate, as well as the freedom to go back to the kind of expansive, complex records we had always dreamed of making, but without fear of selling poorly.

Acrobats love to talk about working without a net like it's the bravest thing in the world. But the thing about working without a net is that if you fall, you die. It's better to work with a net, and to know that you can attempt the tricky maneuver without permanent consequences. It's an answer to the dialogue between Bleek and Shadow in *Mo' Better Blues*, or maybe just a third voice in the conversation. (SCENE: Ahmir pokes head in door. Bleek and Shadow look up. Bleek: "Who's that big fella?" Shadow: "And what the fuck is the deal with his hair?")

Redford Stevens was one kind of young American in crisis, but between the time we finished the record and the time it came out, in December that year, the country started to focus on another kind of young American in crisis: the students and activists who came together around questions of corporate greed and economic frustration and set up camp in Zucotti Park in downtown Manhattan, and then elsewhere around the country. The people in the park were at once hopeful and pessimistic, at once determined and disorganized, with one eye turned toward the policy decisions and institutional factors that were ruining ordinary lives and the other turned toward personal decisions that were doing the same. People liked to say that the Occupy movement was like one big protest song, but the grievances weren't always specific enough for that. Sometimes it sounded to me like one big blues song.

And we went on through the rest of it, too. We recorded an album with Betty Wright, the queen of Miami soul; you could call it her comeback record, but people like her never really went anywhere. Instead, times change around them. I kept waiting for D'Angelo to resurface with the follow-up to *Voodoo*, and for a brief moment, it looked like he might. There was momentum toward the end of 2011, and then he and I had a triumphant appearance at Bonnaroo in the summer of 2012. He was every bit as hypnotic as he had been a decade before. I try to keep track of young artists in all genres, whether it's the ones who show up on Fallon or the ones who show up on my iPod. And I keep thinking about the persistence of hip-hop.

The persistence of hip-hop. It's a funny word, persistence. It means not giving up, but it also means just passing on through time. It's the will to survive but it's also inertia. So which is it? There's still big money in hip-hop for some. There are still acts who come out and top the charts—though topping the charts isn't what it used to be, and people don't seem to stay there very long at any rate. But something has been lost. I say this well aware that I risk seeming like a grumpy old man, the curmudgeon who's always grumbling about the glory days. But at least some of what I say is simply true.

The other day I was listening to some old records, and Public Enemy's "Rebel Without a Pause" came on. It was that Daryl "Hasaan" Jamison trumpet squeal, which ascended and transcended like Coltrane's spiritual longings when it happened back at the dawn of the seventies, in the J.B.'s, but became something much more revolutionary and urgent when the Bomb Squad put it in the Public Enemy song. That's a piece of music that just straightens your goddamn spine. But the real secret to that record is how personal and relatable it is: "No matter what the name, we're all the same / Pieces in one big chess game." So where's the distance between the artist and the listener? There isn't any. That's why you can take it in. That's why it can fill you up. And those are the things that make sense to me, even now, twenty-five years later, at a time when most hip-hop has done away with the personal, the relatable.[33]

We just went through an election, and some of the same issues surfaced there. Think about how Mitt Romney played his hand, how he came out at first swinging his millionaire stick, saying that he wasn't going to apologize for his success. At the same time, he was trying to tell a story that people would understand, or want to take part ownership of. And when it became clear that he was failing at that, he went to phase two, the convention phase, Operation Humanize, which was overshadowed a little bit by Clint Eastwood's chair act but pushed him far enough that he was starting to get some traction again. And then there was the leak of the earlier donor dinner, the comments to money men about "the 47 percent," and much of the goodwill that was starting to build dissipated overnight—not only among people

---

33. Yeah, but one of the recent exceptions to this rule is Kendrick Lamar. His music is personal. He's writing shit about riding around in his mom's van and experiencing his own thoughts and feelings. There's a human behind the persona in his songs. And he's not the only one—Frank Ocean has accessible stories. But it's still different than it was. It's something that can happen now for an individual but it can't be a movement anymore, not really.

who Romney had specifically insulted, but among plenty of people who were undecided. And through all of this, there was the same undercurrent of racism that we had talked about on *Rising Down*, the same reluctance to completely accept a black leader. Donald Trump kept trying to thread the needle with birther accusations. *Maybe this sitting president isn't a real American. Maybe this election—of a man, by the way, who was scrutinized the first time he ran for office—is a case where we need to take a closer look.* This all happens on a more fundamental level than policy disputes. It would be comedy if it wasn't a kind of tragedy. There's a song called "Pimps" by the Coup that takes place in a millionaire party, and Rockefeller and J. Paul Getty are there, and all of a sudden they burst into rap. It's rapped, in character. They talk about their money and power, and how they "make the army go to war for Exxon." At one point, Trump comes up, and they're a little embarrassed by him, and he breaks into this ragga toasting: "Trump, Trump, check out di cash in a-mi trunk." It was hard not to think about that song during the election, and after, as Trump kept mouthing off on Twitter, promoting himself, trying to get more eyeballs for his TV show, *Celebrity Apprentice*. But then it was over and Obama won his second term. That was yet another kind of accomplishment to put next to and in some ways above the first term: he wasn't just a novelty president, someone that America's fickle finger settled on for a second, but he was—he is—a real president.

We're starting work on a new Roots record, which has some ideas attached to it, some jams, some lyrics, though it's subject to change, depending on what happens in the studio, depending on Tariq's ideas, and depending also on the rest of the band: on Captain Kirk and Knuckles and Tuba and James and Kamal and everyone else. It's strange sometimes to think of yourself as an individual, which is something you have to do for sanity's sake, something you have to do to take responsibility for your own thoughts and actions, but to realize at the same time how you've been defined almost entirely by this tapestry you've been woven into for twenty years, and how grateful you should be for that tapestry. It's a sentimental thing to say that I wouldn't exist without the band, but sometimes sentimental things are true. I spent years looking for this commune or that one, the jam sessions on St. Albans or the Soulquarians at Electric Lady, and all the while, Dorothy-style, I could have gone home any time— or rather, I was already home. And yet, at the same time, there's yin and yang. There's such push and pull. Let's say there's an event and people around me get invited and I'm not invited. Some part of me will feel like a failure. How can you not? The real me knows that it's just an event, but doubt enters my mind about why I'm not there. Is it because I'm not good enough? Part of me would just like to relax and have one job that pays me the amount I need to survive. And another part of me wants the creativity that comes out of struggle and frustration and fear. It's a never-ending cycle, which must be how I want it, on some level.

And so that's how it goes. I keep moving through time and time keeps moving through me. And through that process, life takes shape. The question is what shape it is. I'm not the first person to ask this question, or to see how absurd it is to think there's a real answer. Maybe life's a circle. Maybe what goes around comes around. Maybe there's karma and an account ledger that balances off all debts and credits. Part of me believes that: the part of me that remembers that my drums are circles, that turntables are circles. But drumsticks are straight, and there are times when life seems like an arrow that goes in one direction and one direction only, toward a final target that might not be a final reward. Part of me believes that, too: the part of me that sees the "dun" in *undun*, and that believes that the story of that record, the life that ends before it's properly told, the life that has to unspool in reverse to exist at all, is the more common form of life. Music has the power to stop time. When I listen to songs, I'm transported back to the moment of their birth, which is sometimes even before the moment of my birth. Old songs, rock or soul or blues, still connect with me because the human emotions in them, whether jealousy or rage or hope, are recognizably similar to the emotions that I'm feeling now. But I'm feeling all of them, all the time, and so the songs act like a chemical process that isolates certain feelings at certain times: maybe one song helps illuminate the jubilation and one helps illuminate the sorrow and one helps illuminate the resignation. Music has the power to stop time. But music also keeps time. Drummers are timekeepers. Music conserves time and serves time, just as time conserves and serves music. I think I have to believe in circularity, even if I know that the arrow's coming in on the wing. I think I have to cast my lot with cycles, and revolution, with the Beach Boys' "I Get Around" and Chuck Berry's "Around and Around" and James Brown's "World Cycle Inc." Will the circle be unbroken? That's not the only circle that's a question. Every circle is. Lines are statements. Arrows are especially emphatic statements. They divide and they define. They count up and count down. Circles are more careful. They come around again. They overthink. They analyze. They go back to the scene of the crime. They retrace their steps. That's where I end up, definitely maybe, always circumspect, always circumscribed by questions, by curiosity, by a certainty that I need a certain amount of uncertainty.

There's a Tribe Called Quest song called "What" on *Low End Theory*. That word is a statement, a line. The song samples "Uncle Willie's Dream," by Paul Humphrey. That sample is another line. But who was Paul Humphrey? That's a question that makes you circle back around. Paul Humphrey was a session drummer who worked with everyone from Jimmy Smith and Charles Mingus to Frank Zappa and

Marvin Gaye. He was also the drummer for Lawrence Welk's TV show in the late seventies, and his children would sometimes appear with him on the show. Sound familiar? That's another rhetorical question. On the Tribe song, over the (circular) sample, Q-Tip asks a series of questions, one after the other, rapid-fire, staying on the Q tip so vigilantly that there's no time (or space) to answer them—which is okay, because answers seem beside the point anyway. There are many, many questions in that song, but a few remain with me: "What is position if there's no contorting?" "What is a compound without an element?" "What is a war if it doesn't have a general?" and "What is a Quest if the players aren't willing?" Not all of the questions are that philosophical. Some are about pop culture. Some are about sex. Some are about money. Some are about jurisprudence. But they're all questions that move your mind forward and then pull it back: a fish hook, a circle, an orbit. There's a moment just past the halfway point where Q-Tip says "Chill for a minute; Doug E. Fresh said silence," and then there's silence, four seconds of it, and the song is moving along so jauntily at that point, and the momentum of the questions is building so nicely, that it's shocking but also peaceful, a period of forced reflection, a pause that almost refreshes but doesn't give you quite enough time to answer anything before the drum returns and the flood of questions with it. That's sort of how life operates. What does that mean? What doesn't it mean? What is the role of the artist? What is the chance that an artist will actually create something new something lasting? What is the responsibility the artist has, if any, t old forms, to old questions? What is a community? What do you ca the parts of the community if not individuals? What is a band? Wh do you call the parts of a band if not brothers? What is soul? Wh is *a* soul? What is a blues? What is a life? What is a death if not t confirmation of life? What is a sound if not the reminder of silenc

What is the top if not the confirmation of the bottom? What is the bottom if not the confirmation of the Roots? What is the matter with asking again? What is the best way to know why and when? What is the answer? What is the reason? What are they growing when it's growing season... WHAT?!?!

So, like I said...

What's this gonna be, Ahmir?

ACKNOWLEDGMENTS

OK, it's 2:34 a.m. on a Friday night. I'm in New York, in my apartment, looking out my window at the Brooklyn Bridge. I *think* the "A" in the blinking red Watchtower sign just went out, so it's reading "Wtchtower" from where I am. This book is officially over. The hardest part of this process is the one name that I'll forget to mention in the Acknowledgments.

So I would love to thank:

"Your Name Here"

for just being there for me. I know it sounds impersonal and insincere but those who know me know I've got twelve jobs and I'm absentminded when it comes to things like this.

I'd also like to give a shout to those who have all these outlandish Ahmir-back-in-the-day stories that get back to me and wind up being the most hilariously over-bloated versions of my legend. I actually wish that I was as wild and reckless as I'm told I was.

I'mma do my best to remember everyone on this journey. If I forget you, please don't hold it against me more than you already hold it against me.

Roots fans lived for my liner notes in the early years, mostly because there was no social media back in the early nineties. Of course, as time has developed, my notes have become less and less engaging because I save my special zingers for Okayplayer.com and Twitter (well, that and label cost cutbacks on pages in our CDs). And plus, I don't feel like hearing a whole buncha "so why didn't you thank me!!??!" threats in my timeline after these types of projects come out.

My inner circle is pretty conditional on me thanking them for helping me get to where I am today.

I'm kidding.

Am I?

OK…now it's 3:52 a.m. and I've yet to start this list…

THANK YOU TO:

Mom: Thank you for always believing in me when I didn't even believe in myself. Everything I do, I do for you.

Dad: Thank you for always sacrificing and providing for me to ensure that one day I'd be well equipped to live my dream. I remember every lesson you ever taught me.

Donn: Thank you for being my role model. I've tried to emulate every step you took in life. You liked a band, I liked a band. You loved a song, I loved a song. Thanks for being my hero. Thank you for also bringing Jake and Sorren into our crazy family.

Richard Nichols: For being in the lighthouse. Actually, I think you are the lighthouse.

Shawn Gee: For being the shark-proof life preserver. Many days you wanted to kill me for every foolish, reckless purchase I've ever made. You've now made me a productive, responsible businessman...who still makes reckless decision$.

Entire 1992-to-present members:

Josh	Kirk
Yatta	Frank
Hub	Martin
Malik	Tuba
Scott	Owen
Kamal	Dice
Rahzel	Ray
Scratch	and Mark
Ben	

Salute. I know our motto was to never overtly celebrate, for we knew the other shoe was dropping with bad news. But we've made history, fellas. When all is said and done, we made quality history. Hear, hear!

Joseph "AJ Shine" Simmons: You gave us our first big break. Without you, this would not have happened.

Jimmy Fallon: Thank you for giving us a new lease on life. I absolutely appreciate the risk you took in believing in us.

Mike Shoemaker: For all the gray hair I've added to your life, I apologize. It's a learning curve. One day, I'll get it right. Thank you for being fair.

Jonathan Cohen: JC, a lot of the magical music moments were due to your thankless hard work. Let's make more history!

Lorne Michaels: Thanks for having an open mind. It's an honor to have a footnote in your history.

To the entire staff (present and past, too) of *Late Night with Jimmy Fallon*: This is one of the most magical-amazingness experiences ever. There are entirely too many of you to name. Thank you for making this the greatest day job in the world.

Wendy Goldstein: You truly believed in us.

Cara Lewis: You fought for us when no one was fighting for us. And for that, I will be forever grateful.

Ben Greenman and Ben Greenberg: Thanks for confusing the ish outta me with your names. Also, for the patience with my tardiness. I appreciate the opportunity, guys.

Keith McPhee	Paul Klimson
Tina Farris	Bill Clarke
Dominic Keska	Jeff Gussen
Hope Wilson	Munir Nuriddin
Silbert Mani	Rebecca Proudfoot
Nou Ra	Brandon Pankey
Princess	Kimyatta Graham
Toya Day	Christian Diaz
Alexis Rosenzweig	Dana Jackson
Rachel Ghansa	Julie "Tank" Green
Sarah Diebel	Diamon Dyer
Efrem Jenkins	Tierekka "Reek" Walker
Artless Poole	

...all of the people who have helped me, tirelessly, thanklessly. Thank you.

Team Ahmir: A name so ridiculous it stuck:

Steve: My guru and the only dude who gives me real-life advice without judging. Thanks for being a real friend, man.

Zarah: Vice President of Questlove Industries. I never make a move without your permission first. I'm writing these words even as you dial me to make sure that I'll be in my car at 5 a.m. in time for the airport (note: I missed the plane by a minute, so as of this writing, it's 12:10 p.m. in an Atlanta Delta airport and I'm waiting three hours for my flight to Austin).

Crazy Rebecca Pietri: My favorite robot. Stay crazy. Stay organized. Can't thank you enough.

Dawn Englehart: Started off potential jawn material. Wound up running an empire. Let's make meeeeeeelllllllions more, buahhahahahaha muahahahahahah.

William: You are a human flux capacitor capable of getting to 1955 in record time. Thanks for being a great friend.

Yameen Allworld: I hate the way you spell your name so I'm not thanking you.

Yahmeen Allworld: Keep the jokes coming. One day your designated owner will claim you.

Darryl, Sandy, Therese, Maureen, and Ardenia: You keep me alive.

Maisha: You know and I know you purposely shorten my fro because you never wanna leave my side...and I love you for that.

Maria Scali: OUCH!!!!!!!!!!!!!!!!! xxooo

Carleen Donovan and Katie Leggett and the entire Press Here team: Thanks for publicizing me and putting out some of my many fires.

OK. I was just gonna end it there, but since I got hours to kill, I'mma rattle off line-association games.

This is in NO particular order. Just names of people who helped me get here.

Ginny Suss: Ideas and schemes.

Dan Petruzzi: Keeper of a dream.

dream hampton: My greatest muse.

Mwanamke Jordan: My second love.

Madison McFerrin: How did you wind up 4th Nermal?

FWMJ: You hate everything. I love that.

Alan Leeds: My favorite historian.

John Book: The Wax Poet.

James Poyser: Fi Skeen.

Nikki Borges: (((((hug)))))

Stephanie Brown: For the Nico cassette.

JT: Keep that iPod alive.

April Garrett: You started my college mission at Harvard.

Amber Tamblyn and David Cross: Two of the craziest people I know. I should be so lucky to have the honor of knowing you two.

Amy Schumer: "Tonight is your night."

Sasha Grey: Thanks for listening. And for the advice. One of my truest friends.

Steve Higgins: The sharpest, expert-timing-est, wittiest human I know.

Thea Chaloner: So glad we reconnected after all this time. Love u nerd!

Zoë Kravitz: My sizuuuuurp provider.

Fiona: Come out of hiding already.

Brittany Jones-Pugh: Your beautiful scowl is my favorite thing about 6B.

Elita Bradley: So glad we're making this journey together.

The Smolletts: Thanksgiving will never be the same. I pray all your turkey is thawed by at least 2 a.m. next time.

Midi Nichols: Big up, Shmidy.

Steve Hendel: Thank you for bringing Fela into my life.

Joseph Gordon-Levitt: Thank you for your undying support.

Nzingha Stewart: Stay-exy.

Laiya St. Clair: I'm imagining your sigh of relief because you see your name here.

Rusty Gramiak: My first drum teacher.

Hov: Thanks for workin' with a nerd like me.

Damon Bennett: The cat who taught me about breakbeats.

Q-tip: The Leader!

Dave Chappelle: Thanks for letting a guy get his feet wet in TV scoring. It has opened doors for me and I appreciate that.

Dave Matthews: Thanks for sharing your secret with the world.

Thuy-An Julien: The...Apple of my eye? Get It? Tu-pac? LOL.

Nelson George: So amazing that one of my writing heroes is now someone I consider a friend. Amazing to know you.

Dozia Blakey and King Britt: You guys provided me with the playground to practice my skill. Appreciated!

Nick Puzo: My Soul Brother.

Stacey Wilson and Mike Nyce: Thank you for shining a light on a dying art form. Keep the spirit alive in Philly.

Annabella Sciorra: Next lifetime when we are cats.

D: I pray this album comes out before my twentieth book. Thanks for allowing me residency in your crazy world.

Charles Stone III: So glad you are a part of our history.

Fatin and Aja: You showed us, didn't ya?

Kali Hawk: Rice to You.

Bowlegged Lou and Paul Anthony: Two inspirational brothers. Stay strong. Thank you for leading the way.

Gretchen Lieberum and Maya Rudolph: Two purple people who know my pain.

Paul Peterson, Eric Leeds, Jellybean Johnson, Jerome Benton, Susannah Melvoin: The real family.

Bill Johnson: My favorite tastemaker.

Stephen Starr: Here's to a good future.

HouseShoes: Keep his spirit alive. Educate the masses.

Pete Shapiro: Thanks for winning me over.

Jay Pharoah: You keep us in stitches on Thursdays. Stay awesome.

Meta Smith: The world knows our li'l secret. I really named this book after you.

Cyndie Lou Boehm: Never stop practicing.

Danny Swain: Stay the course. Perhaps one day you'll save my life.

Seth Herzog: The man who started my comedy career.

Michelle Trotter: My best intended worst cupid ever. Lol I love you for that.

Touré: My first and best interviewer. We walked this journey together. Thanks for that.

Rachel Goldstein: For impressing all the women who step into my apartment.

Pearl Schaeffer: My first teacher, thank you.

Niclana Tolmasoff: Driving you crazy is fun.

Greg Tate: Hope to reach your plateau one of these days.

Cosmo Baker: My soul funk brother.

Joseph Jazzbo Patel: DMX forever son!

Rashad Smith: Treats galore, man.

Tayyib Smith: I'd vote you into any office.

Salaam Remi: Thank you for Amy.

Doyle Bramhall II: You have turned into a prayer.

Vikter Duplaix: Grandmaster Vik!

John Legend and Chrissy Teigen and Puddy: The first family of balanced zaniness.

Nikki Jean: Never give up.

Bevy Smith: Class class class.

Zuhirah Khaldun: Our earliest supporter. Much love to you.

Alan Light: Words to live by.

Tiarra Mukherjee: You brought the Soulquarians to lite.

Suzanne Mates: I miss our days at Sony.

Aimee Morris: I miss us.

Aaron Halfacre: Keep the treats alive.

Abbey Goodman: You are the secret to my success…and by success…you know where this is goin'.

Adam Blackstone: You got the juice now.

Salee and Kendal Black: My Jewish parents.

MC Paul Barman: The best cockroach of a poet.

Kon and Amir: Always looking for the perfect beat.

The Jazzyfatnastees: For taking over my home.

Colby Colb: You were the first.

DJ Ran: For the support.

Erykah Badu: Stay fearless and creative.

Gabe Tesoriero: Thank you for listening to our crying over the years.

Cosmic Kev: For being on my nuts.

Melody Ehsani: That laugh is one of my favorite sounds of all time.

Wendy and Susannah Melvoin: The muse's muses.

Anthony Tidd: For being sane.

Kobi Wu: Your Zen-like patience.

Harry Allen: Your wisdom.

Sheena Lester: For giving me my first writing job.

Harry Weinger: Thank you for teaching me how to teach.

Christian Bootsey McBride: For the experiments.

Dominique Trenier: Your vision helped make history.

Nicco Ardin: My favorite aural experiment subject.

Tom Moon: Your words meant so much to us.

Hucky Austin: I'm still laughing at the gym story.

Vanessa Wruble: That ingot. Yeah I said it.

Adrianna Allen: You are my inspiration for even thinking that I could write a book.

Jeff Nat: You and King gave us our first debut.

Dawn Baxter: You helped a youngin' realize a dream.

Major Jackson: Your support was invaluable.

Christine Cauble: The truest b-girl of all time.

Suki: For helping expand my record collection.

Jazzy Jeff: My most favorite DJ of all time. You taught me so much.

Maria Jose: Muh x infinity.

The Dreher's: My other family. Save my Thanksgiving spot forever.

Mel D. Cole: I still blame you for making me lose Megan Fox's favorite hoodie of mine.

Jason Brown: Thanks for having that bootleg of *De La Soul Is Dead*. Changed me forever.

Tom Sarig: Those were great times.

Abdul Stone Jackson: We made a miracle that Thanksgiving in '92.

Ashaka Givens: Outfits galore. You turnt me and Com into hippies.

Adam Bomb: My billiard bud and Serato organizer.

Diane Miller: My first jazz punisher. I hated it then but I love it now.

Kaya Davis: Miss you like crazy.

Bill Coleman: The first tastemaker of the press that kept me abreast of music I'd never heard of. Thank you for your knowledge!

Samantha Shipp: You will be the first Supreme Court MC. I'm calling it 2024!

Bill Stephney: You taught me that classic songs and albums are snapshots of your life you will never forget.

Noel "Keeb" Hubler: Salve!

Beverly Reece: Another great teacher.

Anthony Maddox: You reconnected me to my soul.

Khartoon Ohan: You helped me buy my first house! Thank you!

Natasha Ryan: Dream and believe.

Adam Goldstein: You opened my eyes to a whole new sonic possibility.

Rocsi Diaz: I was there first-hand to see you start your dream. Congrats. Don't forget the little people.

Jennifer Gomez: The sexiest drummer.

Paulette Surles: My favorite teacher ever.

Deborah Eptein-Diarena: You are passion times a billion.

Radji Mateen: You helped keep me organized.

Bobby "Z" Rivkin: So glad you are still here. Thank you!

Common: I hope after all this time, you've learned where "the one" is.

Kelley Lowe: My first shoulder in high school.

Axel Niehaus: You unearthed and unleashed the monster by teaching me tricks in mixing the *Things Fall Apart* album.

Rob EST Walker: Coolest role model ever. Philly thanks you.

Paula Quijano: I owe you a mansion.

Shameka Speed: Stop spitting on my love.

Jaguar Wright: Your fearlessness was an inspiration.

Jill Scott: You gave us our first pair of wings. Thank you.

Taara Sultaana: Love you, Groucho.

Heather Boice: So glad we're connected again.

Janina Gavankar: Best shoulder ever.

Faheem Alexander: You kept me sharp.

Dana Holland: My favorite sparring partner.

Prince Paul: Your creativity changed hip hop.

De La Soul: My favorite group changed me.

Kid Sister: One day Mel, you'll consider me worthy of working with you.

Louie Ski Carr: Cutty finger salute!

Chris Dave and John Roberts: Cats that kept me up all night practicing way up after my bedtime.

Kiv Chao: *sigh*

Antoine Green: My OG diggin' in the crates partner.

Larry Gold: Keeping the spirit of lush string culture alive.

Aunt Beth: For your snark (this is where you are like "I...do...not...snark!"). But whoever she's pointing this out to? She DOES!

Tom Hayes: The real king of the walk-on! You are without a doubt my biggest supporter. Thank you!

Steven Savitz: You started my twelve-inch collecting career.

Vernon Reid: My favorite minion.

James Stiles: Bombs/teardrops.

James Gadson: The breaks.

Steve Ferrone: My idol.

Clyde Stubblefield and John "Jabo" Starks: My foundation.

Tika Sumpter: You've come a long way. Proud.

Darryll Brooks: The legacy.

Cynthia Horner: My first source!

Pino Palladino: The steadiest perfect pulse.

Alison Brie: I'm still shaking my head...

Chris Schwartz: You gave an intern the loan that began his professional career. Thank you very much.

Neal Brennan: You are the white Richard Nichols. Next book, you are doing counter footnotes.

Erica Toper: You were the last person to whom I'm doing this impossible mission and I'm running out of names.

Antoniette Costa: The nicest, gentlest human I know. So glad I know you.

Jon Shecter: You gave me the keys.

Rachel Feinstein: Of all my greasees...I loved greasing you up the most.

Corey Shapiro: You've kept more gray hair on my business manager's head than any human being I know. Thank you for my newfound addiction to frame collecting.

Prince and J Dilla: My two musical heroes who built this machine. I hope you are proud of your work.